SUCCESSFUL GARDENING

A–Z of ROCK GARDEN & WATER PLANTS

Staff for *A–Z of Rock Garden & Water Plants* (U.S.A.)
Senior Associate Editor: Theresa Lane
Associate Picture Researcher: James McInnis

Contributors
Editor: Thomas Christopher
Art Editor: Diane Lemonides
Picture Researcher: Barbara Salz
Editorial Assistant: Claudia Kaplan
Consulting Editor: Lizzie Boyd (U.K.)
Consultant: Ruth Rogers Clausen
Copy Editor: Gina E. Grant
Art Assistant: Coralee Storms

READER'S DIGEST GENERAL BOOKS
Editor-in-Chief
Books and Home Entertainment: Barbara J. Morgan
Editor, U.S. General Books: Susan Wernert Lewis
Editorial Director: Jane Polley
Art Director: Evelyn Bauer
Research Director: Laurel A. Gilbride
Affinity Directors: Will Bradbury, Jim Dwyer,
Joseph Gonzalez, Kaari Ward
Design Directors: Perri DeFino, Robert M. Grant, Joel Musler
Business Manager: Vidya Tejwani
Copy Chief: Edward W. Atkinson
Picture Editor: Marion Bodine
Head Librarian: Jo Manning

Library of Congress Cataloging in Publication Data

A–Z of rock garden & water plants
    p.   cm. — (Successful gardening)
ISBN 0-89577-836-X
    1. Rock plants — Encyclopedias.   2. Aquatic plants — Encyclopedias.
I. Reader's Digest Association.   II. Series.
SB421.A2 1995
635.9'672'03 — dc20   95-23107

Printed in the United States of America

Opposite: Rock and water are basic features in nature's landscape. Miniature
versions create ideal habitats for a host of plants.

Overleaf: Water irises and hostas grow into massive clumps in the boggy ground
at the edges of streams and ponds.

Pages 6–7: White-flowered candytufts and purple aubrietas make a colorful
display as they creep over rocks and walls.

THE READER'S DIGEST ASSOCIATION, INC.
Pleasantville, New York / Montreal

A–Z of ROCK GARDEN
& WATER PLANTS

CONTENTS

A rocky niche Common thyme spreads rapidly to a wide mat, while lime-encrusted saxifrage forms a tight rosette.

A–Z of rock garden plants

Rock gardening opens new perspectives to the garden scene, offering exquisite flowers that require minimal space. Rock garden plants range from the plants commonly known as "alpines" — true high-mountain plants that thrive naturally on the peaks, finding shelter in the lee of rocks — to the shrubs and wildflowers that thrive in sunny mountain meadows.

Alpine plants have adapted to harsh conditions to thrive above the tree line, surviving in a minimum of soil among barren rocks and exposed to biting winds and frigid winter frosts. Their blossoms are comparatively large and brilliantly colored, their leaves are small, and their roots penetrate deep into the gravelly subsoil. These plants require fast-draining soil, and they usually demand bright light.

Plants with a dwarf, creeping, or trailing habit can be included in the rock garden, too. These include shrubs and conifers, small bulbs, perennials, annuals, ferns, and succulents. Their requirements are less stringent than those of alpine plants, and they will thrive without fuss in well-drained soil and in open sites.

The miniature mountain landscape that the rock garden represents can take many forms. For example, a large garden — a properly constructed rock garden, with stone outcrops and rocky ledges interspersed with scree beds, alpine meadows, and perhaps a pool — can be impressive. However, if you have limited space, a smaller rock garden — one that is confined to a raised bed or two, a drystone wall (a stone wall without mortar), a concrete trough, one or more large planting containers, or even blocks of tufa rock (a porous limestone) — can be just as effective as its larger counterpart.

To help you determine if a particular plant will thrive in your area, we've given you zones that correspond to the plant-hardiness map on page 176.

ROCK GARDENS
Dwarf perennials, bulbs, shrubs, and conifers for year-round interest can be grown in rock gardens, raised beds, trough gardens, and tufa blocks.

A large, constructed rock garden should be in proportion with the rest of the garden, in an open site, and built on a gentle slope so that it looks like a natural outcrop. If possible, use local stone; embed the rocks vertically and horizontally to expose the different strata and to create ledges for trailing plants and sheltered pockets for rosette-type alpine plants. Good drainage is essential; you can achieve it by mixing gravel or crushed stone into the soil.

Building a naturalistic rock garden display is not essential to the enjoyment and cultivation of rock garden plants. Raised beds are a good alternative, and they bring plants closer to eye level.

Drystone walls can be host to numerous trailing and compact plants, and soil pockets between paving stones can become home to the roots of creeping species.

Concrete troughs are ideal for miniature gardens, complete with dwarf willows or conifers, and they are easy to construct. Make a mold by packing sand into the shape of the trough's interior and covering it with 1 in (2.5 cm) mesh chicken wire. Then mix one part Portland cement, one and a half parts sphagnum peat, and one and a half parts perlite, and moisten the mixture with water until it is wet but still stiff. Using a trowel, apply it to the mold and wire, 1-2 in (2.5-5 cm) thick. To

make drainage holes, insert dowels into what will be the bottom of the trough; once the mixture sets and before it is fully cured, pull out the dowels.

Tufa (available from nurseries that specialize in rock garden plants and supplies) is an ideal planting site for compact, high-mountain specimens, such as *Saxifraga longifolia*. Drill holes into this soft material to make room for the plants.

▼ **Summer rock garden** The blue-flowered *Campanula portenschlagiana* is easy to grow. It blooms throughout summer and spreads to large clumps. It complements the pink of this dianthus.

▲ **Checkerboard planting** A sunny sitting area is paved with stone slabs and gravel, and creeping rock plants have been planted in the crevices. Thyme scents the air, and sempervivums and saxifrages form mounded rosettes.

▶ **Container planting** Shallow pots of colorful sempervivums are sunk in a bed of gravel to ensure perfect drainage. Small pieces of tufa rock heighten the illusion of a high-mountain scene.

▼ **Trough gardens** Stone or concrete troughs are ideal for creating miniature mountain landscapes. They are planted with compact plants and dwarf conifers, interspersed with pieces of rock and mulched with gravel.

◀ **Spring flowers** The peak season for rock garden flowers is late spring, when aubrietas, phlox, and alyssums *(Aurinia saxatilis)* shower themselves with bright blooms. Dwarf rhododendrons on the upper ledges add deeper colors, and miniature and creeping conifers tie the composition together.

▼ **Cascades of color** The top of a dry-stone wall and soil-filled pockets between the stones support a multitude of creeping and trailing rock plants. Their roots gain a foothold in crevices, while the stems hang in ripples of vivid colors.

▲ **Natural container** A hollowed-out tree stump has become home to a collection of high-mountain succulents. The evergreen fleshy-leaved sempervivums form perfect rosettes in shades of green, often flushed or tipped with red. A mulch of pebbles keeps the rosette bases dry.

▶ **Alpine meadow** A scree bed — a gently sloping bed of gravel — fans out into a little summer meadow, covered with a bright carpet of different types of dianthus, thyme, and dwarf irises.

▲ Tufa garden Tufa, a porous lime-stone, is an ideal (if relatively expensive) material for rock gardens. It retains water needed by roots in dry weather, and it has a high calcium content, which is essential to the health of many alpine plants. Tufa's weathered appearance blends well with other rock garden features, such as concrete troughs cast from Portland cement, sphagnum peat, and perlite.

▶ Brilliant color Despite their small size, alpine, or high-mountain, plants produce comparatively large, vivid blossoms in many different colors. Here, spring-flowering alpine plants are shown to their best advantage against a background of dwarf conifers and carpeting evergreens.

Abies

dwarf fir

Abies nordmanniana 'Golden Spreader'

❏ Height up to 3 ft (90 cm)
❏ Spread up to 4 ft (1.2 m)
❏ Foliage shrub
❏ Moist, acid or neutral soil
❏ Full sun or light shade
❏ Hardy zones 3-7

Dwarf firs *(Abies)* provide vertical accents among ground-hugging and trailing flowers. Their evergreen color is a welcome sight in winter. *Abies* includes a number of compact cultivars that are conical in shape and bear an aromatic, needlelike foliage. They take many years to reach their maximum height and produce cones.

Popular species and cultivars
Abies balsamea 'Hudsonia' (dwarf balsam fir) is a round-topped, spreading shrub that grows to 2½ ft (75 cm) high. It is hardy in zones 3-6, and it has a dense foliage of glossy, medium-green needles, each marked underneath with two white bands.
Abies cephalonica 'Meyer's Dwarf' (dwarf Greek fir) has horizontally spreading branches and shiny green needles that are white underneath. It grows to 1 ft (30 cm) tall and 3 ft (90 cm) wide, thrives in alkaline soil, and is hardy to zone 6.
Abies concolor 'Compacta' (dwarf white fir), syn. 'Glauca Compacta,' has an irregular growth habit and gray-blue foliage. It grows 2-3 ft (60-90 cm) tall after 10 years; it is hardy in zones 3-7.
Abies nordmanniana 'Golden Spreader' (dwarf Caucasian fir), syn. 'Aurea Nana,' has wide-spreading branches. The leaves are golden yellow above, pale yellowish white below. It grows 1 ft (30 cm) tall and 3 ft (90 cm) wide; the species is hardy in zones 5-7.

Abies balsamea 'Hudsonia'

Abies concolor 'Compacta'

Abies procera 'Glauca Prostrata' (dwarf noble fir) is 1 ft (30 cm) high and 3 ft (90 cm) wide, with spreading branches and blue-gray leaves; it is hardy in zones 5-7.

Cultivation
Plant in late fall or early spring in slightly acid or neutral, moist but well-drained soil. Full sun is best for golden cultivars, although light shade is acceptable and will give protection from late-spring frost. Avoid exposed positions.
Propagation Home propagation is impractical; it is best to purchase new plants.
Pests/diseases Firs may suffer from dieback or rust or be infested with sap-sucking insects, which create tufts of white, waxy wool on leaves and branches.

Acaena
New Zealand bur

Acaena novae-zelandiae

- ❑ Height 1-6 in (2.5-15 cm)
- ❑ Spread 1½-2½ ft (45-75 cm)
- ❑ Foliage; burs in late summer
- ❑ Any well-drained soil
- ❑ Sun or partial shade
- ❑ Hardy zones 7-10

New Zealand bur *(Acaena)*, a low-growing, carpeting evergreen, is raised for its tiny leaves and its burs — bristly, globular seed heads. The scarlet, red, amber, or purple burs mature in late summer, following insignificant flowers, and they are carried well above the carpet of leaves.

New Zealand burs are sensitive to frost, and they may burn in very hot sun. They thrive along the Pacific Coast. Because New Zealand burs grow vigorously where they are adapted, do not plant them near choice plants — they might become swamped by the New Zealand burs. These are good ground-cover plants and can be planted between paving stones or on drystone walls.

Popular species and cultivars
Acaena 'Blue Haze,' syn. 'Pewter,' has blue-green foliage borne on red stems and bears pale brown burs. It grows 4 in (10 cm) high and 2 ft (60 cm) wide.
Acaena buchananii is just 2 in (5 cm) high, but it spreads to 2 ft (60 cm) wide. It displays pea-green leaves and amber burs.

Acaena 'Blue Haze'

Acaena microphylla, the most commonly raised species, grows to only 2 in (5 cm) high, but it spreads 2 ft (60 cm) wide. It has bronzed foliage and scarlet burs. The cultivar 'Copper Carpet,' syn. 'Kupferteppich,' has coppery leaves and reddish burs.
Acaena novae-zelandiae produces green leaves and purple burs.

Cultivation
Set out young plants in fall or early spring in any well-drained garden soil. New Zealand burs thrive in full sun but can also tolerate some shade.
Propagation Sow seeds in a cold frame between early fall and early spring. Alternatively, divide and replant existing stock in fall or early spring.
Pests/diseases Trouble free.

Acantholimon
prickly thrift

Acantholimon glumaceum

- ❑ Height 6-8 in (15-20 cm)
- ❑ Spread 1 ft (30 cm)
- ❑ Flowers early summer to early fall
- ❑ Any well-drained soil
- ❑ Sunny site
- ❑ Evergreen perennial
- ❑ Hardy to zone 8

Prickly thrift is grown for its mats of needlelike leaves and for its loose spikes of starry flowers produced from early summer to early fall. It is slow-growing but long-lived. The choice species of *Acantholimon* described here come from Armenia and Asia Minor and are the ones most commonly available.

Popular species
Acantholimon glumaceum has dark green, spiked leaves. They form compact mats that reach up to 6 in (15 cm) high. Mauve to rose-pink flowers, ½ in (12 mm) wide, are borne on 4 in (10 cm) long spikes throughout summer. This is the hardiest species.
Acantholimon venustum reaches a height of 6-8 in (15-20 cm). It forms loose tufts of silver-gray foliage; pale rose flowers, about ⅓ in (8 mm) wide, are carried well above the leaves. Persistently wet soil around the roots in winter may cause rot; this species grows best on a drystone wall.

Cultivation
Prickly thrifts thrive in gritty, well-drained soil in an open, sunny position. Plant in spring and deadhead after flowering.
Propagation Sow seeds indoors in late winter. Alternatively, root cuttings of nonflowering basal shoots in a cold frame in summer.
Pests/diseases Trouble free.

Achillea
yarrow

Achillea clavennae

Achillea tomentosa

Achillea × kellereri

❑ Height 4-9 in (10-23 cm)
❑ Spread 8-12 in (20-30 cm)
❑ Flowers late spring to early fall
❑ Any well-drained soil
❑ Full sun
❑ Perennial
❑ Hardy zones 3-10

Dwarf yarrow *(Achillea)* is an easy, reliable rock garden plant grown for its aromatic, gray-green or silver, usually feathery leaves and for its flowers. These may be yellow, flat-topped heads or daisylike white flowers. The plant grows well in poor soil, such as that found in drystone walls or in crevices in paving, where it may live longer and flower more freely than it would in a rich loam.

Popular species and cultivars

Achillea ageratifolia reaches up to 8 in (20 cm) high and bears tight rosettes of narrow, deeply toothed, silver leaves. The white, daisylike flowers bloom in mid and late summer.

Achillea clavennae, syn. *A. argentea,* has oval, irregularly toothed, bright silver leaves. Heads of white, daisylike blossoms grow profusely on 6 in (15 cm) stems in late spring and early summer.

Achillea × kellereri is a hybrid derived partly from *A. clavennae.* It grows 6 in (15 cm) high and 10 in (25 cm) wide and has bright silver leaves that are similar to those of *A. clavennae.* The flower clusters are smaller and tighter.

Achillea × lewisii 'King Edward' is hardy to zone 6. It grows 4-6 in (10-15 cm) high and 8 in (20 cm) wide. It has gray-green leaves and bears lemon-yellow flower heads up to 2½ in (6.25 cm) wide from late spring to early fall.

Achillea tomentosa grows to 9 in (23 cm) high. Its dense mat of downy gray leaves spreads 1 ft (30 cm) wide. The stems bear flat, yellow flower heads from midsummer to early fall.

Achillea umbellata is 6 in (15 cm) high and 12 in (30 cm) wide. It makes a neat, dense mat of felted, silver leaves and bears showy, loose heads of daisylike flowers in summer. It is hardy to zone 6.

Cultivation
Plant yarrows in fall or early spring in any well-drained garden soil in a sunny position. When the flower stems fade in fall, cut them back to the ground.

Propagation In early spring divide the roots into sections, each bearing four to five young shoots, and replant immediately in their permanent positions.

Pests/diseases Trouble free.

Adenophora

ladybells

Adenophora tashiroi

- ❑ Height 8-24 in (20-60 cm)
- ❑ Spread up to 1 ft (30 cm)
- ❑ Flowers in summer
- ❑ Any well-drained soil
- ❑ Full sun or light shade
- ❑ Perennial
- ❑ Hardy zones 3-9

Ladybells *(Adenophora)* are generally grown for their clusters of blue, lavender, or violet-blue, bell-shaped, nodding flowers. The two Asiatic species described here can be grown in a rock garden. Although tall, they are slender and delicate in appearance.

Popular species

Adenophora bulleyana, which comes from western China, grows to a height of 2 ft (60 cm). It produces spikes of pale blue, ½-¾ in (1.25-2 cm) flowers all summer. *Adenophora tashiroi* is smaller than *A. bulleyana* at just 8-10 in (20-25 cm) high, and it is hardy only as far north as zone 7. The flowers are violet-blue and appear either singly or with just a few blooms per spike.

Cultivation

Plant in fall or spring in well-drained soil in full sun or a lightly shaded spot.
Propagation Sow seeds in late spring. Or, in spring, divide large clumps into smaller ones; replant.
Pests/diseases Slugs and snails may eat the leaves.

Adonis

pheasant's-eye

Adonis amurensis

- ❑ Height 9-15 in (23-38 cm)
- ❑ Spread 1 ft (30 cm)
- ❑ Flowers late winter to early spring
- ❑ Any well-drained soil
- ❑ Sun or partial shade
- ❑ Perennial
- ❑ Hardy zones 3-8

The bright yellow flowers of pheasant's-eyes *(Adonis)* appear in late winter and early spring, in time to complement spring bulbs. When the sun is out, the flowers open into shiny bowl shapes set against the neat, round clumps of bright green, feathery leaves. The plants die down in summer.

Pheasant's-eyes are admirable plants in the rock garden and are ideal as an edging to borders.

Popular species

Adonis amurensis is the earliest species to flower. It grows 9-15 in (23-38 cm) high and has single-petaled flowers that open to 2 in (5 cm) wide, displaying a large central boss of stamens. It is hardy to zone 4. 'Florepleno' is a double-flowered form.
Adonis vernalis reaches 9-12 in (23-30 cm) high. It bears bright yellow flowers, 2 in (5 cm) wide, in early spring.

Cultivation

Adonises will grow in any well-drained but moisture-retentive soil. Plant in a sunny or partially shaded spot from midsummer to midfall, setting the crowns 1 in (2.5 cm) below the soil level.
Propagation Divide and replant the roots in fall.
Pests/diseases Trouble free.

Aethionema

stone cress

Aethionema 'Warley Rose'

- ❑ Height 4-9 in (10-23 cm)
- ❑ Spread 1-1½ ft (30-45 cm)
- ❑ Flowers midspring to midsummer
- ❑ Any well-drained soil
- ❑ Full sun
- ❑ Perennial
- ❑ Hardy zones 5-9

Stone cresses *(Aethionema)* form thick mats of evergreen leaves and bear abundant clusters of pink or white flowers. They revel in hot, dry spots and flourish in light, sandy, alkaline soil. Stone cresses are suitable for planting in pockets and crevices in rock gardens or drystone walls.

Popular species and hybrids

Aethionema grandiflorum (Persian stone cress) is a loosely branched species with narrowly oval, gray-green leaves. It may be erect or spreading, growing up to 9 in (23 cm) high. Delicate pink flowers, arranged in domed heads 1½-2 in (3.75-5 cm) wide, appear in profusion from late spring to midsummer.
Aethionema iberideum is hardy as far north as zone 7. It grows 6 in (15 cm) high, with oval, blue-green leaves. The white flowers are produced freely in 2 in (5 cm) terminal clusters from late spring to midsummer.
Aethionema 'Warley Rose' is a hybrid with linear gray-green leaves that makes a handsome, compact mound only 4-6 in (10-15 cm) high. In mid and late spring, deep rose-pink flowers appear in broad spikes 2-3 in (5-7.5 cm) long. This species adapts better to warm climates than most of the other stone cresses do.

Ajuga
bugleweed

Aethionema iberideum

Aethionema grandiflorum

Ajuga reptans 'Multicoloris'

- ❑ Height 4-12 in (10-30 cm)
- ❑ Spread 6-18 in (15-45 cm)
- ❑ Flowers late spring to midsummer
- ❑ Any moist soil
- ❑ Partial shade
- ❑ Perennial
- ❑ Hardy zones 2-10

Bugleweed *(Ajuga)* has attractive leaves and spikes of blue, white, or pink flowers. It flourishes in moist, shady areas.

Popular species

Ajuga pyramidalis grows to 9 in (23 cm) high, with toothed, green leaves and pyramid-shaped spikes of whorled, blue flowers in late spring. It is hardy in zones 2-9.
Ajuga reptans, too invasive for a rock garden, is a good ground cover, hardy in zones 3-10. Cultivars with nice foliage are 'Atropurpurea' ('Purpurea,' purple), 'Burgundy Glow' (purple, bronze, and cream), 'Multicoloris' ('Rainbow,' bronze, pink, and cream), and 'Variegata' (gray-green, cream).

Cultivation

In fall or spring plant in ordinary moisture-retentive soil. Avoid

Cultivation

Plant in any well-drained soil in full sun in fall or early spring. Remove faded stems after flowering.
Propagation You can increase 'Warley Rose' by taking cuttings of green, nonflowering shoots in early or midsummer. Root them in a cold frame or other cool, protected spot. When the cuttings root, pot them up individually and overwinter in the cold frame or a protected spot. Plant them out in their permanent positions in midspring.

Other aethionemas can be increased from seeds sown in a cold frame or indoors in early spring.
Pests/diseases Generally trouble free.

Ajuga reptans 'Atropurpurea'

deep shade for colored-leaved bugleweeds; *A. pyramidalis* thrives in shade.
Propagation Divide and replant in fall or spring.
Pests/diseases Slugs and snails may damage these plants.

Alchemilla

lady's-mantle

Alchemilla erythropoda

- ❑ Height 6-9 in (15-23 cm)
- ❑ Spread 10-12 in (25-30 cm)
- ❑ Flowers in summer
- ❑ Moist but well-drained soil
- ❑ Sunny or partially shaded site
- ❑ Perennial
- ❑ Hardy zones 3-7

The dwarf types of lady's-mantle (*Alchemilla*) are grown mainly for their rounded, deeply divided leaves. A central depression in the leaves catches drops of rainwater, which sparkle like many-faceted diamonds. Their small, round flower clusters are pleasant but unremarkable, unlike those of their relative *Alchemilla mollis,* a border perennial with lime-green flowers.

Popular species
Alchemilla alpina grows to 9 in (23 cm) high, with neat tufts of rounded, silvery-green leaves divided into narrow leaflets. The flower clusters are green.
Alchemilla erythropoda is hardy only as far north as zone 7. This species grows to 6 in (15 cm) high, and its leaves have a bluish tinge. The small, round flower heads are yellow, and they turn russet-red as they age.

Cultivation
Plant lady's-mantle in fall or early spring in a sunny or partially shaded site in any moist but well-drained soil. The plants are suitable for large rock gardens, as edging, and as ground cover.
Propagation Sow seeds in early spring. Or divide and replant established plants in fall or spring.
Pests/diseases Trouble free.

ALKANET — see *Anchusa*

Allium

ornamental onion

Allium moly

- ❑ Height 6-15 in (15-38 cm)
- ❑ Spread 6 in (15 cm)
- ❑ Flowers spring and summer
- ❑ Any well-drained soil
- ❑ Sun or partial shade
- ❑ Bulb
- ❑ Hardy to zone 4

Ornamental onions *(Allium)* are related to ordinary onions. Some species have the typical flower clusters borne singly on stiff, upright stems; most have the familiar onion smell. The strap-shaped leaves form low, tufted clumps.

Popular species
Allium karataviense grows to 6 in (15 cm) high, with broad leaves tinted metallic red. The globular flower heads, 4 in (10 cm) wide, are a soft gray-pink and are borne in late spring.
Allium moly grows 1 ft (30 cm) high and is an invasive species. It has gray-green leaves and bears loose clusters of bright yellow, star-shaped flowers in late spring.
Allium oreophilum, syn. *A. ostrowskianum,* will grow 6-12 in (15-30 cm) high, with small tufts of leaves at ground level. The cerise-pink blossoms are carried in dense heads in late spring. The cultivar 'Zwanenburg' has exceptionally richly colored flowers.

Allium oreophilum

Allium roseum is hardy only to zone 5. It is 12-15 in (30-38 cm) high, has long, broad leaves, and displays clusters of pink, star-shaped flowers in late spring.

Cultivation
In fall or spring plant ornamental onions in a sunny spot in any well-drained soil. Cover the bulbs to three or four times their own depth. Deadhead the flowers, leaving the stalks to feed the bulbs. Leave clumps untouched until they become congested.
Propagation Split clumps in fall or as growth starts in spring, and replant.
Pests/diseases Young plants may be eaten by slugs.

Alyssum

alyssum, basket-of-gold

Alyssum saxatile

- ❏ Height 2-12 in (5-30 cm)
- ❏ Spread 1-1½ ft (30-45 cm)
- ❏ Flowers late spring to midsummer
- ❏ Any well-drained soil
- ❏ Sunny site
- ❏ Perennial
- ❏ Hardy zones 3-10

Alyssum is vigorous and so free-flowering that the leaves are often totally hidden. This long-lived plant thrives in sunny rock gardens or tumbling over drystone walls and banks.

Popular species
Alyssum montanum is hardy in zones 3-9 and grows about 6 in (15 cm) high, forming a dense mat of gray, hairy, oblong-oval leaves. It bears scented yellow flowers in early and midsummer.
Alyssum saxatile has been reclassified as *Aurinia saxatilis*. It forms bold clumps of gray-green, tapering leaves, grows 9-12 in (23-30 cm) high, and is hardy in zones 4-10. The dense clusters of yellow flowers are borne from mid spring to early summer. Cultivars include 'Citrinum' (lemon-yellow flowers), 'Compacta' (only to 6 in/15 cm high; golden yellow flowers), 'Dudley Neville' (buff-yellow flowers), and 'Plenum' (golden yellow double flowers).
Alyssum serpyllifolium is prostrate, growing no more than 2 in (5 cm) high but trailing and spreading to 12 in (30 cm). It bears gray leaves; clear yellow flowers appear in early summer.
Alyssum tortuosum forms a tangled mat of twisted woody stems

Alyssum saxatile 'Dudley Neville'

and neat, silver-gray foliage 3 in (7.5 cm) high and 12 in (30 cm) wide. Yellow flowers bloom in early summer. It is hardy to zone 7.

Cultivation
Plant alyssums in full sun in any well-drained soil in early fall or early spring. Cut them back hard after flowering to encourage compact growth.
Propagation To increase cultivars mentioned here, take cuttings in early summer; root them in a cold frame or other protected spot. The species are easy to grow from seeds sown in early spring.
Pests/diseases Young plants are vulnerable to slugs and flea beetles. Downy mildew may cause the leaves to curl.

Anacyclus

Mount Atlas daisy

Anacyclus depressus

- ❏ Height 2 in (5 cm)
- ❏ Spread 1 ft (30 cm)
- ❏ Flowers early summer
- ❏ Any well-drained soil
- ❏ Sunny site
- ❏ Perennial
- ❏ Hardy zones 6-10

Mount Atlas daisy *(Anacyclus depressus)* is a colorful little plant. Its red buds contrast with the open, daisylike white flowers, and both are set off by delicate, gray-green, ferny foliage. It grows as a low mat only 2 in (5 cm) high and up to 1 ft (30 cm) wide. Flowering in early summer, the blossoms have petals that are white above and red on the underside.

Cultivation
Plant Mount Atlas daisy in a sunny spot in well-drained, gritty soil in fall or early to mid spring. Deadhead after flowering. This plant will not tolerate a site that remains soggy in wintertime.
Propagation Take cuttings of nonflowering shoots in early to mid spring or mid to late summer and root in a cold frame or other protected spot. Plant spring cuttings in early fall, summer ones the following spring.
Pests/diseases Black or green aphids may infest the foliage, and their sticky secretions may attract sooty mold.

Anchusa
alkanet, bugloss

Anchusa capensis

- ❏ Height 16-18 in (40-45 cm)
- ❏ Spread 12 in (30 cm)
- ❏ Flowers in spring
- ❏ Well-drained, gritty soil
- ❏ Sunny site
- ❏ Perennial
- ❏ Hardy to zone 7

Alkanet, or bugloss, *(Anchusa)* produces flowers of a clear blue — a relatively rare hue in the flower garden. While most species will grow too large for the average-size rock garden, the ones listed here grow to a size reasonable for most rock gardens.

Popular species
Anchusa capensis, the Cape forget-me-not, is a biennial species that may be started indoors from seeds in early spring and treated as an annual. It grows to a height of 18 in (45 cm) and produces blue funnel-shaped flowers that are similar to those of *A. leptophylla* ssp. *incana* (however, in the case of the cultivar 'Pink Bird' the flowers are pink). This is a useful plant for filling in gaps

that are left in the rock garden by earlier-flowering perennials.
Anchusa leptophylla ssp. *incana*, grows to a height of 16 in (40 cm). This species bears narrow, dark green leaves that form a loose rosette. In springtime the rosette is crowned with an attractive cluster of funnel-shaped flowers that are azure-blue.

Cultivation
Plant *A. leptophylla* ssp. *incana* in a sunny position in well-drained, gritty soil anytime in fall or early spring.
Propagation Because of its long root system, this species cannot be propagated by division. Instead, take root cuttings in mid or late winter and plant them in a cold frame or other protected spot; they should root and be ready for setting out in a nursery bed by late spring. Transfer them to their permanent positions from midfall onward.
Pests/diseases Generally trouble free.

Andromeda
bog rosemary

Andromeda polifolia

- ❏ Height 6-18 in (15-45 cm)
- ❏ Spread 1 ft (30 cm) or more
- ❏ Flowers late spring to early summer
- ❏ Acid, moist soil
- ❏ Semishaded site
- ❏ Evergreen shrub
- ❏ Hardy zones 2-6

Bog rosemary *(Andromeda polifolia)* grows wild in peat bogs and marshy places from Newfoundland to Minnesota and New Jersey. It is suitable for cool, shady places in the rock garden. Like other members of the heath family, it thrives only in acid soil.

While bog rosemary can grow up to 18 in (45 cm) high, several compact-growing forms are available. Notable cultivars include 'Grandiflora Compacta' and the pink-flowered 'Macrophylla,' both of which will eventually form dense hummocks. 'Nana Alba' is a white-flowered cultivar.

Bog rosemary has wiry stems and leathery, narrow, oval leaves. The pale pink, bell-shaped flowers are borne freely in tight clusters on the tips of the shoots in late spring and early summer.

Cultivation
Plant bog rosemary in rich, moist, acid soil in fall or spring in a cool, partially shaded site.
Propagation To increase, lift and divide mature plants in fall or early spring. Alternatively, layer long shoots in fall, or increase by taking hardwood cuttings.
Pests/diseases Trouble free.

21

Androsace

rock jasmine

Androsace sarmentosa

❏ Height 1-4 in (2.5-10 cm)
❏ Spread 4-24 in (10-60 cm)
❏ Flowers late spring to midsummer
❏ Very well-drained soil
❏ Sunny site
❏ Perennial
❏ Hardy to zone 3, depending on
   the species

Rock jasmines *(Androsace)* are true high-mountain, or alpine, plants. Many of its species perform best in upland areas of the western states, where they thrive in the temperate summers with low humidity, and where they have adapted well to the dry winters. Those described here can be grown in a well-drained rock garden or in a concrete trough even in the Northeast.

Rock jasmines are prized for their dainty tufts — formed where the compact roots raise the plant in a clump above ground level — or as ground-hugging mats of leaves. These plants are also appreciated for their tiny, primroselike flowers that are carried singly or in dense clusters.

Popular species

Androsace carnea is a relatively moisture-tolerant plant that is hardy to zone 5. It grows to 3 in (7.5 cm) high, forming a clump of dark green, needlelike leaves. The small pink or white flowers are displayed in small clusters on erect stalks in early summer. The variety *A. c. laggeri* bears small clusters of deep pink flowers in late spring.

Androsace lanuginosa is a prostrate, trailing plant that is ideal for growing high up in crevices on the shady side of a rock garden. It is hardy to zone 6. The silver-leaved stems can spread 1-1½ ft (30-45 cm). Clusters of pink flowers appear in summer.

Androsace sarmentosa is hardy to zone 3. It forms a mat of leaf rosettes 4 in (10 cm) high and up to 2 ft (60 cm) wide that turn from medium green in summer to a woolly gray-green in winter. The clusters of pink flowers bloom profusely from midspring to early summer. This species is the best choice for eastern gardens, since it is relatively tolerant of summer humidity and less prone to rot during wet winters.

Androsace sempervivoides, hardy to zone 6, grows in 2 in (5 cm) tall rosettes of overlapping leathery green leaves. This species produces short, erect flower stems that display pink blossoms in early summer.

Androsace villosa produces tufts of small, gray-green leaves clustered at the ends of hairy, often red runners, and it grows into mats about 2 in (5 cm) high and 9-12 in (23-30 cm) wide. The flowers, which bloom in early summer, are white or pale pink with a red eye. The species is hardy to zone 5.

Cultivation

In early to mid spring plant rock jasmines in gritty, very well drained soil in an airy, open site. An east- or north-facing slope is best, since full summer sun may burn rock jasmines.

Propagation Detach rosettes in early summer and root in a cold frame or other cool, protected spot. Overwinter in pots and plant the following midspring. Take 2 in (5 cm) basal shoots of *A. lanuginosa* and treat in the same way as you do the rosettes.

Alternatively, sow seeds in mid or late winter and leave outdoors for two weeks; freezing temperatures will hasten germination.

Pests/diseases Aphids and mealybugs may check the plants' growth.

Antennaria
everlasting, pussytoes

Anthemis
anthemis, dog fennel, chamomile

Anthemis marschalliana

❑ Height 3-12 in (7.5-30 cm)
❑ Spread up to 3 ft (90 cm)
❑ Flowers spring to late fall; foliage
❑ Any well-drained soil
❑ Sunny site
❑ Perennial
❑ Hardy zones 4-10

Low-growing anthemis species are grown as much for their feathery, aromatic foliage as for their daisylike flowers. Common chamomile, formerly *A. nobilis,* is now classified as *Chamaemelum nobile.* It is included in this entry because of its similarity to the anthemis species. Common chamomile, a hardy plant, may be used as a lawn substitute or planted between paving stones.

Popular species
Anthemis cupaniana is a spreading, cushion-forming plant that grows up to 1 ft (30 cm) high and 1½-3 ft (45-90 cm) wide. It has silvery, feathery foliage. Large, white, daisylike flowers, borne singly on long stems, brightly accent the garden from late spring until early fall. This species is hardy in zones 5-10.
Anthemis marschalliana, syn. *A. biebersteiniana,* has filigreed silver foliage and yellow, daisylike flowers displayed on 9 in (23 cm) stems in summer. The foliage grows 6 in (15 cm) high.
Anthemis montana, syn. *A. macedonica,* is hardy to zone 6. It forms 6 in (15 cm) high mats of small green leaves and bears a profusion of small white flowers in early summer.
Chamaemelum nobile (common chamomile) is somewhat invasive

Antennaria dioica 'Minima Rubra'

❑ Height 1-6 in (2.5-15 cm)
❑ Spread up to 1½ ft (45 cm)
❑ Flowers late spring to early summer
❑ Any well-drained soil
❑ Sunny site
❑ Perennial
❑ Hardy to zone 4

Everlastings *(Antennaria)* are suitable ground-cover plants for carpeting areas where spring bulbs have been planted and for growing in cracks between paving stones. In regions of mild winters, it will perform as a perennial.

Popular species
Antennaria dioica, syn. *A. tomentosa,* grows into woolly mats of narrow, silver-gray foliage 1 in (2.5 cm) high and 1½ ft (45 cm) wide. The erect stems are 2-6 in (5-15 cm) tall and display small heads of white, pink-tipped, tufted flowers in late spring and early summer. Cultivars include 'Nyewood' (syn. 'Nyewood Variety'; 3 in/7.5 cm tall; deep pink blossoms), 'Rosea' (6 in/15 cm high; green and silver foliage; rose-pink flowers), and 'Minima Rubra' (2 in/5 cm tall; deep pink flowers).

Antennaria parvifolia

Antennaria parvifolia, syn. *A. aprica,* has silver-gray leaves and bears silver-white blossoms in early summer.

Cultivation
Plant in any well-drained soil in a sunny spot in fall or early spring.
Propagation Divide and replant established plants in early spring.
Pests/diseases Trouble free.

Anthyllis

anthyllis

Anthyllis montana

❑ Height 4-18 in (10-45 cm)
❑ Spread up to 1 ft (30 cm)
❑ Flowers mid to late summer
❑ Any well-drained soil
❑ Sunny site
❑ Shrubby perennial
❑ Hardy to zone 5

Anthemis cupaniana

and is most commonly seen as the double-flowered 'Flore-pleno.' It carpets the ground with tiny green leaves and pompon-shaped white flowers on 3 in (7.5 cm) stems all summer long.

The nonflowering cultivar 'Treneague' makes a mossy, aromatic, emerald-green carpet that reaches up to 9 in (23 cm) high. This is the cultivar that is commonly planted for a chamomile lawn. It needs no regular mowing, just an occasional light trim. Chamomile lawns will withstand a modest amount of foot traffic, although they are not as resilient as grass lawns. When the leaves are bruised underfoot, they release a delicate fragrance.

Cultivation
Plant anthemis in any well-drained soil in a sunny site in fall or early spring. To grow a chamomile lawn, set young plants of *C. nobile* 'Treneague' 6 in (15 cm) apart in an open position in early to mid spring.
Propagation Divide and replant established plants. Or take cuttings of basal shoots (lateral shoots of *C. nobile*) in spring and root in a cold frame or other protected spot. Plant in early fall.
Pests/diseases Trouble free.

Although some species grow too tall for use in the rock garden, anthyllis deserves a place there because it continues to flower into late summer, when many rock garden plants are past their prime. It has attractive feathery foliage and pealike flowers.

Popular species
Anthyllis montana is hardy to zone 5. It forms a closely knit carpet of gray leaves covered with fluffy silver hairs and reaches a height of 4-6 in (10-15 cm) or more. It bears cloverlike, rose-red flowers; 'Rubra' has flowers of an exceptionally deep pink.
Anthyllis vulneraria (ladies'-fingers) is hardy to zone 7. This species can grow to 1½ ft (45 cm) tall, though it is usually shorter. It produces flowers that range from cream or yellow to orange or red. The cultivar *A. vulneraria* 'Rubra' bears clusters of rich vermilion blossoms.

Cultivation
Plant anthyllis in full sun in any well-drained soil in fall or early spring. It grows best in alkaline soil and flourishes among hot, sunny rocks.
Propagation Take softwood cuttings and root them in a cold frame or other protected spot in early to late summer.
Pests/diseases Aphids may infest the foliage.

Chamaemelum nobile 'Treneague'

ANTIRRHINUM — see *Asarina*

Aquilegia
columbine

Aquilegia caerulea

Aquilegia flabellata 'Nana Alba'

- ❏ Height 4-24 in (10-60 cm)
- ❏ Spread 6-12 in (15-30 cm)
- ❏ Flowers late spring to midsummer
- ❏ Well-drained, moist soil
- ❏ Sunny or lightly shaded site
- ❏ Perennial
- ❏ Hardy zones 3-10

Columbines have divided gray-green leaves and spurred, funnel-shaped, often bicolored flowers.

Popular species
Aquilegia alpina is 1 ft (30 cm) high and wide. It bears blue or blue-and-white blossoms in late spring; hybrids can produce other colors. 'Mini Star,' a dwarf cultivar, has pink-and-white blooms. *Aquilegia bertolonii* has large, deep blue flowers borne singly on 4 in (10 cm) long stems in late spring. It is hardy only to zone 6. *Aquilegia caerulea* grows 8-24 in (20-60 cm) tall. Its light to deep blue flowers may be bicolored with white. 'Biedermeier Dwarf,' 12 in (30 cm) tall, has clusters of blue, pink, lilac, or cream blooms. *Aquilegia canadensis* grows up to 2 ft (60 cm) high. It bears red-and-yellow flowers. 'Nana' does not exceed 1 ft (30 cm). *Aquilegia flabellata,* 10 in (25 cm) high, has purple-blue flowers

Aquilegia flabellata

from late spring to midsummer. The dwarf 'Nana' has lilac and cream flowers; 'Nana Alba' is even smaller, with white flowers.

Cultivation
In fall or spring plant in sun or partial shade in any fertile, moist but well-drained soil. Deadhead after flowering.
Propagation Sow seeds in summer; divide plants in fall or spring.
Pests/diseases Leaf miners and aphids may infest the plants.

Aquilegia alpina 'Mini Star'

25

Arabis
rock cress

Arabis caucasica 'Compinkie'

❑ Height 4-9 in (10-23 cm)
❑ Spread 9-24 in (23-60 cm)
❑ Flowers late winter to summer
❑ Any well-drained soil
❑ Partial shade
❑ Evergreen perennial
❑ Hardy zones 4-10

Rock cress (Arabis) is deservedly one of the most popular rock garden plants. It is easy to grow, covers the ground with dense hummocks of gray-green foliage, and bears a profusion of attractive flowers over long periods.

Popular species and cultivars
Arabis blepharophylla is hardy in zones 6-9. It grows 4 in (10 cm) high and 9 in (23 cm) wide. This plant bears tufts of stiff leaves with hairy margins and, from early to late spring, pink, white, or rose-purple flowers.
Arabis caucasica, syn. A. albida, is hardy in zones 4-10. It reaches 9 in (23 cm) high and spreads up to 2 ft (60 cm). Clusters of white flowers are produced from late winter until early summer. The species is an aggressive spreader but is easily contained by planting in a wall. The cultivar 'Plena' is more compact; it is less free-flowering but has double blooms.
Other compact cultivars include 'Compinkie' and 'Rosabella,' both of which produce pink flowers. 'Variegata' is a slow-growing cultivar. It has gold-and-silver-marked foliage and bears

Arabis caucasica 'Plena'

Arabis ferdinandi-coburgi 'Variegata'

flowers that are white, sometimes flushed with pink.
Arabis ferdinandi-coburgi 'Variegata' grows only 4 in (10 cm) high and 9 in (23 cm) wide. It bears white flowers in late spring and green leaves attractively striped with cream all year round. This species is hardy as far north as zone 7.

Cultivation
Set the plants out in well-drained soil in partial shade in early to mid fall or in early spring. Trim A. caucasica and its cultivars back hard after flowering.
Propagation Root nonflowering leaf rosettes in a cold frame or other protected spot from early to mid summer. Transplant to the garden in early spring. You can also divide and replant A. caucasica in early fall. A. blepharophylla can be raised only from seeds.
Pests/diseases Generally trouble free.

Arctostaphylos
bearberry

Arctostaphylos uva-ursi

❑ Height 4-6 in (10-15 cm)
❑ Spread up to 4 ft (1.2 m)
❑ Flowers late spring; edible fall berries
❑ Acid, moist soil
❑ Full sun or light shade
❑ Evergreen shrub
❑ Hardy zones 2-6

Bearberry, a member of the heath family, thrives in light shade or sun. It can be grown in a rock garden, but it makes a better ground-cover plant. Bearberry will not tolerate alkaline soil; it requires acid soil and plenty of room to ramble. The one species in cultivation is Arctostaphylos uva-ursi, a near-prostrate subshrub that spreads rapidly, rooting where it touches the ground to form a dense mat, 4-6 in (10-15 cm) high, of shiny, leathery oval leaves. In spring it produces pendent, urn-shaped white flowers flushed with pink. The flowers are followed by glistening, scarlet, edible berries in fall.

Cultivation
Plant bearberry in early fall or midspring. It thrives in poor or sandy, cool, moist, acid soil and in sun or partial shade.
Propagation Layer long shoots in early spring and separate them from the parent plant after one year. Alternatively, take heel cuttings in late summer.
Pests/diseases Trouble free.

Arenaria

sandwort

Arenaria montana

Armeria

thrift

Armeria maritima 'Alba'

❏ Height 1-6 in (2.5-15 cm)
❏ Spread up to 1½ ft (45 cm)
❏ Flowers spring and summer
❏ Any very well-drained soil
❏ Sunny or partially shaded site
❏ Evergreen perennial
❏ Hardy to zones 5 and 6

Sandworts *(Arenaria)* are inconspicuous plants, but they are valuable in the rock garden for their ability to creep over rocks. They are evergreen, with leaves so tiny that the plants have a mosslike appearance. Small, usually white flowers cover the plant in spring and summer. *Arenaria* is sometimes confused with the closely related genus *Minuartia* (see p.91).

Popular species

Arenaria balearica (Corsican sandwort) is hardy to zone 6. This plant is ideal for a shady rock garden with moist soil. It is prostrate, growing only 1 in (2.5 cm) in height but spreading to 1½ ft (45 cm). Tiny white flowers are borne abundantly on 1 in (2.5 cm) high stems from early spring to midsummer.

Arenaria ledebouriana forms a 1 in (2.5 cm) high, 8 in (20 cm) wide pincushion of foliage that is studded with brilliant white flowers in summertime. This species is easy to grow, prefers full sun, and is hardy to zone 6.
Arenaria montana thrives in full sun and is hardy to zone 5. It grows 6 in (15 cm) high, with clouds of glistening white flowers produced in early summer above dark green leaf mats. To show it off to its best advantage, plant it in narrow rock crevices; it will eventually cascade over the rocks.

Cultivation
Plant in sun or shade, according to the species, in well-drained, gritty soil in late spring. In wintertime waterlogged soils will cause plants to rot.
Propagation Divide and replant *A. balearica* in early to mid spring. Start *A. ledebouriana* and *A. montana* from seeds sown in pots of gritty soil in late fall; place the pots in a cold frame or other protected spot over the winter.
Pests/diseases Generally trouble free.

❏ Height 3-24 in (7.5-60 cm)
❏ Spread 6-12 in (15-30 cm)
❏ Flowers midspring to midsummer
❏ Any well-drained soil
❏ Sunny site
❏ Evergreen perennial
❏ Hardy zones 3-10

Thrifts *(Armeria)* are delightful in a rock garden or as edgings to a flower border. They grow in small, neat, grassy clumps, with globular blooms on short, sturdy stalks. The flowers are usually pink or white, and they can be so profuse that the foliage can hardly be seen. Miniature species are very effective in concrete troughs.

Popular species
Armeria caespitosa, syn. *A. juniperifolia,* is a compact species that reaches only 3 in (7.5 cm) high, with a maximum spread of 9 in (23 cm). The pink flower heads are almost stemless and are borne from mid to late spring. The leaves are gray-green. The cultivar 'Bevan's Variety' produces deep pink flowers with dark green foliage.
Armeria maritima is native to northwestern Europe and Iceland, flourishing from seacoast to mountain peaks. It is extremely hardy and grows up to 1 ft (30 cm) high, with globular pink flower heads produced in profusion from late spring to midsummer.

Arnica
arnica

Arnica montana

Armeria maritima 'Dusseldorf Pride'

Among the popular cultivars are 'Alba' (white flowers), 'Bee's Ruby' (shocking-pink flowers), 'Bloodstone' (deep-red flowers), 'Dusseldorf Pride' (crimson-magenta blossoms), 'Laucheana' (rich pink flowers), and 'Vindictive' (rich, glowing red flowers). *Armeria pseudarmeria* (pinkball thrift), syn. *A. cephalotes* and *A. grandiflora,* is hardy only to zone 6. It forms a vigorous clump of foliage up to 2 ft (60 cm) tall and 1 ft (30 cm) wide. In summer it bears bright pink flowers, in heads 1-1¾ in (2.5-4.5 cm) wide.

Cultivation
Set young plants in ordinary, well-drained soil in full sun in fall or early to mid spring. Deadhead after flowering.

Thrifts are hardy plants and tolerate both poor soil and seaside conditions.

Propagation Divide and replant in early to mid spring. Alternatively, sow seeds in a cold frame in early to mid spring. Pot the seedlings singly and plunge (with the lip of the pot just above the soil) in an outdoor nursery bed until ready to plant in permanent positions in fall. Or take cuttings of basal shoots during mid to late summer and root in a cold frame.

Pests/diseases Generally trouble free.

- Height 8-24 in (20-60 cm)
- Spread 6-12 in (15-30 cm)
- Flowers in late spring to summer
- Any well-drained soil
- Partially shaded or sunny site
- Perennial
- Hardy zones 2-9

Arnicas have showy flowers. They produce attractive rosettes of slender oval leaves and large, daisylike flowers on tall stems. Arnicas are not easy to grow, but they may spread aggressively in a hospitable spot.

Popular species
Arnica cordifolia, hardy to zone 2, is 8-12 in (20-30 cm) tall. In June and July it bears yellow, daisylike blooms, each one framed by a pair of opposing heart-shaped leaves. It prefers a partially shaded site and is difficult to transplant.

Arnica montana reaches 1-2 ft (30-60 cm) high and 1 ft (30 cm) wide. In late spring or summer, yellow to orange flowers spring from the basal rosette of oblong, hairy leaves. This species prefers full sun; it is hardy in zones 6-9.

Cultivation
Plant in well-drained soil during fall or spring. Arnicas succeed in all types of soil, but *A. montana* flourishes in acid soil.

Propagation Divide and replant in midspring.

Pests/diseases Trouble free.

Artemisia

Artemisia

Asarina

asarina

Artemisia schmidtiana 'Nana'

Asarina procumbens

❑ Height up to 2 in (5 cm)
❑ Trails to 1½ ft (45 cm) or more
❑ Flowers summer and early fall
❑ Any well-drained soil
❑ Partially shaded site
❑ Evergreen perennial
❑ Hardy to zone 7

❑ Height 2-5 in (5-13 cm)
❑ Spread 9 in (23 cm)
❑ Foliage plant
❑ Any well-drained soil
❑ Sunny site
❑ Evergreen subshrub
❑ Hardy zones 4-10

Miniature versions of the familiar silver-leaved artemisia that is often grown in flower borders fulfill the same function in the rock garden — they supply a cool background for other, more colorful plants. When crushed, the evergreen leaves have a sharp but pleasant fragrance.

Popular species and cultivars
Artemisia pedemontana, syn. *A. lanata,* grows up to 2 in (5 cm) high, forming shiny, silvery cushions that spread to 9 in (23 cm). Tiny yellow flowers appear from midsummer to early fall. This species is hardy only as far north as zone 5.
Artemisia schmidtiana 'Nana' has finely cut, glistening, silvergray leaves that grow in a neat dome 3-5 in (7.5-13 cm) high. Dull yellow flowers that are enclosed

in round, woolly, silver bracts appear in early fall.
Artemisia stellerana 'Silver Brocade' forms mats of deeply lobed, felted, gray leaves. This cultivar makes an excellent ground cover.
Artemisia umbelliformis, syn. *A. mutellina* and *A. laxa,* forms a mat of silver-gray leaves that reaches only 2 in (5 cm) high. The pale yellow flower spikes are tall, up to 8 in (20 cm) high, but you should remove them so that the foliage can be seen at its best.

Cultivation
Plant artemisias in spring in any well-drained soil in full sun.
Propagation In late summer take semihardwood heel cuttings and root in a cold frame. Pot rooted cuttings and place outdoors in a sheltered bed; move them to their permanent positions the following spring.
Pests/diseases Aphids may settle on the leaves. The leaves may also be attacked by rust, pale brown spots on the undersides that develop into almost-black pustules.

Asarina procumbens, syn. *Antirrhinum asarina,* is a trailing plant with rounded or broadly heart-shaped, softly hairy, graygreen leaves. The leaves are 2 in (5 cm) long and borne on sticky stems. The plant grows no more than 2 in (5 cm) high but can spread and trail to 1½ ft (45 cm).

Throughout summer and early fall it displays a succession of attractive snapdragonlike, creamyyellow flowers that often have a pinkish flush.

Asarinas will grow in a minimum of soil and are excellent for planting in crevices in a drystone wall or in the angles between walls and paving. However, make sure to site it on the wall's shady side, as this plant likes cool soil in which to spread its roots.

Cultivation
In fall or spring plant asarinas in a partially shaded site in any well-drained soil or in crevices in a wall or between paving stones.
Propagation Root stem cuttings in late summer; the plants selfseed freely.
Pests/diseases Trouble free.

Asperula
woodruff

Asperula suberosa

Asplenium
spleenwort

Asplenium trichomanes

❑ Height 6-12 in (15-30 cm)
❑ Spread 6-12 in (15-30 cm)
❑ Foliage plant
❑ Well-drained, moist, rich soil
❑ Shady site
❑ Evergreen fern
❑ Hardiness varies with species

The graceful evergreen fronds of spleenwort make a good contrast to mat- or clump-forming plants grown in the rock garden. You can grow it in vertical crevices on the north side of walls or rocks.

Popular species
Asplenium adiantum-nigrum (black spleenwort) is hardy to zone 6. It grows up to 9 in (23 cm) high, with pairs of glossy, black-stemmed, triangular fronds.
Asplenium scolopendrium, syn. *Phyllitis scolopendrium* (hart's-tongue fern), is hardy to zone 5. It grows to 12 in (30 cm) high and wide, forming a tuft of shiny light green fronds.
Asplenium trichomanes (maiden-hair spleenwort), hardy to zone 3, grows 10 in (25 cm) tall. Its wiry, arching, black-stalked fronds bear many pairs of rounded pinnae.

Cultivation
Plant in spring or fall in good, moist but well-drained soil in light shade. *A. trichomanes* needs alkaline soil.
Propagation Sow the dustlike spores in early spring. Or divide and replant plants in spring.
Pests/diseases Slugs and scale insects may attack the fronds.

❑ Height 1-3 in (2.5-7.5 cm)
❑ Spread 4-9 in (10-23 cm)
❑ Flowers early to mid summer
❑ Moist, well-drained soil
❑ Sunny site
❑ Perennial
❑ Hardy zones 5-9

One of the prettiest ground-cover plants, woodruff *(Asperula)* forms low cushions of green or gray-green leaves that are smothered with delicate pink, tubular flowers from early to mid summer. Given a well-lit site in moisture-retentive soil, most species are usually easy to grow.

Popular species
Asperula gussonii reaches 1 in (2.5 cm) tall and 8 in (20 cm) wide. It forms a tufted mat of tiny, emerald-green leaves and displays delicate pink flowers in stemless clusters. This species grows well in scree beds or trough gardens.
Asperula suberosa, syn. *A. athoa,* is hardy only to zone 7. It grows 2-3 in (5-7.5 cm) high and about 9 in (23 cm) wide in low carpets of gray, hairy leaves. The flowers are a soft shell-pink. The plant is intolerant of wet soil in wintertime and flourishes in a sunny crevice, scree bed, or trough.

Cultivation
Plant woodruff in mid to late fall or early spring in any well-drained but moist soil in a sunny site. Cut back *A. suberosa* by one-third after flowering in order to promote compact growth. A perfectly drained soil and a mulch of crushed rock or pebbles is necessary to protect this plant from rotting during wintertime in rainy regions.
Propagation Take soft cuttings of nonflowering basal shoots in mid to late spring. Root in a cold frame, then pot up rooted cuttings singly. Grow on in an outdoor nursery bed. Plant out in their permanent positions in spring of the following year.
Pests/diseases Generally trouble free.

Aster
aster

Aubrieta
aubrieta

Aubrieta deltoidea 'Borsch's White'

❑ Height 3-4 in (7.5-10 cm)
❑ Spread 2 ft (60 cm) or more
❑ Flowers early spring to early summer
❑ Well-drained, alkaline soil
❑ Sunny site
❑ Evergreen perennial
❑ Hardy zones 4-9

Aster alpinus

❑ Height 6-24 in (15-60 cm)
❑ Spread 1-1½ ft (30-45 cm)
❑ Flowers early summer to early fall
❑ Any good, well-drained soil
❑ Sunny, open site
❑ Perennial
❑ Hardy zones 4-9

Alpine or dwarf asters are as popular in the rock garden as their larger cousins are in the flower border. These plants are easy to grow, hardy, and extremely free-flowering. As a rule, the smaller species flower earlier than their taller relatives — most bloom from early summer onward.

These asters' soft gray-green leaves are a perfect color contrast to the daisylike flowers that appear in shades in the pink-to-red and blue-to-purple range, each with a prominent golden center.

Popular species
Aster alpinus grows 6 in (15 cm) high in clumps that can spread to 1½ ft (45 cm). The gray-green leaves are narrow and lance-shaped. The flowers, up to 1½ in (3.75 cm) wide, come in varying shades of mauve, blue-purple, and white, with bright orange-yellow centers. They are at their height in midsummer.

Numerous cultivars include 'Albus' (pure white flowers), 'Goliath' (soft blue flowers), 'Happy End' (semidouble, lavender flowers), and 'Trimix' (large flowers in shades of white, blue, or pink). *Aster sericeus* is a North American native that grows up to 2 ft (60 cm) tall. It needs full sun and well-drained soil and is hardy to zone 4. In late summer and early fall it bears large, daisylike blossoms with purplish, curved petals and a yellow, disk-shaped center. *Aster tibeticus,* which is hardy to zone 4, reaches a height of 6 in (15 cm). It has slender, medium green leaves and bears purple-blue flowers, 1-2 in (2.5-5 cm) wide, in early summer.

Cultivation
In fall or early spring plant asters in any fertile, well-drained soil in a sunny, open position. Cut faded flower stems back to soil level after flowering.
Propagation You can divide and replant the roots in midfall or early spring.
Pests/diseases Powdery mildew may appear on the leaves. Aster wilt may be troublesome.

The sight of clumps of aubrietas tumbling over garden walls and rocky ledges is one of the great joys of early spring. Because it is such a common plant and so easily grown, aubrieta is sometimes undervalued, but it is a plant no rock garden should be without. However, it does need to be cut back hard once its glorious flowering display is over. If it is not, it will sprawl all over its neighbors, smothering more choice and delicate plants before they can put on their own show.

Only one species, *Aubrieta deltoidea,* is in general cultivation, but there are many cultivars. The plants grow 4 in (10 cm) high and 2 ft (60 cm) wide or more, in loose mounds or mats that may trail just a little. The leaves are slightly downy and medium to deep green or sometimes variegated. The species itself bears purple, cross-shaped flowers, but the cultivars offer a range of shades: lavender, purple, mauve, crimson, and pink. The individual, four-petaled flowers are no more than ³/₄ in (2 cm) wide but are produced in dazzling profusion.

Aubrieta deltoidea

Bolax
bolax

Bolax gummifera

- ❑ Height ½-2 in (1.25-5 cm)
- ❑ Spread 6-9 in (15-23 cm) or more
- ❑ Foliage plant
- ❑ Well-drained soil
- ❑ Sunny site
- ❑ Evergreen perennial
- ❑ Hardy to zone 7

Bolax gummifera, syn. *Azorella trifurcata,* is an uncommon plant, more of a curiosity than a beauty, although when it flowers in full sun, it gives the impression of molten gold.

The plant grows to 2 in (5 cm) high and forms hard, evergreen hummocks or rosettes of leathery, glossy, light apple-green leaves divided into three oval lobes. The tiny, golden-yellow flowers are stemless and borne in clusters of four. An even smaller cultivar, 'Nana,' grows only ½ in (1.25 cm) high. It is suitable for trough gardens and for planting into cracks in pavement.

Cultivation
Plant bolax in fall or spring in any well-drained soil in full sun.
Propagation Take cuttings of basal shoots in summer and root in a cold frame. Pot up in early spring; plant in permanent sites in fall. Or divide plants in spring.
Pests/diseases Trouble free.

BONNET BELLFLOWER — see *Codonopsis*
BROOM — see *Cytisus, Genista*
BROOM, HEDGEHOG — see *Erinacea*

Popular cultivars
Among the numerous cultivars available are 'Borsch's White' (white flowers), 'Gurgedyke' (deep purple flowers), 'Hendersonii' (violet flowers), 'Leichtlinii' (carmine-pink flowers), 'Purple Gem' (royal purple flowers), 'Royal Cascade' (flowers in shades of red), and 'Variegata' (gray-green leaves edged with creamy yellow).

Cultivation
Plant aubrietas in fall or early spring in well-drained, preferably alkaline soil in a sunny site. Cut rock garden plants back hard after flowering to prevent them from becoming straggly. You can allow aubrietas that trail over walls to grow unchecked.
Propagation Sow seeds indoors in late winter or early spring. Pot the seedlings when well rooted and plunge the pots outside, with the lips of the pots above the soil. Transfer the plants to their permanent positions in fall. Alternatively, root basal-shoot cuttings from established plants in a cold frame or other protected spot.
Pests/diseases Downy mildew may affect the leaves.

AURICULA — see *Primula*
AURINIA SAXATILIS — see *Alyssum saxatile*
AVENS — see *Geum*
AVENS, MOUNTAIN — see *Dryas*
BABY'S BREATH — see *Gypsophila*
BASKET-OF-GOLD — see *Alyssum*
BEARBERRY — see *Arctostaphylos*
BELLFLOWER — see *Campanula*
BELLFLOWER, TRAILING — see *Cyananthus*
BLOODROOT — see *Sanguinaria*
BLUEBERRY — see *Vaccinium*
BLUET — see *Houstonia*
BOG ROSEMARY — see *Andromeda*

Bruckenthalia
spike heath

Bruckenthalia spiculifolia

- ❏ Height 6-8 in (15-20 cm)
- ❏ Spread 1 ft (30 cm)
- ❏ Flowers late spring to early summer
- ❏ Well-drained, acid soil
- ❏ Sunny site
- ❏ Evergreen shrub
- ❏ Hardy zone 6

There is only one species of spike heath: *Bruckenthalia spiculifolia*. It is easy to grow, but because it is a member of the heather family, it needs acid soil. The plant is grown for its 1 in (2.5 cm) long spikes of bell-shaped flowers that are borne between late spring and early summer. They are white in bud, opening to a very pale pink. The leaves are typically heatherlike — vivid green, small, narrow, and bristle-tipped. The plant grows up to 8 in (20 cm) high and 1 ft (30 cm) wide, forming a thick, ground-covering mat.

Cultivation
Plant spike heath in mid to late spring or mid to late fall in well-drained but moisture-retentive, acid soil in a sunny position.
Propagation Divide established plants in spring when they become straggly. Replant rooted portions 1 ft (30 cm) apart. Or take semihard cuttings in late summer and root in a cold frame.
Pests/diseases Trouble free.

BUGLEWEED — see *Ajuga*
BUGLOSS — see *Anchusa*

Bulbocodium
spring meadow saffron

Bulbocodium vernum

- ❏ Height 4-6 in (10-15 cm)
- ❏ Spread 2-4 in (5-10 cm)
- ❏ Flowers early spring
- ❏ Well-drained soil
- ❏ Sunny site
- ❏ Bulbous perennial
- ❏ Hardy zone 6

Spring meadow saffron *(Bulbocodium vernum,* syn. *Colchicum bulbocodium)* is a striking sight when in flower. The almost stemless blossoms appear before the leaves, which gives them the appearance of being scattered on the ground instead of growing from it. The plant is related to *Colchicum,* the fall crocus, which also bears flowers well before it grows leaves.

Each corm produces a cluster of up to three pinkish or violet, funnel-shaped flowers in early spring. The leaves are narrow and straplike, and the plants die back by early summer. They look charming in the rock garden.

Cultivation
Plant the corms 3 in (7.5 cm) deep during early fall in any well-drained soil in a sunny site.
Propagation Lift the clusters of corms every three to four years in early fall. Split them up and replant in new positions immediately. Unless the corms are lifted and split up regularly, flowering will be impaired.
Pests/diseases Trouble free.

BUTTERCUP, ALPINE — see *Ranunculus*

Calamintha
calamint

Calamintha grandiflora

- ❏ Height 4-9 in (10-23 cm)
- ❏ Spread 6-12 in (15-30 cm)
- ❏ Flowers spring and summer
- ❏ Any well-drained soil
- ❏ Sunny site
- ❏ Perennial
- ❏ Hardy zones 5-10

Calamint *(Calamintha)* forms neat hummocks of mintlike, aromatic leaves covered for long periods with small flowers.

Popular species
Calamintha grandiflora grows up to 9 in (23 cm) high and produces bright lavender-pink, tubular flowers throughout summer. The cultivar 'Variegata' has leaves spotted with a creamy white.

Cultivation
Plant calamint in any well-drained soil in a sunny site during fall or spring. This plant flourishes in a warm spot.
Propagation Divide and replant in fall. Or take cuttings in late spring and root in a cold frame or other protected spot.
Pests/diseases Mint rust may affect young shoots.

Calceolaria

slipper flower, pocketbook flower

Calceolaria biflora

- Height 2-12 in (5-30 cm)
- Spread 1-1½ ft (30-45 cm)
- Flowers late spring to early fall
- Any well-drained, moist soil
- Full sun or partial shade
- Perennial
- Hardy zone 6 or 7

The slipper, or pocketbook, flower (*Calceolaria*) is familiar to the plant lover as a potted plant from the florist's shop. Dwarf forms, some of which reach just 2 in (5 cm) high, make an intriguing addition to the rock garden. The pouch-shaped flowers, borne from late spring into early fall, are beautifully marked and mottled.

The dwarf slipper flowers are not winter hardy in the northern states. But they can be treated as annuals and started indoors in late winter or planted in troughs and overwintered in a sheltered, frost-free spot.

Popular species and cultivars

Calceolaria biflora grows 6-12 in (15-30 cm) high from a basal rosette of oval leaves. The 1 in (2.5 cm) long flowers are yellow and are borne on 1 ft (30 cm) high stems in mid to late summer. It is hardy to zone 6.

Calceolaria falklandica, hardy to zone 7, is only 2-4 in (5-10 cm) high. It has narrow, oval leaves. The bright yellow flowers, 1-1½ in (2.5-3.75 cm) long, are spotted chestnut-brown and have a white band across the lower lip. They appear in early summer.

Calceolaria fothergillii is hardy to zone 7. This species has soft,

Calceolaria 'John Innes'

hairy leaves and smaller flowers that are sulfur-yellow spotted with crimson.

Calceolaria 'John Innes' is hardy to zone 7. It is 4-6 in (10-15 cm) high and bears lance-shaped, pale to medium green leaves. In late spring erect stems display one or two 1½ in (3.75 cm) long yellow flowers spotted with brown.

Calceolaria lagunae-blancae is a mat-forming species with trailing stems that root as they grow. It is hardy to zone 7 and reaches a height of only 4 in (10 cm). Bright yellow flowers bloom from late spring to early fall.

Calceolaria polyrrhiza is a creeping species hardy to zone 6. It grows 3-4 in (7.5-10 cm) high, with lance-shaped, medium green leaves. The 1 in (2.5 cm) long yellow flowers appear in early and mid summer.

Cultivation

Calceolarias require fertile, well-drained but moisture-retentive soil. Plant them in mid to late spring. Although the plants prefer a sunny site, they will tolerate partial shade.

Remove faded flower stems after flowering. In the North plant in pots or troughs and overwinter in a cool but frost-free spot.

Propagation Sow seeds in midsummer and place in a cold frame or other protected spot. Pot up the seedlings singly and overwinter in a cool but frost-free location. They should be ready for planting out in their permanent positions in midspring of the following year. Alternatively, you can divide and replant mature specimens in spring.

Pests/diseases Aphids and slugs may cause problems. Red spider mites may also infest calceolarias.

CALIFORNIA FUCHSIA — see *Zauschneria*
CALIFORNIA LILAC — see *Ceanothus*

Campanula

bellflower

Campanula carpatica

- ❏ Height 2-12 in (5-30 cm)
- ❏ Spread 6-24 in (15-60 cm)
- ❏ Flowers late spring to early fall
- ❏ Any well-drained soil
- ❏ Sun or partial shade
- ❏ Herbaceous and semievergreen perennials
- ❏ Hardy zones 3-10

Bellflowers *(Campanula)* form a vast genus, including many tall plants to 4 ft (1.2 m) high; these are best suited to a flower border. However, dwarf species and cultivars are ideal for planting in rock gardens, drystone walls, paving, and troughs and for planting as edgings to beds and borders. Like their taller relatives, dwarf bellflowers are adaptable, thriving in sun or partial shade and producing blue flowers for long periods.

The flower is often bell-shaped, usually pendent, but sometimes erect. Some species have open,

cup-shaped blooms, and others have starlike ones. The leaves are heart-shaped with toothed edges.

Popular species

Campanula alpestris, syn. *C. allionii,* is hardy to zone 5. It spreads by means of underground stems, from which rosettes of narrow, slightly hairy leaves grow. It grows 2-3 in (5-7.5 cm) high and 6 in (15 cm) wide and bears large, purple-blue flowers.

Campanula arvatica is hardy to zone 7. Its leaves form creeping mats of small rosettes. Each rosette produces a stem that carries star-shaped, upturned, deep violet-blue flowers. The plant grows only 2 in (5 cm) high but spreads to 12 in (30 cm).

Campanula carpatica, hardy in zones 3-10, is 6-12 in (15-30 cm) high and spreads in clumps up to 15 in (38 cm) wide. The plant is

Campanula garganica

Campanula cochleariifolia

Campanula portenschlagiana

Campanula raineri

This species is best grown in partial shade. The leaves form broad tufts of shiny, medium green rosettes. Pendent, bell-shaped purple flowers appear in early summer. It is hardy to zone 6.
Campanula raineri is hardy to zone 6. It produces tufts of gray-green leaves 3-4 in (7.5-10 cm) high and bears erect, bell-shaped china blue flowers in midsummer. *Campanula rotundifolia* (hare-bell) is hardy to zone 3. It grows 6-12 in (15-30 cm) high and up to 1½ ft (45 cm) wide. Bell-shaped slate-blue to purple-blue flowers appear from early to late summer. *Campanula saxatilis* is hardy to zone 8. It forms tufts of foliage and, in summertime, bears loose clusters of pale blue bells on stems up to 8 in (20 cm) high.

Cultivation
Plant bellflowers in fall or early to mid spring in any fertile, well-drained soil. (*C. alpestris* does better in neutral to acid soil.) Most plants will do well in sun or light shade.
Propagation Divide and replant clump-forming species in early spring. Alternatively, raise plants from seeds sown in midfall or spring in a cold frame or other protected spot.
Pests/diseases Slugs and snails may damage the plants.

invasive and more suitable for edging. The large, cup-shaped flowers are blue, purple, or white and appear from early summer to early fall. Among its cultivars are 'Blue Clips' (violet-blue), 'China Doll' (lavender-blue), and 'White Clips' (white).
Campanula cochleariifolia (fairy's thimble), syn. *C. pusilla,* is hardy in zones 6-10. This species grows 3-6 in (7.5-15 cm) high but spreads to 12 in (30 cm). The small, pendent, bell-shaped blue or white flowers are borne from early summer to early fall.
Campanula garganica is hardy to zone 6. It grows 6 in (15 cm) high and 12 in (30 cm) wide, producing profuse sprays of star-shaped

blue flowers from late spring to early fall. The cultivar 'Major' displays dark gray flowers.
Campanula portenschlagiana, syn. *C. muralis,* reaches just 6 in (15 cm) high but spreads to 2 ft (60 cm) and is invasive. Deep blue-purple, bell-shaped flowers are borne between mid summer and late fall. It does best in shade, in the crevices in paving or dry-stone walls. It is hardy to zone 5.
Campanula poscharskyana is hardy to zone 3. It grows to 10 in (25 cm) tall and 2 ft (60 cm) wide. Its star-shaped lavender flowers appear between early summer and early fall.
Campanula pulla reaches just 3-4 in (7.5-10 cm) high and wide.

CAMPION — see *Lychnis, Silene*
CANDYTUFT — see *Iberis*

Cardamine
cardamine

Cardamine pratensis 'Flore Pleno'

❑ Height 4-10 in (10-25 cm)
❑ Spread 12 in (30 cm)
❑ Flowers early to mid spring
❑ Any moist soil
❑ Sun or partial shade
❑ Perennial
❑ Hardy zones 3-9

Cardamines belong to the cress family and are moisture-loving plants. Some have watercresslike leaves. The species most often grown is *Cardamine pratensis,* which grows wild in damp meadows. It is suitable for cool, shady rock gardens and is a good choice for wild and woodland gardens.

Popular species
Cardamine pratensis (cuckooflower, lady's-smock) reaches up to 10 in (25 cm) or more high and spreads to 12 in (30 cm). The medium green leaves are divided into rounded leaflets. The white or pale lilac flowers are borne in loose sprays in early spring. The cultivar 'Flore Pleno' is taller than the species, with larger, double flowers.

Cultivation
Plant cardamines in any moist soil in partial shade or sun during spring or fall. They flourish in wet places besides streams or ponds, and the delicate flowers are at their best in such a situation.
Propagation Divide and replant established plants after flowering.
Pests/diseases Trouble free.

Carlina
stemless thistle

Carlina acaulis

❑ Height 1-4 in (2.5-10 cm)
❑ Spread 6-9 in (15-23 cm)
❑ Flowers in summer
❑ Any well-drained soil
❑ Sunny site
❑ Perennial
❑ Hardy zones 5-9

The most famous member of the thistle clan is, of course, an obnoxious weed, but a few of its relatives are actually grown as ornamental plants. *Centaurea* (cornflower) is one example; *Carlina acaulis* (stemless thistle) is another. The latter is the only thistle that is suitable for the rock garden.

Stemless thistle comes from the European Alps and the Pyrenees and prefers a cool, dry climate, such as that found in the Rocky Mountain states. It does not thrive in hot, damp regions, and it prefers alkaline soil, another common feature of gardens in western North America.

The plant grows only 1-4 in (2.5-10 cm) high, occasionally more, and has spreading rosettes of long, deeply divided, spiny, grayish leaves up to 6 in (15 cm) long. The off-white or pale brown flowers are 2-4 in (5-10 cm) wide, almost stemless, and stud the leaf rosettes throughout summer.

Cultivation
Plant stemless thistle in well-drained, nutrient-poor soil in a sunny site in spring or fall.
Propagation Increase by sowing seeds in fall.
Pests/diseases Generally trouble free.

Ceanothus

California lilac, New Jersey tea

Ceanothus americanus

- ❏ Height 4-48 in (10-120 cm)
- ❏ Spread 2-16 ft (0.6-4.9 m)
- ❏ Flowers spring or early summer
- ❏ Well-drained, nutrient-poor soil
- ❏ Sun or shade
- ❏ Evergreen or deciduous shrubs
- ❏ Hardy zones 4-8

Indigenous exclusively to North America, the large genus of *Ceanothus* includes many natives of the Pacific Coast region, as well as a few from the eastern states. There are many fine shrubs among the ceanothuses, but most are too large for the rock garden. Because they thrive in poor, rocky soil and need little irrigation even in the arid West, ceanothuses can be valuable as large-scale ground cover or as a background to more refined plantings.

Popular species

Ceanothus americanus (New Jersey tea) forms a broad but compact shrub 3-4 ft (90-120 cm) high and 3-5 ft (90-150 cm) wide. The dark green, ovate, and deciduous leaves measure 2-3 in (5-7.5 cm) long, and the small, white flowers are displayed in 2 in (5 cm) long bunches at the branch tips in early summer. This species is hardy in zones 4-8.

Ceanothus gloriosus, a prostrate shrub, forms a mat of leathery leaves. It is 4-18 in (10-45 cm) high and 12-16 ft (3.7-4.9 m) wide and is hardy to zone 7. It has deep blue to purplish flowers in spring. *Ceanothus prostratus* (squaw carpet or Mahala mat) is native to the coastal mountains from Washington to California. It is hardy to zone 7 and forms a mat 1 ft (30 cm) high and 8 ft (2.4 m) wide. It bears deep to light blue clusters of flowers from mid to late spring. It does not thrive in summer heat and humidity.

Cultivation

Plant in well-drained, average to rocky soil in spring or fall. Almost all species prefer sun; *C. americanus* will tolerate partial shade. Avoid irrigation after the first year following transplanting.
Propagation Take cuttings of green or mature wood in July or August and root in a cold frame or other moist and protected spot.
Pests/diseases Aphids and whiteflies can be problems.

CELANDINE, LESSER — see *Ranunculus*

Celmisia

celmisia

Celmisia coriacea

- ❏ Height 1-12 in (2.5-30 cm)
- ❏ Spread 1-2 ft (30-60 cm)
- ❏ Flowers late spring and early summer
- ❏ Rich, moist, acid soil
- ❏ Sunny or lightly shaded, sheltered site
- ❏ Evergreen perennial
- ❏ Hardy zones 7-9

Celmisias are often grown for their white, daisylike flowers with golden centers and for their handsome foliage. Many have thickly felted, silvery leaves. The majority of celmisias come from New Zealand and are sometimes called New Zealand daisies. They do best in cool and moist climates, such as those found along coastal Northern California and the Pacific Northwest.

Popular species

Celmisia bellidioides forms creeping mats 1-3 in (2.5-7.5 cm) high and 1 ft (30 cm) wide. One of the easiest species to grow, it bears glossy, dark green, round, and leathery leaves. The flowers appear in early summer.
Celmisia coriacea grows 9-12 in (23-30 cm) high and wide. The sword-shaped leaves are silver above and thickly felted underneath. The flowers appear in early summer. The leaves of the cultivar 'Stricta' are narrower and more silvery than those of the species.
Celmisia sessiliflora is tiny, forming 1 in (2.5 cm) high mats of needlelike, gray-green leaves that

Centaurea
knapweed

Centaurea simplicaulis

❑ Height 10-24 in (25-60 cm)
❑ Spread 10-24 in (25-60 cm)
❑ Flowers late spring to early fall
❑ Well-drained soil
❑ Sunny site
❑ Perennial
❑ Hardy zones 3-10

Some of the knapweeds *(Centaurea)* are large for the rock garden. Still, their adaptability and length of bloom make them a worthy background planting.

Popular species
Centaurea montana (mountain bluet) is hardy in zones 3-10. It grows 1-2 ft (30-60 cm) high and 2 ft (60 cm) wide. The leaves are covered with silvery hairs. The bright purple-blue flowers open from early summer to early fall. *Centaurea simplicaulis,* hardy to zone 4, is a fine ground cover for small bulbs. It is 10 in (25 cm) high and wide. The leaves are dark green above, with silvery undersides. The pink-mauve flowers, borne in late spring and early summer, are followed by attractive, fluffy seed heads; do not deadhead them.

Cultivation
In fall or spring plant knapweeds in any well-drained soil in a site with full sun.
Propagation Increase by sowing seeds or by division.
Pests/diseases Trouble free.

Celmisia walkeri

display short-stemmed flowers in early summer.
Celmisia walkeri, syn. *C. webbii,* grows about 9 in (23 cm) high and forms mounds, up to 2 ft (60 cm) wide, of narrow, leathery, gray-green leaves that are white and hairy on the undersides. In early summer large, finely rayed, daisylike flowers are produced on thin, wiry stems that are 12-15 in (30-38 cm) high.

Cultivation
In fall or spring plant New Zealand daisies in rich, preferably acid, moist but well-drained, gritty soil. Select a site that is sheltered from both summer heat and winter cold. The plants should receive plenty of light, but do not allow them to dry out during hot weather. Of all these species,

C. bellidioides is the most tolerant and hardy.
Propagation You can sow seeds in spring and germinate them in a cold frame or other protected spot. Because seeds lose vitality rapidly, sow them as soon as possible while they are fresh.

Division and taking cuttings in summer are more reliable methods. Once plants are established, take cuttings from side rosettes and root in a cold frame.
Pests/diseases Generally trouble free.

Centaurium

centaurium

Centaurium scilloides

- ❏ Height 3 in (7.5 cm)
- ❏ Spread up to 6 in (15 cm)
- ❏ Flowers late spring to summer
- ❏ Well-drained soil
- ❏ Sun
- ❏ Perennial
- ❏ Hardy to zone 8

Centaurium scilloides is a delightful little plant. It grows in 3 in (7.5 cm) high tufts of small, round, shiny, green leaves. Short stems carry a mass of clear lilac-pink flowers from late spring throughout summer. When fully open to the sun, the flat-faced flowers resemble those of the spring gentian *(Gentiana verna)*, but they are pink instead of blue.

Centauriums are not reliably perennial, but they set seed freely. Once a group has taken root in the garden, new plants will grow from these seeds and replace the old plants. Centauriums are also ideal for trough gardens.

Cultivation
Plant centauriums in fall or spring in any well-drained soil in a sunny position.
Propagation Increase by division in spring or fall. However, the plant is often short-lived, and propagation by sowing seeds is a more reliable method.
Pests/diseases Generally trouble free.

Cerastium

cerastium, mouse-ear chickweed

Cerastium alpinum

- ❏ Height 2-6 in (5-15 cm)
- ❏ Spread 9-24 in (23-60 cm) or more
- ❏ Flowers late spring to late summer
- ❏ Any well-drained soil
- ❏ Sunny site
- ❏ Evergreen perennial
- ❏ Hardy zones 2-10

Cerastium is a popular rock garden plant, but choose and site the species with care, as some are extremely vigorous and invasive. Such rampant species are more suitable as ground covers.

Cerastiums have soft silver-gray leaves and small, delicate white blooms. Some plants flower so profusely that they appear to turn white, earning the common name snow-in-summer.

Popular species
Cerastium alpinum is hardy to zone 2. It grows 2-4 in (5-10 cm) high and 9 in (23 cm) wide, forming mats of gray to pale green, lance-shaped leaves. Clusters of white, star-shaped flowers, ³/₄ in (2 cm) wide, bloom from late spring through summer.
Cerastium biebersteinii (snow-in-summer) grows 4-6 in (10-15 cm) high and spreads to 2 ft (60 cm) or more. The slender, lance-shaped leaves are a woolly silver-gray. The white, cup-shaped flowers, which appear in early summer, are ³/₄-1 in (2-2.5 cm) wide.
Cerastium lanatum is so similar to *C. alpinum* that it is usually classified as a subspecies. It forms attractive woolly, silver tufts, with insignificant flowers.

Cerastium tomentosum

Cerastium tomentosum (snow-in-summer) grows 4-6 in (10-15 cm) high and rapidly spreads to 2 ft (60 cm) or more. It closely resembles *C. biebersteinii,* but the leaves are less woolly and silvery. The flowers are slightly smaller and starlike.

Cultivation
In early to mid spring or in early fall, plant cerastiums in any well-drained soil in a sunny site. The woolly-leaved *C. lanatum* is especially vulnerable to wet and is liable to decay during cold, damp winters.
Propagation Divide and replant in early to mid spring.
Pests/diseases Trouble free.

Chamaecyparis
dwarf false cypress

Chamaecyparis obtusa 'Nana'

Chamaecyparis pisifera 'Filifera Aurea'

❑ Height 6-36 in (15-90 cm)
❑ Spread up to 4 ft (1.2 m)
❑ Foliage shrub
❑ Any well-drained soil
❑ Sun or light shade
❑ Dwarf evergreen conifer
❑ Hardy zones 5-8

False cypresses *(Chamaecyparis)* are hardy, evergreen conifers that are native to North America, Japan, and Taiwan. They differ from true cypresses in that their foliage sprays are flattened.

While the species can reach a height of 40 ft (12 m) or more, there are numerous dwarf cultivars, many with golden foliage, that are suitable for the rock garden. Some of these eventually do become too tall, but because they grow very slowly, this takes many years to happen.

Dwarf cypresses are particularly useful in rock gardens, as they provide year-round interest and color with their conical, globular, or prostrate shapes and foliage that contrasts well with colorful flowering rock plants. The heights given are those a plant can be expected to reach after 10 years.

Popular species and cultivars
Chamaecyparis lawsoniana (Lawson's cypress) cultivars are, in general, narrowly conical, with a pointed top and leading shoots

that droop. They are reliably hardy through zone 6. 'Minima' grows to 1 ft (30 cm) high, forming a globular, or round-topped, plant. 'Nana' is taller, about 2 ft (60 cm), and broadly conical. A similar, blue-green cultivar is 'Minima Glauca.' 'Minima Aurea' and 'Aurea Densa' are attractive golden forms. Because 'Tamariscifolia' reaches a height of 28 in (70 cm) and spreads up to 4 ft (1.2 m), it is suitable only for placement among large rocks;

however, it forms an elegant, uniform, flattened globe.
Chamaecyparis obtusa (Hinoki cypress) is a Japanese species often used for bonsai. It is hardy in zones 5-8. This species has produced numerous dwarf forms, including some of the smallest conifers known. 'Nana' reaches 6-8 in (15-20 cm) high, with dark green foliage carried in tight, rounded sprays. 'Nana Gracilis' grows more quickly than 'Nana,' with larger, shell-like sprays of very dark green. 'Nana Aurea' is a golden form of similar size. 'Pygmaea' has flat, fan-shaped branchlets. It grows into a semi-prostrate shrub 6-8 in (15-20 cm)

Chamaecyparis lawsoniana 'Minima Aurea'

Chiastophyllum
lamb's tail

Chiastophyllum oppositifolium

- Height 4-6 in (10-15 cm)
- Spread up to 1 ft (30 cm)
- Flowers late spring to early summer
- Well-drained, gritty soil
- Sunny or partially shaded site
- Evergreen perennial
- Hardy to zone 7

Chamaecyparis pisifera 'Plumosa Flavescens'

high and 2 ft (60 cm) wide. The foliage is bronze-green, tinged reddish brown in winter.

Chamaecyparis pisifera (Sawara cypress) is hardy in zones 5-8. It includes a number of dwarf cultivars of widely differing appearance. 'Boulevard' is fairly large at 3 ft (90 cm) high but is worth growing for its pyramid of silvery-blue foliage that is at its brightest in light shade. 'Nana,' an extremely slow-growing cultivar, forms a dense, flat-topped dome of dark green foliage sprays. Both 'Aurea Variegata' and 'Nana Aureovariegata' have bright gold new growths, which fade in winter. 'Plumosa Flavescens' forms a dense, compact shrub; it has soft, dark green foliage sprays that are pale golden when young.

The 'Filifera' types of the species have thin, threadlike foliage. 'Filifera' is the tallest, reaching up to 2½ ft (75 cm) high. 'Filifera Aurea' is smaller and grows into a bright gold, domed shrub that retains its color year-round if planted in a sunny site. 'Filifera Nana' is a slow-growing shrub and forms a compact, flat-topped mound.

Cultivation
Dwarf cypresses will flourish in any well-drained soil in an open,

sunny position or in moderate shade. Grow golden cultivars in full sun to preserve their color.

Plant container-grown specimens in midfall in light soil, in midspring in heavy soil. This ensures that the roots remain moist during their settling-in period.

As dwarf conifers do not grow deep roots, when they grow too large for the rock garden you can sometimes transplant them to other sites. Afterward, water them liberally during dry spells.

Some conifers may fork, producing two leading shoots. Some forms of *C. lawsoniana* are especially prone to this. If forking occurs, prune away the weaker shoot as soon as possible.

Propagation Dwarf conifers are grown from cuttings grafted onto a proven rootstock. Home propagation is difficult.

Pests/diseases None serious, although root-rot fungi may occur.

CHAMOMILE, COMMON — see *Anthemis*
CHECKERBERRY — see *Gaultheria*
CHEIRANTHUS — see *Erysimum*

Lamb's tail *(Chiastophyllum oppositifolium,* syn. *Cotyledon oppositifolia)* is an evergreen grown as much for its flowers as for its fleshy, rounded, coarsely toothed leaves. It belongs to the Crassula family. The succulent leaves form low, compact rosettes that spread to mats 1 ft (30 cm) or more wide. The yellow flowers are displayed in arching sprays in late spring and early summer.

Lamb's tail — so named for the appearance of its flower sprays — is suitable for growing in walls and crevices, where the sprays can arch freely without touching the ground. It thrives in sun, but the roots should be protected with some form of shade.

Cultivation
In fall plant lamb's tail in fast-draining, gritty soil in a sunny spot and surround it with a mulch of gravel. Or plant it in partial shade in rock crevices or walls.

Propagation Take tip cuttings in early summer. Allow the cut surfaces to heal before setting them into the rooting medium. Alternatively, separate and replant offsets.

Pests/diseases Mealybugs may show as unsightly tufts of white, waxy wool on new growth.

Chionodoxa
glory-of-the-snow

Chionodoxa luciliae

- ❑ Height 4-8 in (10-20 cm)
- ❑ Spread 2-4 in (5-10 cm)
- ❑ Flowers late winter to late spring
- ❑ Ordinary, well-drained soil
- ❑ Sunny or partially shaded site
- ❑ Bulb
- ❑ Hardy to zone 4

Glory-of-the-snow *(Chionodoxa)* is a hardy, bulbous plant. Its blue, starlike flowers bring color to the rock garden from late winter to late spring.

Popular species
Chionodoxa luciliae bears light blue flowers with white centers. They appear in late winter to early spring and are borne about 6 in (15 cm) above the ground. The cultivar 'Gigantea' reaches 8 in (20 cm) high and produces violet-blue flowers with white eyes. 'Blue Giant' bears bright blue flowers and is 6 in (15 cm) high. A white-flowered cultivar, 'Alba,' and a pink-flowered cultivar, 'Pink Giant,' are also available. *Chionodoxa sardensis* has slender stems that carry nodding, sky-blue flowers with tiny white centers from early to late spring. It grows 4-6 in (10-15 cm) high.

Cultivation
Plant the bulbs in fall in any well-drained soil in sun or partial shade; set them 2-3 in (5-7.5 cm) deep and 4 in (10 cm) apart.
Propagation Glory-of-the-snow self-seeds freely. Or divide when leaves die down after flowering.
Pests/diseases The plants may be damaged by slugs.

Chrysanthemum
alpine chrysanthemum

Chrysanthemum hosmariense

- ❑ Height 6-10 in (15-25 cm)
- ❑ Spread 12-15 in (30-38 cm)
- ❑ Flowers late spring to early fall
- ❑ Well-drained soil
- ❑ Sunny site
- ❑ Perennial or subshrub
- ❑ Hardy zones 6-9

Dwarf chrysanthemums enliven the rock garden with attractive foliage and flowers. Botanists have assigned many of the species to other genera; some are found here because many gardeners know them as chrysanthemums.

Popular species
Chrysanthemum alpinum (now *Leucanthemosis alpina*), hardy to zone 6, is a short-lived perennial. It is 6 in (15 cm) high and 12 in (30 cm) wide, with dissected, deep green foliage. Large, white, daisylike flowers are borne on short stalks in mid and late summer. *Chrysanthemum haradjanii* (now *Tanacetum haradjanii;* often listed as *T. densum* 'Amani'), hardy to zone 8, is 10 in (25 cm) high and 15 in (38 cm) wide. It has silvery, fernlike foliage and clusters of yellow blooms in late summer. *Chrysanthemum hosmariense* (now *Pyrethropsis hosmariense*) is hardy to zone 9. It grows 6-8 in (15-20 cm) high and 12 in (30 cm)

Chrysanthemum haradjanii

wide, with silver-green foliage. It bears white, yellow-centered blossoms in late spring to early fall.

Cultivation
In fall or early to mid spring, plant in any well-drained soil in full sun.
Propagation In early to mid summer take 2-3 in (5-7.5 cm) long cuttings; root in a cold frame or other protected spot. Or divide and replant in fall or spring.
Pests/diseases Trouble free.

CINQUEFOIL — see *Potentilla*
CLOVER — see *Trifolium*

Codonopsis
bonnet bellflower

Codonopsis ovata

- ❑ Height 9-24 in (23-60 cm)
- ❑ Spread 12 in (30 cm)
- ❑ Flowers in summer
- ❑ Well-drained, fertile soil
- ❑ Sunny or lightly shaded position
- ❑ Perennial
- ❑ Hardy zones 5-9

Bonnet bellflowers *(Codonopsis)* are lax climbing plants and ideal for trailing over a rocky ledge or scrambling through other plants.

Popular species
Codonopsis clematidea reaches 1-2 ft (30-60 cm) high — tall for a rock garden plant if supported; however, it is more effective when its stems trail over a ledge or wall. In early to mid summer this species produces white, blue-tinged, bell-shaped flowers with brownish-gold and black markings inside. The small oval leaves are medium green.
Codonopsis ovata has oval, hairy, light green leaves. In mid to late summer it bears pale blue flowers with orange-purple markings. The plant grows 9 in (23 cm) high and 12 in (30 cm) wide.

Cultivation
Plant in fall or early to mid spring in fertile, well-drained soil in a sunny or lightly shaded position.
Propagation Take cuttings of basal shoots in spring and root in a cold frame. Alternatively, sow seeds in early spring in a cold frame or other protected spot and plant out in midfall.
Pests/diseases Trouble free.

COLCHICUM — see
Bulbocodium
COLUMBINE — see *Aquilegia*

Convolvulus
ground morning glory

Convolvulus sabatius

- ❑ Height 6-8 in (15-20 cm)
- ❑ Spread 1-2 ft (30-60 cm)
- ❑ Flowers late spring and summer
- ❑ Well-drained, preferably sandy soil
- ❑ Sheltered, sunny site
- ❑ Perennial
- ❑ Hardy zones 8-10

Because of their invasive habit, most *Convolvulus* species spread rampantly over their neighbors and soon become serious pests. A more manageable species is suitable for growing in the rock garden. This is *Convolvulus sabatius*, syn. *C. mauritanicus*, a delightful little plant from North Africa.

It will not tolerate much frost and needs a warm, sunny, sheltered rock crevice where its trailing stems can form a mat to 6 in (15 cm) high and 2 ft (60 cm) wide. It bears a succession of blue, trumpet-shaped flowers with white throats from late spring into summer and has round, soft gray-green, hairy leaves.

Cultivation
In mid to late spring plant in well-drained, preferably sandy soil in a warm, sunny, and sheltered position. Prune back hard before new growth begins in the spring.
Propagation In summer take 1½-2 in (3.75-5 cm) heel cuttings of basal shoots or side shoots and root in a well-ventilated cold frame or other protected spot. Pot up rooted cuttings, overwinter in a frost-free cold frame or sun porch; plant out in late spring.
Pests/diseases Trouble free.

Corydalis
corydalis

Corydalis cheilanthifolia

- ❑ Height 4-12 in (10-30 cm)
- ❑ Spread 4-12 in (10-30 cm)
- ❑ Flowers midspring to midfall
- ❑ Well-drained soil
- ❑ Sunny site
- ❑ Perennial
- ❑ Hardy zones 5-10

The dainty corydalis species are enchanting plants for rock gardens, drystone walls, and cracks in paving. All have delicate, fern-like foliage and a long display of tubular, spurred flowers.

Popular species and cultivars
Corydalis ambigua reaches 4-6 in (10-15 cm) high and wide. In late spring and early summer it displays blue, purple, or white flowers with upturned spurs. The leaves, composed of rounded leaflets, appear in pairs. The plant is hardy to zone 6 and dies down by midsummer.
Corydalis cheilanthifolia is one of the most popular rock garden plants. It is hardy to zone 6 and grows about 10 in (25 cm) high. This species bears bold tufts of ferny leaves and produces bright yellow flowers throughout late spring and early summer. It makes an excellent ground-cover or edging plant, and it will self-seed freely.
Corydalis flexuosa 'Blue Panda' is hardy to zone 6. It bears electric blue flowers from spring to late summer. It is 6-12 in (15-30 cm) high, forming a compact clump of ferny foliage with flowers emerging on long stems. It prefers partial or dappled shade and is a good choice for a woodland garden with neutral to acid soil.
Corydalis lutea (common yellow corydalis) blooms for several

Crassula
crassula

Crassula multicava

Corydalis wilsonii

months at a stretch and thrives when rooted into the crevices of an old wall or stone paving. It bears dainty, light blue-green, ferny leaves. Yellow flowers, borne on arching stems 1 ft (30 cm) high, appear from midspring to midfall. It self-seeds freely and is hardy in zones 5-10.

Corydalis wilsonii has blue-green, prostrate rosettes of ferny leaves and upright spikes of bright canary-yellow flowers in summer. It is hardy to zone 7 and grows up to 10 in (25 cm) high and wide.

Cultivation
Plant corydalis in early spring in any fertile, well-drained soil in a sunny site. *C. lutea* tolerates some shade, and *C. flexuosa* requires it.

Propagation *C. cheilanthifolia* and *C. lutea* self-seed freely. Sow seeds of other species in a cold frame or other protected spot in late winter to early spring or early to mid fall. Prick out the seedlings, overwinter in a cold frame, and plant out in early to mid spring.

Pests/diseases Generally trouble free.

- ❏ Height 1-12 in (2.5-30 cm) or more
- ❏ Spread 6-15 in (15-38 cm)
- ❏ Flowers in winter, spring, or summer; attractive foliage
- ❏ Very well-drained soil
- ❏ Sunny, sheltered position
- ❏ Evergreen perennial and subshrub
- ❏ Hardy zones 9-10

The *Crassula* genus is best known for its houseplants, but a few of the species are suitable for the rock garden, as long as they are planted in a sheltered area and the garden is located in an area with mild winters. Crassulas have succulent leaves and small star-shaped flowers.

Popular species
Crassula excilis ssp. *cooperi*, syn. *Crassula cooperi*, forms a dense, spreading cushion of small, pointed leaves arranged in whorls. It produces white flowers tinged with pink.

Crassula multicava (fairy crassula) is woody at the base with upright or trailing stems that may reach a height and spread of 1 ft (30 cm). It has glossy, dark green oval leaves that measure 1-3 in (2.5-7.5 cm) long. In late winter or early spring, this species displays delicate clusters of four-petalled flowers that are white tinged with pink; they sit atop pink stems. This is a free-spreading plant with branches that root where they touch the soil; it also drops tiny

plantlets from pollinated flower clusters. The species is hardy in zones 9-10.

Crassula rupestris is called the necklace vine. It is not actually a vine but a sprawling perennial. The leaves, borne on opposite sides of the shoots, connect at the base to give the foliage the appearance of a string of beads. The flowers are pinkish and borne in short terminal clusters. It is hardy in zones 9-10.

Crassula setulosa, syn. *Crassula milfordae*, forms dense cushions of tiny, gray-green rosettes that are 1 in (2.5 cm) tall and 12-15 in (30-38 cm) wide. In winter the leaves are tinted bronze. Crimson buds open into small, white flowers in summer.

Cultivation
Plant in spring in very well-drained soil in full sun.

Propagation Take leaf cuttings in spring or summer. Or raise new plants from seeds in spring.

Pests/diseases Poor drainage promotes fungal infections.

CRANE'S BILL — see *Geranium*

CREEPING JENNIE — see *Lysimachia*

Crepis
hawkweed

Crepis aurea

- ❏ Height 4-9 in (10-23 cm)
- ❏ Spread 9-12 in (23-30 cm)
- ❏ Flowers in summer
- ❏ Any well-drained soil
- ❏ Sunny site
- ❏ Perennial
- ❏ Hardy zones 6-10

Hawkweeds *(Crepis)* will grow in the poorest of soil. Many species are persistent weeds, but those listed here are decorative perennials for the rock garden or the front of a border. They bear dandelionlike flowers in summer.

Popular species
Crepis aurea is hardy to zone 6. It forms basal tufts of oblong, light green leaves; orange-bronze flowers are borne on short stems from midsummer on. The plant grows 4-8 in (10-20 cm) high.
Crepis incana bears rosettes of narrow gray-green leaves covered with soft hairs. The numerous soft pink blooms are borne on 9 in (23 cm) high stems from early to late summer. The species is hardy in zones 7-10.

Cultivation
Plant in well-drained soil in a sunny site in fall or spring. These

Crepis incana

plants do not thrive in hot, humid conditions.
Propagation In midspring sow seeds in shallow pots of seed-starting mix in a cold frame or other protected spot. Prick out the seedlings into individual pots; transplant to permanent sites in late summer or early fall. Or lift, divide, and replant established clumps in mid to late spring.
Pests/diseases Trouble free.

CRETAN DITTANY — see *Origanum*

Crocus
crocus

Crocus vernus

- ❏ Height 2½-4 in (6.25-10 cm)
- ❏ Spread 3-4 in (7.5-10 cm)
- ❏ Flowers spring, fall, or winter
- ❏ Well-drained soil
- ❏ Sunny site or dappled shade
- ❏ Corm
- ❏ Hardy zones 4-9

These dwarf bulbs or corms are a welcome source of spring and fall color in rock and trough gardens. In addition to a large number of true species of crocuses in cultivation, hundreds of cultivars are available with flowers in a wide range of colors.
Unless otherwise stated, the species and cultivars listed here grow 3-4 in (7.5-10 cm) high.

Popular species and cultivars
Crocus angustifolius, syn. *C. susianus,* is hardy to zone 4. Its flowers, just 2½-3 in (6.25-7.5 cm) high, are bronze outside and golden yellow inside. They appear in winter.
Crocus biflorus, hardy to zone 4, bears white flowers flushed with purple-blue in late winter and early spring.
Crocus chrysanthus is hardy to zone 4. It has golden-yellow flowers. Depending on the local climate, it blooms in the open in late winter or early spring.
This species is parent to numerous cultivars. Among them are 'Advance' (yellow-and-violet), 'Blue Bird' (violet-and-white), 'Cream Beauty' (cream), 'E.A. Bowles' (yellow-and-bronze), 'Elegance' (brown-and-gold), 'Goldilocks' (yellow with a bronze-purple base), 'Gypsy Girl' (gold-and-brown), 'Lady Killer'

Crocus chrysanthus 'Lady Killer'

Crocus chrysanthus 'Goldilocks'

Crocus chrysanthus

(purple and pale lilac), 'Princess Beatrix' (blue with a yellow base), 'Snow Bunting' (white), and 'Zwanenburg Bronze' (bronze and golden yellow).

Crocus goulimyi flowers in early fall, bearing pale to deep purple blossoms. It is hardy to zone 7.

Crocus imperati, hardy to zone 7, flowers as early as midwinter in milder regions. The outer petals are buff streaked with purple; the inner ones are satiny purple.

Crocus kotschyanus, syn. *C. zonatus,* is hardy to zone 5. It has lilac-blue flowers spotted with bright orange at the base. They appear in early to mid fall before the leaves form.

Crocus sieberi, hardy to zone 7, bears pale mauve flowers with a yellow base in late winter and early spring. Cultivars include 'Bowles' White' (pure white), 'Tricolor' (deep lilac-blue with white bands and a yellow base), and 'Violet Queen' (violet-blue).

Crocus speciosus, hardy to zone 4, flowers in midfall, bearing lilac blooms with yellow anthers and scarlet stigmas. It is one of the easiest crocuses to grow, and several popular cultivars have been developed, including 'Albus' (white) and 'Cassiope' (aniline blue with a yellow base).

Crocus tomasinianus is hardy to zone 5. It produces lilac flowers in late winter or early spring. The blooms of 'Ruby Giant' and 'Whitewell Purple' are in shades of purple.

Crocus vernus, syn. *C. napolitanus,* is hardy to zone 4. It has variable flowers that may be white, lilac, or purple and sometimes striped. The variety 'Vanguard' is light blue. This species produces flowers in early spring and is one of the parents of the larger-flowered Dutch crocuses.

Cultivation

Plant the corms as soon as they are available: spring-flowering species in fall and fall-flowering species in early summer. Crocuses grow in any well-drained soil in sun or dappled shade. Set the corms in groups 2-3 in (5-7.5 cm) deep and 3-4 in (7.5-10 cm) apart.

Both early-spring- and winter-flowering species are excellent for growing in pots in a cold greenhouse or in the home. Plant the corms in shallow containers of potting soil. You can place about six to eight corms in each 6 in (15 cm) pot.

Do not remove dead flowers when they fade, and allow the leaves to turn brown and die down naturally.

Propagation After the leaves die down, lift the corms and remove any cormels; then replant. *C. tomasinianus* and *C. vernus* increase naturally.

Pests/diseases Mice eat corms in the ground, and bulb mites may infest and destroy corms stored in warm, humid places.

CUCKOOFLOWER — see *Cardamine*

Cyananthus
trailing bellflower

Cyananthus lobatus

❑ Height 2-4 in (5-10 cm)
❑ Spread 1-1½ ft (30-45 cm)
❑ Flowers late summer and fall
❑ Well-drained but moist, acid soil
❑ Sunny site
❑ Perennial
❑ Hardy to zone 4 or 5

The bright blue, funnel-shaped flowers of this plant are reminiscent of gentians. Trailing bellflowers *(Cyananthus)* are worthy of a place in the rock garden and are prized for their fall display.

Popular species
Cyananthus lobatus is hardy to zone 5 and bears bright blue flowers at the tips of its creeping stems in late summer and early fall. It is 4 in (10 cm) high and has a spread of 12-15 in (30-38 cm). 'Albus' produces ivory-white flowers; 'Dark Seedling' displays deep violet flowers.
Cyananthus microphyllus, syn. *C. integer,* the easiest species to grow, is hardy to zone 4. It has small-leaved, trailing stems that spread to 1 ft (30 cm), and it bears blue-purple flowers in early fall. It grows 3 in (7.5 cm) high.

Cultivation
Plant in early to mid spring in rich, neutral to acid soil in a sunny position. The fleshy roots require good drainage and constant moisture.
Propagation Between mid-spring and early summer, take 1½-2 in (3.75-5 cm) long cuttings of basal shoots and root them in a cold frame.
Pests/diseases Trouble free.

Cyclamen
cyclamen

Cyclamen coum

❑ Height 4-6 in (10-15 cm)
❑ Spread 4-6 in (10-15 cm)
❑ Flowers midsummer to late spring
❑ Well-drained, rich soil
❑ Sheltered, shady site
❑ Bulbous plants
❑ Hardy zones 6-9

Tiny cyclamens are ideal for providing color when little else is in flower. They thrive in shady rock gardens and under trees. One or two species are hardy in the North, but none will survive a bitter winter. Most cyclamens do better in mild climates, such as those of the coastal areas in the Pacific Northwest.

Popular species
Cyclamen africanum is hardy to zone 9. It is 4 in (10 cm) high and has broad, dark green leaves splashed with silver-gray. This plant bears pink flowers with crimson mouths in fall.
Cyclamen balearicum is hardy to zone 8. The white flowers, flushed pink at the base, appear in spring after the leaves. It grows 4-6 in (10-15 cm) high.
Cyclamen coum, hardy to zone 6, is 4 in (10 cm) tall. It flowers from early winter to early spring in regions with mild climates. Its medium green leaves are marbled with silver. 'Album' is white; 'Pewter' has pink flowers.

Cyclamen hederifolium (ivy-leaved cyclamen), syn. *C. neapolitanum,* is hardy to zone 6. It bears a profusion of rose-pink flowers in fall, followed by deep green leaves with silver markings that persist until late spring. 'Album' has white flowers.
Cyclamen libanoticum is hardy to zone 9. It is 6 in (15 cm) high and has green, ivy-shaped leaves with a white zone. It has pink flowers in late winter and early spring.
Cyclamen purpurascens, syn. *C. europaeum,* hardy to zone 6, bears carmine flowers from midsummer to early winter. The medium green leaves have silver markings. It is 4 in (10 cm) high.
Cyclamen repandum, syn. *C. vernale,* is hardy to zone 7. It is 4 in (10 cm) high, with medium green leaves marbled silver. Pink, scented flowers appear in midspring.

Cultivation
Plant cylamens in late summer to early fall. Set them in groups 6 in (15 cm) apart, 1-2 in (2.5-5 cm) deep. They require well-drained, humus-rich soil in a shady, sheltered site. In the East even hardy species may succumb to winter weather if they are not protected.
Propagation Increase by sowing seeds.
Pests/diseases Mites may infest greenhouse species.

Cytisus

broom

Cytisus scoparius 'Moonlight'

Cytisus x kewensis

- ❏ Height 6-72 in (15-180 cm)
- ❏ Spread 12-72 in (30-180 cm)
- ❏ Flowers midspring to early summer
- ❏ Any well-drained soil
- ❏ Sunny site
- ❏ Deciduous shrub
- ❏ Hardy zones 5-8

While brooms (*Cytisus*) are not generally long-lived shrubs, they will tolerate poor, dry soil, and these plants are spectacular when in full bloom from midspring to early summer. The flowers, which are borne in profusion, are similar in form to those of sweet peas. The wild-type brooms display flowers that are typically golden yellow, but there are a number of fine cultivars available that bear flowers of several other colors.

The brooms listed here are not small shrubs. Although most of them are too large to plant among the more delicate high-mountain (or alpine) rock garden plants, they are excellent for planting into a rocky outcrop, where the springtime blossoms can cascade down over the boulders.

Popular species and cultivars

Cytisus decumbens is prostrate, growing about 6 in (15 cm) high and 12 in (30 cm) wide. It is hardy to zone 5. The solitary flowers are rich yellow and are produced in profusion during late spring and early summer.

Cytisus × kewensis grows 1-2 ft (30-60 cm) high and is hardy to zone 6. It has a lax, drooping habit and can spread up to 4 ft (1.2 m). The three-lobed leaves are medium green. In late spring cream-white or soft yellow flowers, about ½ in (1.25 cm) long, bloom in great profusion. They are borne singly or in twos or threes in the axils of the previous year's shoots.

Cytisus scoparius is the most commonly available species. The plant is hardy in zones 5-8, and it will grow 5-6 ft (1.5-1.8 m) high, with an equal or even greater spread. The stems are grass-green and attractive in winter. This species has trifoliate leaves that are light to medium green. The flowers are a glowing yellow and appear at the bases of the leaves along the stems.

Among the popular cultivars are 'Burkwoodii' (bushy, compact plant; 1½ ft/45 cm high; garnet-red flowers), 'Dorothy Walpole' (rose-pink and crimson flowers), 'Lena' (3-4 ft/90-120 cm high; ruby-red and pale yellow flowers), 'Lilac Time' (reddish-purple flowers), 'Moonlight' (grows into a low, wide, mounding shrub; cream-white blossoms), and 'Red Favorite' (upright and compact shrub; bold red flowers).

Cultivation

Plant brooms in any well-drained soil in a warm, sunny site in fall or early spring. They will tolerate alkaline soil, although they may be short-lived in such a situation. Buy container-grown plants, as brooms are particularly sensitive to root disturbance.

Prune straggly growth immediately after flowering to encourage new shoots to sprout. Do not cut back into old wood, because this often causes the branches to die back.

Propagation Take 3 in (7.5 cm) long heel cuttings of young side shoots in late summer and root in a cold frame or other protected spot. Alternatively, sow seeds in pots in spring and germinate in a cold frame.

Pests/diseases Generally trouble free, but leaf spot and blight may attack plants; they appear as irregular spots on the foliage and enlarge rapidly to form blotches of diseased tissue.

Daphne
daphne

Daphne cneorum 'Eximia'

❑ Height 3-36 in (7.5-90 cm)
❑ Spread up to 6 ft (1.8 m)
❑ Flowers midspring to early summer
❑ Good, well-drained soil
❑ Sunny or partially shaded site
❑ Deciduous or evergreen shrub
❑ Hardy zones 4-9

Daphnes are fragrant, colorful flowers that appear in late spring and early summer. They are tubular at the base, expanding into four lobes, and are often borne in clusters. Dwarf and mat-forming species are ideal for the rock garden or the front of a border.

Popular species

Daphne alpina is a deciduous species, hardy to zone 5. It is 1½ ft (45 cm) high and 16 in (40 cm) wide. In late spring gray-green leaves and white blooms appear; they are followed by red berries.
Daphne arbuscula is evergreen and hardy to zone 6. It grows 6 in (15 cm) high and 12 in (30 cm) wide. Shiny, leathery, dark green leaves are crowded together at the ends of the branches. It bears rose-purple flowers in clusters in late spring and early summer.
Daphne blagayana, an evergreen species, forms a mat 6 in (15 cm)

Daphne arbuscula

Daphne blagayana

high and 6 ft (1.8 m) wide. Leathery, medium green leaves are crowded toward the tips of the branches, giving the plant a sparse appearance. Creamy-white flowers are borne in clusters in late spring. It is hardy to zone 5.
Daphne cneorum (garland flower) is hardy to zone 4. It reaches a height of 6 in (15 cm) and spreads 2-3 ft (60-90 cm). It is evergreen and the most widely grown daphne, although it may prove difficult to establish in the garden. The slender stems bear small, oval, deep green leaves and dense terminal clusters of rose-pink flowers. 'Alba' has white flowers and is less vigorous. 'Eximia' is a particularly fine cultivar, larger than the species. *D. cneorum* var. *pygmaea* is fully prostrate and free-flowering.
Daphne genkwa, hardy to zone 5, is a tall species, reaching a height of up to 3 ft (90 cm). It may prove difficult to establish in the garden. It is deciduous and bears lavender-blue, lightly scented flowers in mid to late spring.
Daphne jasminea is hardy only to zone 9. It forms a dwarf, semi-prostrate shrub just 1 ft (30 cm) high or even less. The blue-green leaves are 3-4 in (7.5-10 cm) long and evergreen. It bears reddish-purple flowers in clusters at the branch tips in spring.
Daphne tangutica, syn. *Daphne retusa,* is an evergreen, bushy shrub of rounded habit. It slowly reaches a height of 3 ft (90 cm),

Daphne tangutica

with a 1½-2 ft (45-60 cm) spread. It is hardy to zone 6 and has leathery, lustrous, dark green leaves. Pale pink to purple flowers appear in late spring and early summer; they are followed by bright red berries in fall.

Cultivation

Plant daphnes in early fall or early to mid spring in fertile, well-drained soil, including alkaline soil, in sun or partial shade.
Propagation Take heel cuttings from midsummer to early fall and root in a cold frame or other protected spot; grow on and transplant to permanent positions one or two years later.
Pests/diseases Aphids, mealybugs, and scale may infest stems and foliage. Leaf spot may attack foliage, and crown rot may kill whole plants, especially those in shady sites. Viruses may distort young leaves.

Dianthus
pink

Dianthus deltoides   *Dianthus sylvestris*

❑ Height 3-18 in (7.5-45 cm)
❑ Spread 6-24 in (15-60 cm)
❑ Flowers late spring to fall
❑ Any well-drained soil
❑ Sunny site
❑ Evergreen perennial
❑ Hardy zones 3-10

No rock garden should be without pinks *(Dianthus)*. These charming plants have neat clumps of grassy evergreen foliage and dainty flowers that are almost always scented. Numerous species and cultivars are available.

Popular species and hybrids
Dianthus × allwoodii (modern rock pinks), hardy in zones 4-10, are hybrids with complex parentage. They flower profusely, usually in early summer and again in fall, and have gray-green leaves. Among the compact cultivars that reach 10-12 in (25-30 cm) high are 'Aqua' (double, white), 'Danielle Marie' (double, coral-pink), 'Doris' (semidouble, salmon-pink with darker eye; fragrant), 'Helen' (double, salmon-pink), 'Her Majesty' (double, pure white), and 'Pike's Pink' (6 in/15 cm high; double, pink).

Dianthus alpinus forms medium to deep green mats of foliage 4 in (10 cm) high and 6 in (15 cm) wide. The large flowers vary in color from pale pink to purple, with a pale eye ringed with purple spots. 'Albus' is cream-white. This species is hardy to zone 3.

Dianthus arenarius is hardy to zone 3. This 8-12 in (20-30 cm) high plant forms a dense mat, up to 12 in (30 cm) wide, of green or gray-green leaves. White flowers with fringed petals and a green eye appear in summer.

Dianthus deltoides (maiden pink) is hardy in zones 3-10. It grows up to 9 in (23 cm) high, bearing medium to deep green leaves, sometimes tinged with purple. Flowers are borne from early summer to fall. Popular cultivars include 'Albus' (single, white), 'Brilliant' (double, bright crimson), and 'Fanal' (crimson double flowers; bronze foliage).

Dianthus gratianopolitanus, syn. *D. caesius* (Cheddar pink), grows 4-12 in (10-30 cm) tall and 9-12 in (23-30 cm) or more wide. The leaves are gray-green. The flowers are soft pink with fringed petals and appear in summer. The cultivar 'La Bourboulle' (syn. 'La Bourbille') is 6 in (15 cm) wide, with blue-gray foliage and scented pink flowers. This species is hardy to zone 3.

Dianthus monspessulanus, syn. *D. × arvernensis* (Auvergne pink), grows to a height and spread of only 6 in (15 cm). It is hardy to zone 4, has gray leaves, and bears numerous rose-pink flowers from late spring to midsummer.

Dianthus alpinus

Dicentra
Dutchman's-breeches

Dicentra cucullaria

Dianthus gratianopolitanus

Dianthus superbus

Dianthus pavonius (glacier pink), syn. *D. neglectus,* forms dense gray-green tufts of foliage 3 in (7.5 cm) high and 9 in (23 cm) wide. It bears pale pink to deep crimson flowers in summer. This species is hardy to zone 4.

Dianthus superbus (fringed pink) grows 9-18 in (23-45 cm) high and produces white or lavender-pink, fringed flowers in summer. It is hardy in zones 4-9.

Dianthus sylvestris (wood pink) is hardy to zone 5. It forms clumps of silvery-gray foliage. In early and mid summer the single, luminous pink, fringed flowers are borne on wiry stems that reach 4-10 in (10-25 cm) high.

Cultivation
Plant pinks in full sun in any well-drained soil in spring or fall. Troughs, retaining walls, and gaps between paving stones are good sites.

Propagation Only the species will breed true to their type from seeds; they are easily germinated in late spring or early summer. Or take cuttings of side shoots in summer and root in a cold frame or other protected spot.

Pests/diseases Powdery mildew, aphids, and root aphids may be troublesome.

❑ Height 3-6 in (7.5-15 cm)
❑ Spread 3-6 in (7.5-15 cm)
❑ Flowers midspring to early summer
❑ Rich, well-drained soil
❑ Sheltered, shady site
❑ Perennial
❑ Hardy to zone 5

Dutchman's-breeches is the unromantic name given to *Dicentra cucullaria,* a small species related to the bleeding heart (*D. spectabilis*), a popular border plant. The common name refers to the flowers, which are divided into two and vaguely resemble pairs of baggy breeches hanging up to dry.

The plant has a height and spread of 3-6 in (7.5-15 cm), with fleshy, pale to medium green, deeply dissected leaves. The flowers are up to 1 in (2.5 cm) long and white or pale pink with yellow tips. They droop gracefully along the flower stalks from mid or late spring to early summer.

Cultivation
Plant Dutchman's-breeches in well-drained but moist, humus-rich soil in fall or early spring. Choose a shady site sheltered from late-spring frosts and strong winds. Leave the plants undisturbed once planted, as the roots are brittle.

Propagation If plants are crowded, divide and replant between fall and spring. Or take root cuttings in spring; root in a cold frame or other protected spot.

Pests/diseases Trouble free.

Dionysia
dionysia

Dionysia aretioides

- ❑ Height 2-4 in (5-10 cm)
- ❑ Spread 6-12 in (15-30 cm)
- ❑ Flowers spring and early summer
- ❑ Well-drained, gritty soil
- ❑ Sunny site
- ❑ Evergreen perennial
- ❑ Hardy to zone 7

A native of dry limestone mountains in the Middle East, dionysia can withstand frost, but it cannot tolerate weather that is both cold and wet. This fact is not a concern among rock gardeners in the western United States, because dionysia has naturally adapted to the arid climate. In the eastern states, however, growing dionysia can be quite a challenge for rock gardeners.

In the East, provide dionysia with a very well-drained, preferably alkaline soil, and take care to keep the garden free of dropped leaves in fall. If left in place, the leaves soak up rainfall and pack around the plants to provide just the sort of chilly bath that is fatal.

As soon as temperatures consistently drop below freezing during the day, cover the garden with a loose blanket of evergreen boughs. Such a mulch will keep the plants from thawing on sunny afternoons and refreezing at nightfall, a sequence that greatly increases the likelihood of damage to the plants.

Popular species
Dionysia aretioides is the only species of this genus that is commonly available in the United States. It forms dense cushions, 2-4 in (5-10 cm) high and 6-12 in (15-30 cm) wide, of packed rosettes with soft, hairy, gray-green leaves that are slightly toothed at the upper edges. Each rosette produces an almost stemless, yellow, primroselike, scented flower in such profusion that the entire plant is covered with flowers in spring and early summer. It is a variable species; 'Gravetye' is a popular cultivar.

Cultivation
Grow dionysia in a sunny spot in very gritty, well-drained soil that contains some humus. Mulch around the plants with fine limestone gravel and take care not to wet the foliage when watering. Do not overwater.
Propagation Divide mature plants or grow from seeds.
Pests/diseases Generally trouble free, other than the difficulty of cultivation.

DITTANY — see *Origanum*

Dodecatheon
shooting star

Dodecatheon hendersonii

- ❑ Height 4-24 in (10-60 cm)
- ❑ Spread 6-12 in (15-30 cm)
- ❑ Flowers midspring and early summer
- ❑ Rich, moist soil
- ❑ Partial shade
- ❑ Perennial
- ❑ Hardy zones 4-9

Dodecatheon has cyclamenlike flowers with upward-curving petals, which accounts for the plant's common name of shooting star. The flowers range in color from pale pink to crimson and reddish purple. The plant — like its relative, primula — carries its flowers in loose clusters on tall, straight stems rising from low rosettes of large oval leaves.

All but one species of *Dodecatheon* are native to North America. The species described here are suitable for large rock gardens.

Popular species
Dodecatheon alpinum is hardy to zone 6 and grows 4 in (10 cm) or more high and 6 in (15 cm) wide. The flowers, which are reddish purple with a yellow tube and purple ring in the throat, appear in early summer.
Dodecatheon dentatum, hardy to zone 5, grows 6 in (15 cm) high and wide. This species has heart-shaped leaves with serrated edges. It carries white flowers with prominent dark anthers in drooping clusters in late spring and early summer.

Dodecatheon pulchellum

Dodecatheon hendersonii is hardy to zone 6. It reaches 1 ft (30 cm) high from clumps of kidney-shaped leaves. The flowers are deep pink to pale violet and borne on sturdy stalks in late spring.
Dodecatheon jeffreyi is hardy in zones 5-9. This tall species grows 2 ft (60 cm) high and 1 ft (30 cm) wide. It produces unusually large leaves — up to 1 ft (30 cm) long. The flowers, borne in late spring and early summer, are reddish purple with purple stamens.
Dodecatheon meadia is the best-known species and is hardy in zones 4-9. It is 1 ft (30 cm) high and wide and forms pale green leaf rosettes. Flower clusters are borne in late spring and early summer; they consist of numerous rose-pink flowers with white bases and bright yellow anthers.
Dodecatheon pulchellum, syn. *D. pauciflorum,* hardy to zone 5, grows 9-12 in (23-30 cm) high and 6 in (15 cm) wide. In mid and late spring bright lilac-pink flowers are borne in loose clusters, with wavy purple rings in the throats. The cultivar 'Red Wings' displays magenta-crimson flowers. The plants die down by early summer.

Cultivation
Plant shooting stars in rich, moisture-retentive soil in fall or early spring. They flourish in partial shade but will tolerate sun if the soil remains moist.
Propagation In spring or fall divide mature plants. Or sow seeds in spring and germinate in a cold frame or other protected spot.
Pests/diseases Trouble free.

DOROTHEANTHUS — see *Mesembryanthemum*

Douglasia
douglasia

Douglasia montana

❑ Height 1-3 in (2.5-7.5 cm)
❑ Spread up to 1 ft (30 cm)
❑ Flowers late spring and early summer
❑ Any well-drained soil
❑ Sunny site
❑ Perennial
❑ Hardy to zone 5

A small, cushion-forming or creeping plant, *Douglasia* is closely related to *Androsace* and is often confused with it. The species are sometimes listed under *Vitaliana.* The plants grow best in scree beds or troughs or in crevices between rocks, where water can drain away freely. These plants thrive where winters are not excessively wet.

Popular species
Douglasia laevigata forms dense clumps, up to 3 in (7.5 cm) high and 1 ft (30 cm) wide, of small, glossy green leaf rosettes. Dense clusters of bright crimson blooms are carried on 1 in (2.5 cm) stems in late spring and early summer. This species does not do well in alkaline soil or in hot sun.
Douglasia montana is similar to *D. laevigata,* but it produces larger, bright pink flowers that bloom singly or in pairs above the foliage in late spring and early summer.
Douglasia nivalis, syn. *D. dentata,* grows in loose tufts of pale gray rosettes of small, spoon-shaped leaves that are irregularly toothed at the tips. The violet, primroselike flowers appear on 1 in (2.5 cm) high stems in late spring and early summer.

Douglasia vitaliana

Douglasia vitaliana, syn. *Androsace vitaliana* and *Vitaliana primuliflora,* is a mat-forming species, 2 in (5 cm) high and 9 in (23 cm) wide. Bright yellow flowers are borne in early summer above tufts of gray-green foliage.

Cultivation
Plant douglasia in good, well-drained, gritty soil in a sunny site in fall or early spring. Protect the plant from hot summer sunshine; partial afternoon shade may be beneficial.
Propagation To increase, take cuttings in early summer, divide established plants in spring, or sow seeds in spring.
Pests/diseases Generally trouble free, but aphids may infest leaves in summer.

Draba
draba, whitlow grass

Draba rigida

- ❑ Height 1-4 in (2.5-10 cm)
- ❑ Spread 3-9 in (7.5-23 cm)
- ❑ Flowers early spring to early summer
- ❑ Any well-drained soil
- ❑ Sunny site
- ❑ Evergreen perennial
- ❑ Hardy to zone 4, depending on the species

Of the many species of whitlow grass *(Draba)*, a handful are suitable for a rock or trough garden. Those described here form neat hummocks or small tufts of closely packed leaves that are evergreen and decorative year-round. In spring and summer they are covered with yellow, cross-shaped flowers carried on short stems.

Popular species
Draba aizoides is hardy to zone 4 and grows 4 in (10 cm) high. It bears tightly packed rosettes of bristly, dark green leaves. Large clusters of flowers appear on sturdy stems in early to mid spring.
Draba bruniifolia grows only 2 in (5 cm) high, with loose tufts of hairy leaves. The flower clusters are borne on 4 in (10 cm) stems in midspring. It is hardy to zone 7.
Draba mollissima is hardy to zone 6. This species grows just 1 in (2.5 cm) high and 6 in (15 cm) wide. Its hairy, pale gray-green leaves are packed into numerous tiny, tightly crowded rosettes. Bright yellow flower sprays appear in early summer.
Draba polytricha, hardy to zone 7, grows 2 in (5 cm) high and forms hard cushions of gray-green

Draba bruniifolia

leaves covered with small white hairs. The flowers, which bloom in midspring, are pale yellow.
Draba rigida is hardy to zone 7. It grows 3-4 in (7.5-10 cm) high in compact, medium green cushions formed by minute rosettes of leaves. It produces yellow flowers in midspring. *Draba rigida* var. *bryoides* forms a green cushion, 2 in (5 cm) high and 3 in (7.5 cm) wide, of small, rigid leaves; in midspring a few flowers are borne on thin, wiry stems. *D. rigida* var. *bryoides imbricata* is similar but bears showier flowers.

Cultivation
Plant drabas in gritty, very well drained soil in a sunny site in early to mid spring. Avoid wetting the foliage when watering.
Propagation Detach nonflowering rosettes in summer; root in a cold frame or other protected spot.
Pests/diseases Trouble free.

Dryas
mountain avens

Dryas octopetala

- ❑ Height 2-4 in (5-10 cm)
- ❑ Spread 9-36 in (23-90 cm)
- ❑ Flowers in late spring to summer
- ❑ Well-drained soil
- ❑ Sunny site
- ❑ Evergreen subshrub
- ❑ Hardy to zone 2

Mountain avens *(Dryas)*, a mat-forming evergreen plant, is useful as a ground cover planted with bulbs. Anemonelike flowers are followed by fluffy seed heads.

Popular species and cultivars
Dryas octopetala has prostrate, woody stems and oaklike leaves, dark green above and silvery beneath. White, saucer-shaped flowers appear in late spring.
Dryas octopetala 'Minor' grows 2 in (5 cm) high and 9 in (23 cm) wide, with small, oblong, toothed leaves. White blooms, 1 in (2.5 cm) wide, appear in early summer.

Cultivation
Plant dryases in well-drained soil in a sunny site in fall or early spring. Leave undisturbed; they do not tolerate root disturbance.
Propagation Take heel cuttings in summer and root in a cold frame or other protected spot.
Pests/diseases Trouble free.

DUTCHMAN'S-BREECHES — see *Dicentra*
EDELWEISS — see *Leontopodium*

Edraianthus

edraianthus

Edraianthus pumilio

- ❏ Height 1-6 in (2.5-15 cm)
- ❏ Spread 6-9 in (15-23 cm)
- ❏ Flowers late spring to midsummer
- ❏ Any well-drained soil
- ❏ Sunny site
- ❏ Perennial
- ❏ Hardy to zone 6, depending on the species

Edraianthus, which is related to campanula, bears a profusion of rich purple or purple-blue, up-turned, bell-shaped flowers. It thrives in rock and trough gardens, but it is often short-lived.

Popular species
Edraianthus dalmaticus is hardy to zone 6 and grows 3 in (7.5 cm) high and 6 in (15 cm) wide. It forms tufted rosettes of lance-shaped, gray-green leaves. Purple flowers are borne on semipros-trate stems in midsummer.
Edraianthus graminifolius is hardy to zone 8. It forms rosettes of bristly, needle-shaped, gray-green leaves that measure 3 in (7.5 cm) high and 9 in (23 cm) wide. It displays purple flowers from late spring to midsummer.
Edraianthus pumilio is hardy to zone 6. It grows 2-3 in (5-7.5 cm) high in compact clumps. This species bears strap-shaped gray-green leaves, and purple-blue flowers cover the plant from late spring to midsummer.
Edraianthus tenuifolius is hardy to zone 7. It forms tufts of narrow leaves up to 6 in (15 cm) high and

wide. In late spring and summer the plant produces blue-violet flowers in heads composed of as many as 15 blooms.

Cultivation
Plant edraianthus in deep, well-drained soil in a sunny site in fall or early spring. *E. pumilio* is very vulnerable to cold, wet winter weather; give it a spot with perfect drainage and good aeration.
Propagation Take cuttings of nonflowering basal shoots in mid to late summer and root in a cold frame or other protected spot. Or sow seeds in early spring.
Pests/diseases Slugs may feed on young leaves and flowers.

Edraianthus dalmaticus

Epilobium

alpine willow herb

Epilobium obcordatum

- ❏ Height ½-9 in (1.25-23 cm)
- ❏ Spread 1-3 ft (30-90 cm)
- ❏ Flowers early summer to early fall
- ❏ Any well-drained soil
- ❏ Sunny site
- ❏ Perennial
- ❏ Hardy zones 3-9

Epilobium offers a number of mat-forming species ideal for the rock garden. The flowers are shallowly funnel-shaped.

Popular species
Epilobium crassum is hardy to zone 8. It forms a mat of succulent, bronze-brown leaves, ½ in (1.25 cm) tall. The small white blooms are veined with pink.
Epilobium dodonaei is hardy in zones 3-9. It has 2-3 ft (60-90 cm) long stems; narrow, glossy leaves; and clusters of deep-rose flowers from early to late summer.
Epilobium fleischeri is hardy to zone 5. It has sprawling stems, up to 18 in (45 cm) long, but grows only 3½ in (8.75 cm) tall. Its flowers are light or dark purple.
Epilobium obcordatum is hardy to zone 3. It is 6 in (15 cm) tall and bears a profusion of bright rose-purple flowers in summer. 'Strawberry' has smaller leaves and larger flowers than the species.

Cultivation
Plant epilobiums in well-drained soil in full sun in fall or spring.
Propagation Take basal cuttings in spring; root in a cold frame.
Pests/diseases Trouble free.

Eranthis
winter aconite

Eranthis hyemalis

- ❑ Height 3-8 in (7.5-20 cm)
- ❑ Spread 3-4 in (7.5-10 cm)
- ❑ Flowers late winter to early spring
- ❑ Well-drained, moist soil
- ❑ Sun or partial shade
- ❑ Tuberous perennial
- ❑ Hardy to zone 5

The winter aconites *(Eranthis)* are prized for their yellow, buttercuplike flowers, which appear on naked stems above a ruff of deep green leaves. The flowers are borne one to a stem.

Popular species
Eranthis hyemalis is hardy to zone 5. It grows 4 in (10 cm) high, bearing lemon-yellow flowers in late winter. Good for naturalizing, this plant self-seeds freely — in a few years it will be surrounded by a host of offspring.

Cultivation
As soon as the tubers are available in late summer, plant them in well-drained but moisture-retentive soil. The tubers actually begin their growth in early fall, so it is important to get them into the ground as soon as possible. Select a site in sun or partial shade; beneath a deciduous shrub is ideal. Soak the tubers overnight in warm water before planting; set them in groups 1 in (2.5 cm) deep and 3 in (7.5 cm) apart.
Propagation Lift the tubers as the plants begin to die down in late spring; break them into sections and replant immediately.
Pests/diseases Mice and chipmunks may eat the tubers; protect new plantings by scattering moth crystals over the soil.

Erigeron
fleabane

Erigeron x hybridus

- ❑ Height 3-24 in (7.5-60 cm)
- ❑ Spread 6-15 in (15-38 cm)
- ❑ Flowers late spring to late summer
- ❑ Moist, well-drained soil
- ❑ Sunny site
- ❑ Perennial
- ❑ Hardy zones 4-10

The large genus *Erigeron* (fleabane) includes a number of low-growing species that will enliven the rock garden for long periods with their colorful, daisylike flowers. All fleabanes have flowers with large yellow centers that contrast vividly with the outer ring of orange, pink, mauve, blue, or white ray petals. There are also cultivars with semidouble and double flowers.

Popular species and hybrids
Erigeron aurantiacus is hardy to zone 6. This species grows 9-10 in (23-25 cm) high and wide, forming a mat of velvety gray-green leaves. Solitary, bright orange-yellow flowers are displayed on stout, leafy stems from early to late summer.
Erigeron aureus forms clumps that reach just 3-4 in (7.5-10 cm) high, with spoon-shaped, medium green leaves. This species bears orange-yellow flowers on violet, hairy stems in mid to late summer. It is hardy in zones 4-10
Erigeron borealis grows to 12 in (30 cm) tall, forming tufts of narrow, rounded, soft hairy leaves. The daisylike flowers are purple. The species is hardy to zone 6.
Erigeron compositus is hardy to zone 5. It reaches a height of about 3 in (7.5 cm) and forms tiny tufts of deeply cut, gray-green, woolly leaves. This plant displays purple flowers in summer.

Erinacea
hedgehog broom

Erigeron karvinskianus

Erinacea anthyllis

❑ Height 10 in (25 cm) or more
❑ Spread 10 in (25 cm)
❑ Flowers late spring and early summer
❑ Deep, well-drained soil
❑ Sunny, sheltered site
❑ Evergreen subshrub
❑ Hardy to zone 8

Erigeron flettii is hardy to zone 5. It forms 6 in (15 cm) tufts of gray-green, 1 in (2.5 cm) wide leaves. It displays white blossoms in May and is suitable for a trough or scree garden.

Erigeron × hybridus is hardy to zone 6. It can grow 2 ft (60 cm) high, but there are more compact cultivars that make good rock garden plants. Among them are 'Prosperity' (18 in/45 cm tall; lavender-blue flowers) and 'Rose Jewel' (15-18 in/38-45 cm; lilac-rose flowers).

Erigeron karvinskianus, syn. *E. mucronatus,* is 9-10 in (23-25 cm) tall and produces numerous tiny flowers that vary in color from white to rich pink. It is hardy in zones 9-10. This is a creeping species that is ideal for walls and crevices in paving. It can become invasive, as it self-seeds readily.

Erigeron linearis grows up to 6 in (15 cm) high, with a spread of up to 12 in (30 cm). Its leaves are gray, hairy, and linear. Solitary, bright yellow blossoms appear in early summer. This species is hardy to zone 4.

Erigeron simplex grows up to 8 in (20 cm) high and 12 in (30 cm) wide. It carries gray, hairy leaves. In early and mid summer, this species produces pure white flowers. It is hardy to zone 4.

Cultivation
Plant fleabanes in mid to late fall or early spring in moist but very well drained soil. Good drainage is especially important in the eastern states; there fleabanes are best suited to planting on a gravelly slope, such as a scree.

Fleabanes usually require a sunny site. Some of the species, however, will find a south-facing slope too hot. *E. aureus,* for example, thrives best when set on a cooler, north-facing slope.

Deadhead the plants regularly to prevent the spread of self-sown seedlings and to encourage further flowering later in the season. Cut the stems down to ground level in fall.

Propagation Divide and replant the roots between midfall and early spring. Alternatively, sow seeds in mid to late spring in pots placed in a cold frame. Prick out the seedlings into flats, then into a nursery bed. You can transfer the plants to their permanent positions in fall.

Pests/diseases Generally trouble free.

Hedgehog broom *(Erinacea anthyllis,* syn. *Erinacea pungens)* bears profuse clusters of violet-blue pea flowers in late spring and early summer. It forms a dome-shaped mound of hard, many-branched, smooth, gray-green stems that are tipped with sharp spines. The slender, lance-shaped, gray-green leaves are covered with silky hairs. These leaves are sparse and quickly fall.

In its natural habitats in Spain, France, and North Africa, hedgehog broom can grow 3 ft (90 cm) high, but it is extremely slow-growing. A cultivated specimen will take several years to reach a height of 9 in (23 cm).

Cultivation
Plant hedgehog broom in alkaline soil in a sunny scree bed. Unless it has bright light and excellent drainage, it will rot. Once established in the garden, it should not be transplanted; this plant does not tolerate root disturbance.

Propagation Take softwood cuttings in late spring or early summer; root in a propagation unit.

Pests/diseases Aphids may infest young growth.

Erinus

erinus

Erinus alpinus

- Height 3-4 in (7.5-10 cm)
- Spread 6 in (15 cm)
- Flowers early spring to late summer
- Any well-drained soil
- Sunny site
- Evergreen perennial
- Hardy to zone 6

Erinus alpinus produces a mass of tiny, starry flowers that appear from early spring to late summer. These flowers almost smother the medium green, spoon-shaped, deeply toothed leaves.

Although it is not a long-lived plant, erinus self-seeds freely. It is a good plant to grow in a drystone wall, in the cracks in paving, or in troughs or scree beds. As it is evergreen and has a long flowering period, it provides interest year-round.

Popular cultivars include 'Albus' (white flowers), 'Dr. Hanelle' (carmine-red flowers), and 'Pikos de Europa' (light pink flowers on prostrate stems).

Cultivation

Plant erinus in a drystone wall, a paved area, trough garden, or scree bed in fall or early spring in well-drained soil in a sunny site.
Propagation Collect ripe seeds from mature plants and scatter them where the plants are to grow. Alternatively, plant seeds in pots of seed-starting mix placed in a cold frame or other protected spot. The cultivars given here do not come true from seeds; instead, you should divide and replant clumps of established plants in early spring.
Pests/diseases Trouble free.

Erodium

heron's-bill, storksbill

Erodium glandulosum 'Roseum'

- Height 1-9 in (2.5-23 cm)
- Spread 9-15 in (23-38 cm)
- Flowers midspring to early fall
- Well-drained, preferably alkaline soil
- Sunny site
- Perennial
- Hardy zones 6-10

Heron's-bill *(Erodium),* or storksbill, belongs to a large genus that is closely related to the true geranium, or cranesbill. It is similar in many respects, although this plant is more wiry and elegant in its growth habit. Several species are small and compact; they have attractive five-petaled, saucer-shaped flowers. These plants are ideal for the rock garden.

Popular species

Erodium absinthoides is hardy in zones 6-10. It grows about 6 in (15 cm) high and has deeply cut, gray-green foliage. Loose heads of rosy-lilac flowers are carried on upright stems in summer.
Erodium cheilanthifolium forms a mound of foliage and flowers 8 in (20 cm) tall and 10 in (25 cm) wide. Its light gray foliage gleams with silvery highlights in full sun. The plant bears white flowers veined with cerise and stained with a purple-black blotch. It is hardy to zone 6. The cultivar 'White Pearls' is pure white.
Erodium chrysanthum is hardy to zone 7. It grows 4-6 in (10-15 cm) tall and 12 in (30 cm) wide, forming tufts of deeply divided, fernlike, silvery foliage. It bears small sprays of sulfur-yellow flowers from late spring through summer.
Erodium glandulosum, syn. *E. macradenum,* is hardy to zone 6. It grows up to 9 in (23 cm) high, with deeply divided, fernlike green foliage. The lilac flowers, which are borne throughout summer, have dark violet blotches on the two upper petals. The cultivar 'Roseum' has rose-colored flowers with darker veining and is the only generally available form.
Erodium reichardii, syn. *E. chamaedryoides,* hardy to zone 7, is exceptionally low-growing — reaching a height of just 1-2 in (2.5-5 cm). It forms a spreading

Erysimum
wallflower

Erodium glandulosum

Erysimum pulchellum

mat of round-toothed green leaves. The flowers, borne from early to late summer, are white with pink veins. 'Roseum' has pink flowers with crimson veins, and 'Album' has white blooms.

Cultivation
In midspring plant heron's-bills in well-drained soil in full sun. They do better in alkaline soil than in acid soil and grow particularly well in tufa.

Propagation In early spring take root cuttings of *E. reichardii* from the thickest parts of the root. Leave them in a cold frame and pot when three or four leaves have formed. Take basal-shoot cuttings from other species in midspring; root in a cold frame.

Pests/diseases Plants may be infested with aphids.

Erodium reichardii 'Roseum'

❑ Height 5-12 in (13-30 cm)
❑ Spread 4-12 in (10-30 cm)
❑ Flowers midspring to summer
❑ Any well-drained soil
❑ Sunny site
❑ Perennial
❑ Hardy zones 5-10

Wallflowers *(Erysimum)* are dainty versions of their large border cousin *Cheiranthus.* The species described here are all perennials and suitable for a rock garden. They are fairly short-lived but self-seed freely, and they thrive in poor and chalky soil.

Popular species
Erysimum capitatum, syn. *Cheiranthus capitatus,* is a subshrubby species hardy to zone 6. It grows 8-10 in (20-25 cm) high and bears dark green, lance-shaped leaves. Large heads of scented, cream-white flowers appear in mid and late spring and occasionally at other times of the year.
Erysimum helveticum, syn. *E. pumilum,* grows in neat tufts; 3 in (7.5 cm) high stems carry fragrant, yellow flowers in flat heads in late spring and early summer. It is hardy to zone 6.
Erysimum hieraciifolium, syn. *Cheiranthus alpinus,* is hardy to zone 7. It is 6 in (15 cm) high,

with lance-shaped foliage. Sulfur-yellow flowers in loose clusters appear in late spring.
Erysimum kotschyanum, hardy to zone 6, grows 5 in (13 cm) high and 8 in (20 cm) wide. It forms tufts of rigid, narrow leaves and bears short-stemmed heads of large yellow flowers in summer.
Erysimum linifolium is hardy in zones 5-10 and will grow 9-12 in (23-30 cm) high. It is subshrubby and semievergreen, with narrow blue-gray leaves and clusters of pale lilac flowers in early summer.
Erysimum pulchellum, hardy to zone 6, is 12 in (30 cm) tall. It produces spoon-shaped or oblong leaves. Sulfur-yellow flowers are borne in early summer.

Cultivation
In mid to late fall or early spring, plant wallflowers in full sun. They thrive in any soil, even a poor or alkaline one.

Propagation Take heel cuttings in mid or late summer and root in a cold frame. Pot singly and overwinter in the cold frame or other protected spot; transplant to permanent sites in midspring.

Pests/diseases Trouble free.

Euryops
euryops

Euryops acraeus

❏ Height up to 12 in (30 cm)
❏ Spread 12 in (30 cm) or more
❏ Flowers late spring and early summer
❏ Well-drained but moist soil
❏ Sunny site
❏ Evergreen shrub
❏ Hardy to zone 7

Euryops acraeus, syn. *E. evansii*, is the only species of this genus of evergreen shrubs hardy enough to be grown in the temperate regions of the United States. It is a dwarf shrub suitable for a sunny rock garden. It forms a compact, low-growing mound of woody stems that carry narrow, silver-gray leaves. In late spring and early summer it is covered with a profusion of bright yellow, daisy-like, 1 in (2.5 cm) wide flowers.

Euryops comes from the Drakensberg Mountains in South Africa, but it is winter hardy through zone 7, provided it is given a position in full sun.

Cultivation
Plant euryops in well-drained but moist, gritty, even poor soil in a sunny site in midspring. Set out container-grown plants to minimize root disturbance. Deadhead regularly to encourage successive flowering. Prune straggly or badly placed shoots in spring in order to maintain shape.
Propagation Take cuttings of semimature branches in summer and root them in a cold frame.
Pests/diseases Trouble free.

EVENING PRIMROSE — see *Oenothera*
FALSE CYPRESS (DWARF) — see *Chamaecyparis*
FESCUE GRASS — see *Festuca*

Festuca
fescue grass

Festuca glauca

❏ Height 3-9 in (7.5-23 cm)
❏ Spread 4-6 in (10-15 cm)
❏ Ornamental evergreen grass
❏ Any well-drained soil
❏ Sunny site
❏ Hardy to zone 5

Fescue grasses *(Festuca)* form dense domes of slender evergreen leaves topped in summer by blue-gray flower spikes. They provide year-round color to rock gardens and edgings.

Popular species
Festuca alpina reaches a height of 4-6 in (10-15 cm). This species produces bright green, threadlike leaves in dense tufts. The pale green flower spikes are borne in late summer.

Festuca glauca will grow 6-9 in (15-23 cm) high as dense clumps of tough blue-gray leaves.

Cultivation
Plant festuca in well-drained soil in a sunny site in fall or early to mid spring. Cut off the flower spikes before they develop or the clumps will lose their neat shape.
Propagation Sow seeds in mid-spring in an outdoor nursery bed. Or divide clumps in fall.
Pests/diseases Trouble free.

FIR, DWARF — see *Abies*
FLAX — see *Linum*
FLEABANE — see *Erigeron*
FORGET-ME-NOT — see *Myosotis*

Frankenia
sea heath

Frankenia thymifolia

❏ Height 2-3 in (5-7.5 cm)
❏ Spread 2 ft (60 cm)
❏ Flowers mid to late summer
❏ Any well-drained soil
❏ Sunny site
❏ Evergreen perennial
❏ Hardy to zone 8

Sea heath *(Frankenia)* belongs to a small genus of evergreen plants that grow wild along seacoasts in temperate and subtropical regions. The species recommended here is native to Spain and North Africa. It is a creeping and mat-forming plant that is useful for year-round ground cover, and it is not too rampant. Sea heaths are ideal plants for covering the gaps left in plantings by spring bulbs when their foliage dies down in early summer.

Popular species
Frankenia thymifolia has creeping 3 in (7.5 cm) high stems. They are clothed with gray-green, downy leaves and tinted crimson-red in early fall. As the plant's name suggests, the foliage is heatherlike. Rose-pink flowers appear during midsummer in numerous tiny, stemless clusters. Though not hardy in the North, this plant makes a fine addition to a trough or other type of container garden that can be moved to a protected spot in winter.

Cultivation
In fall to spring plant sea heath in any well-drained, ideally sandy soil in a sunny site.
Propagation Divide plants in midspring and root in a cold frame until reestablished.
Pests/diseases Generally trouble free.

Fritillaria
fritillary

Fritillaria verticillata

❏ Height 6-24 in (15-60 cm)
❏ Spread up to 8 in (20 cm)
❏ Flowers mid to late spring
❏ Rich, well-drained soil
❏ Sunny or partially shaded site
❏ Bulbous perennial
❏ Hardy zones 4-7

Fritillaries are members of the charming lily family. They carry linear or slender, lance-shaped leaves, singly or in pairs, along upright, slender stems and bear pendent, bell-shaped, subtly colored flowers. Fritillaries can be difficult to grow, and many species do not thrive in the wet, cold winters of the eastern states. Those described here are suitable for growing in groups in a sunny rock garden. The plants die down by midsummer.

Popular species
Fritillaria acmopetala, one of the easiest species to grow, reaches 15-18 in (38-45 cm) high. Its strap-shaped leaves are medium green. Two or three bell-shaped flowers appear in midspring, with three pale green outer petals surrounding three smaller inner petals that are purple-brown outside and yellow-green veined with brown inside. It is hardy to zone 7.
Fritillaria pallidiflora, 12-15 in (30-38 cm) high, has stout stems with lance-shaped gray-green leaves. In midspring clusters of greenish-yellow bell-shaped flowers appear at the tips of the stems. It is hardy to zone 5.
Fritillaria pudica grows to 8 in (20 cm) high, with strap-shaped leaves scattered along the stems. Pendent, bell-shaped, deep yellow and orange-tinged flowers usually appear singly in midspring. This species is hardy to zone 4.
Fritillaria pyrenaica grows 6 in (15 cm) or more high. Its slender stems are set with narrow, lance-shaped, gray-green leaves. The bell-shaped, drooping flowers are borne singly at the tips of the stems in midspring; they are deep brown or purple-black and checkered. It is hardy to zone 5.
Fritillaria verticillata is hardy to zone 6 and grows to 2 ft (60 cm) high. It carries slender, lance-shaped leaves in opposite pairs or in whorls along the stems. In mid and late spring the white,

Fuchsia
trailing dwarf fuchsia

Gaultheria
wintergreen

Fuchsia 'Tom Thumb'

- ❏ Height 2-9 in (5-23 cm)
- ❏ Spread 2 ft (60 cm)
- ❏ Flowers summer and fall
- ❏ Fertile, well-drained soil
- ❏ Full sun or light shade
- ❏ Deciduous shrub
- ❏ Hardy to zone 9

Gaultheria miqueliana

- ❏ Height 2-12 in (5-30 cm)
- ❏ Spread up to 3 ft (90 cm)
- ❏ Flowers late spring to late summer
- ❏ Moist, acid soil
- ❏ Partial shade
- ❏ Evergreen shrub
- ❏ Hardy zones 4-9

Fritillaria pallidiflora

pendent, bell-shaped flowers, with green markings, are borne in loose spikes.

Cultivation
Plant fritillaries from early to late fall in a sunny site as soon as the fleshy bulbs are available. Plant them in well-drained, fertile soil. Make sure you handle the bulbs carefully — they are easily bruised and are damaged by prolonged exposure to air. Plant the bulbs 4-6 in (10-15 cm) deep, placing them on their sides so that the hollow crowns do not retain water. Alternatively, surround the bulbs with coarse sand.

Do not disturb the bulbs for at least four years. You should cut the stems to ground level when they die down in summer.
Propagation Buy seeds, or collect them when ripe from plants; sow at once in a cold frame. Because it takes six years for young plants to reach flowering size, it is better to buy new bulbs. Or take offsets from parent bulbs and grow them in pots or a cold frame until they reach flowering size.
Pests/diseases Trouble free.

Though generally intolerant of frost, the fuchsias include a few hardier cultivars; several dwarf types are good for a rock garden.

Popular species and hybrids
Fuchsia hybrids will grow 6-9 in (15-23 cm) high. They bear pendent, tubular flowers that expand into wide bells with prominent stamens. While the flowers may be one color, they are often bicolored; they bloom throughout summer. Popular types include 'Alice Hoffman' (red and white), 'Pumila' (scarlet and violet), and 'Tom Thumb' (carmine-pink and purple; hardy to zone 6).
Fuchsia procumbens is a prostrate plant. Only 2 in (5 cm) high, it will spread and trail up to 2 ft (60 cm). Each tiny flower consists of a yellow tube with backward-curving green-and-purple sepals.

Cultivation
Plant fuchsias in any humus-rich, well-drained soil in sun or light shade once any danger of spring frost is past. In cold regions cut the plants down completely in late fall and cover with a mulch.
Propagation Take nonflowering tip cuttings in spring and root in a propagation unit.
Pests/diseases Fuchsias are particularly attractive to whiteflies.

FUCHSIA, CALIFORNIAN — see *Zauschneria*

Wintergreens *(Gaultheria)* are useful ground-cover plants. Some species grow only a few inches high; others are much taller. They are decorative year-round; urn-shaped, white or pink flowers are followed by globular berries in the fall. All wintergreens spread by means of underground runners. They are ideal for large rock gardens and peat beds and as ground cover on banks.

Popular species
Gaultheria hispidula, a procumbent shrub that forms a creeping mat, is hardy to zone 6. The tiny leathery leaves are hairy beneath. Solitary white flowers appear from late spring into summer and are followed by white berries.
Gaultheria humifusa is hardy to zone 6. Of a dense, compact habit, it grows just 2 in (5 cm) high. It bears rounded, wavy-edged foliage. Bell-shaped pinkish-white flowers are borne in summer and followed by small, scarlet berries.
Gaultheria miqueliana, hardy to zone 6, grows 1 ft (30 cm) high and 3 ft (90 cm) wide. The leaves are dark green, toothed, and oval-shaped. Clusters of small white flowers appear in early summer, followed by globular white berries often flushed with pink.

Gaultheria procumbens

Gaultheria nummularioides is hardy only to zone 9. A densely hairy prostrate shrub, it reaches 6 in (15 cm) tall and 8 in (20 cm) wide. The branches are clothed with rows of leathery, oval leaves. White, pink-flushed flowers are carried in late spring and early summer; the berries that follow are blue-black.

Gaultheria procumbens (checker-berry, partridgeberry), a creeping species, grows 3-6 in (7.5-15 cm) high and spreads to 3 ft (90 cm) or more. Hardy to zone 4, it has toothed oval leaves that are a shiny dark green and clustered at the tips of reddish, hairy stems. Tiny white or pink flowers are carried in short terminal sprays during mid to late summer. They are followed by bright red globular berries.

Gaultheria pyroloides, syn. *G. pyrolifolia,* is hardy to zone 6. A prostrate, creeping plant of tufted habit, it forms dense mats of slender stems just 4 in (10 cm) high. The leaves are glossy bright green above, hairy underneath, with toothed edges. White flowers flushed with pink appear from late spring to midsummer; the berries that follow are black.

Cultivation
Gaultherias require a moist, acid soil enriched with peat or other acidic organic matter. Plant in early fall or in mid to late spring in partial shade but away from overhanging trees, which may drip and damage the leaves.

Propagation Take heel cuttings of lateral shoots in mid to late summer and root in a cold frame or other protected spot. Pot the following spring and plunge in soil outdoors. Plant out in fall.

Pests/diseases Trouble free.

Genista
broom

Genista sylvestris

❑ Height 1-36 in (2.5-90 cm)
❑ Spread up to 6 ft (1.8 m)
❑ Flowers late spring to late summer
❑ Any well-drained soil
❑ Sunny site
❑ Deciduous shrub
❑ Hardy zones 2-9

The brooms *(Genista)* are valued for their golden-yellow pea flowers and make handsome shrubs for borders or specimen planting. Several species are small enough to be planted in a rock garden.

Popular species
Genista lydia is commonly grown in borders, where it reaches a height of 2-3 ft (60-90 cm) and spreads up to 6 ft (1.8 m). It is useful for covering banks or for trailing over rock ledges in large rock gardens. Arching branches carry narrow gray-green leaves. Bright yellow flowers are borne freely in 3 in (7.5 cm) long sprays on spine-tipped shoots in late spring. It is hardy in zones 7-9.

Genista sagittalis forms prostrate mats of winged stems that bear a few dark green leaves. It spreads to 12 in (30 cm). Closely packed golden flowers appear in terminal clusters in early summer. This species is hardy to zone 4.

Genista sylvestris (Dalmatian broom), syn. *G. dalmatica,* is hardy to zone 6. It is 6 in (15 cm) high and 2-3 ft (60-90 cm) wide, forming compact hummocks with narrow, dark green leaves. Bright yellow flowers in densely set terminal sprays appear in early to mid summer. This plant makes an excellent ground cover.

Genista tinctoria (dyer's green-weed) is a variable species, ranging from a prostrate plant just 6 in (15 cm) high to an upright shrub with slender, grooved stems that is 3 ft (90 cm) high and 6 ft (1.8 m) wide. This outstandingly cold-tolerant plant is hardy to zone 2. The slender lance-shaped leaves are dark green. It flowers from early to late summer. The popular cultivars include 'Golden Plate' (up to 12 in/30 cm high; of spreading habit) and 'Plena' (about 8 in/20 cm high; with golden double flowers).

Cultivation
In fall or early to mid spring, plant container-grown young specimens in any well-drained soil in full sun. Do not feed or mulch, as they grow best in poor, dry soil.

Propagation Take heel cuttings of lateral shoots in late summer and root in a cold frame or other protected spot.

Pests/diseases Trouble free.

Genista lydia

Gentiana
gentian

Gentiana clusii

Gentiana acaulis 'Alba'

- ❑ Height 3-10 in (7.5-25 cm)
- ❑ Spread up to 18 in (45 cm)
- ❑ Flowers spring to summer or fall
- ❑ Rich, moist, well-drained soil
- ❑ Sun or partial shade
- ❑ Evergreen perennial
- ❑ Hardy zones 3-9

Gentians have perhaps the most brilliant blue flowers of any garden plant, and no rock garden would be complete without them. There are two basic types — the European species, which start to flower in spring, and the Asiatic species, which are generally fall-flowering. The typical gentian bloom is trumpet-shaped, but bell or star shapes also occur. The exquisite gentians are exacting in their demands — the European species usually tolerate alkaline soil, while the Asiatic species, which are easier to grow, flourish in acid soil.

Most gentians have narrow lance-shaped leaves. Those described here are invaluable in rock gardens, raised beds, and troughs; Asiatic species do well in beds heavily enriched with peat.

Popular species
Gentiana acaulis, syn. *G. excisa,* a European species, is hardy to zone 3. It grows 3 in (7.5 cm) high and forms an 18 in (45 cm) wide mat of glossy, deep green leaves. Brilliant deep blue flower trumpets, speckled green inside, are

Gentiana saxosa

borne in late spring and early summer; the flowering habit is often unpredictable. The cultivar 'Alba' has white flowers.
Gentiana clusii is a European species hardy to zone 6. Rosettes of stiff, leathery, glossy leaves form tufts 6 in (15 cm) high. It bears large azure-blue flowers that may be spotted with green inside. The plant prefers alkaline soil and a sunny site.
Gentiana dinarica, a European species, is hardy to zone 6. It forms tufts up to 5 in (13 cm) high and wide. A free-flowering

species, it bears large bright blue flowers in early summer. It flourishes in full sun in alkaline soil.
Gentiana frigida, another European species, is hardy to zone 5. Erect stems rise from a basal rosette of thick, pale green leaves to form a tuft 6 in (15 cm) tall and wide. It displays solitary creamy-yellow flowers streaked and freckled with purple. This species does not tolerate alkaline soil.
Gentiana saxosa, a New Zealand species, is hardy only through zone 8. It produces 4 in (10 cm) high tufts of shiny green leaves

65

Gentiana verna

Gentiana septemfida

that are spoon-shaped. Small cup-shaped white flowers are borne in late summer.

Gentiana septemfida is an Asiatic species that is hardy in zones 3-9. This species, which grows to 8 in (20 cm) high and 12 in (30 cm) wide, is extremely hardy, free-flowering, and easy to grow in any soil. It forms compact domes of medium green leaves. Clusters of bell-shaped violet-blue flowers appear in summer.

Gentiana sino-ornata is an Asiatic, fall-flowering species that is hardy to zone 6. Easy to grow and free-flowering in acid soil, it reaches a height of 6 in (15 cm), with a spread of 12 in (30 cm). It bears rosettes of slender, medium green leaves. Trumpet-shaped, 2 in (5 cm) long, rich blue flowers appear in fall. The cultivar 'Mary Lyle' has creamy-white flowers.

Gentiana verna (spring gentian) is a European species, usually represented by the cultivar 'Angulosa.' Hardy to zone 5, this is a dainty plant, only 3 in (7.5 cm) high and 6 in (15 cm) wide. It carries tufts of medium green, ovate leaves. The intense blue, starry flowers appear from late spring to midsummer. This species is usually short-lived.

Cultivation

Plant gentians in fall or early spring in fertile soil enriched with organic matter; select a sunny or

Gentiana acaulis

partially shaded site. All gentians need moisture-retentive but well-drained soil, which should be acidic for the Asiatic species. Water in summer.

Divide *G. sino-ornata* every two to three years in spring.

Propagation Most gentians can be increased by dividing and re-planting mature plants in early spring. *G. acaulis* is the exception; it is best lifted in early summer. Alternatively, take cuttings from basal shoots in late spring

and root in a cold frame or other protected spot. *G. verna* 'Angulosa' is best raised from seeds sown as soon as they are ripe; stem cuttings can also be taken immediately after flowering.

Pests/diseases Gentians are usually free of pests, but they can be infected by root-rot fungi, particularly in poorly drained soil.

Geranium

geranium, cranesbill

Geranium dalmaticum

Geranium sanguineum var. striatum

Geranium renardii

- ❏ Height 3-18 in (7.5-45 cm)
- ❏ Spread 6-24 in (15-60 cm)
- ❏ Flowers late spring to midfall
- ❏ Any well-drained soil
- ❏ Sun or partial shade
- ❏ Herbaceous or semievergreen perennial
- ❏ Hardy zones 4-10

Dwarf forms of the true geranium, or cranesbill, are as important to the rock garden as the large geraniums are to the flower garden. Dwarf geraniums are compact or carpeting plants, often with semievergreen leaves;

some have attractive fall coloring. These dwarf plants often bloom longer than their larger counterparts; flowers range in color from white to pale lilac to magenta-pink and crimson-purple. Their common name comes from the shape of the seed heads.

Popular species and cultivars

Geranium cinereum is hardy to zone 5. It grows 4-6 in (10-15 cm) high and 12 in (30 cm) wide. Its round to kidney-shaped gray-green leaves are divided into five or seven wedge-shaped lobes.

Crimson-magenta flowers with almost black centers appear from late spring to midfall. Popular cultivars include 'Apple Blossom' (pale pink), 'Ballerina' (lilac-pink with dark centers and red veins), 'Giuseppii' (crimson-purple), 'Lawrence Flatman' (pink flowers marked with crimson), and 'Splendens' (salmon-pink). The variety *subcaulescens* is 4-6 in (10-15 cm) tall, with round, lobed gray-green leaves. A profusion of bright crimson-magenta, black-centered flowers appears from late spring to midfall.

Geranium dalmaticum is hardy to zone 5. It grows 6 in (15 cm) high and forms a dense, low cushion of deeply cut, rounded, glossy, medium green leaves that are tinted red in fall. Delicate clusters of pale pink flowers appear from early to late summer. The cultivar 'Album' has white flowers.

Geranium nodosum is hardy to zone 6 and grows 18 in (45 cm) high. Its deeply divided leaves have unevenly toothed margins; those along the stems are a shiny bright green. This species bears

Geranium sanguineum 'Alpenglow'

Geranium cinereum var. subcaulescens

Geranium cinereum 'Ballerina'

lilac-rose flowers over a long period in summer.

Geranium orientalitibeticum, syn. *G. stapfianum,* is hardy to zone 8. It grows to 6 in (15 cm) high and 12 in (30 cm) wide. It has bright green, silver-marbled foliage and bears pink flowers with white centers in June. This is an excellent species for a scree bed.

Geranium renardii is hardy in zones 4-10 and reaches up to 9 in (23 cm) high and 2 ft (60 cm) wide. It has soft gray-green, deeply lobed round leaves. Pale lavender, purple-veined flowers are borne from late spring to midsummer. The species will thrive in poor soil.

Geranium sanguineum (bloody cranesbill) is hardy in zones 4-10. It grows 6-10 in (15-25 cm) high and spreads to 1½ ft (45 cm) and makes an effective ground cover. The leaves are dark green and deeply lobed. Crimson-magenta flowers are displayed from early summer to early fall. 'Album' is a slightly smaller cultivar with white flowers; the low-growing 'Alpenglow' has rose-red flowers. The variety *striatum* has rose-pink flowers with darker veins.

Geranium tuberosum is hardy in zones 6-9 and reaches a height of 10 in (25 cm), with a spread of up to 8 in (20 cm). The finely cut snowflakelike leaves emerge from tuberous roots in early spring. Big rosy-purple to violet flowers appear in May. This plant dies back to the ground in summer.

Cultivation

In early fall to early spring, plant geraniums in any well-drained soil in a site with sun or partial shade. If the site is not sheltered and sunny, *G. cinereum* is best planted in early spring. You can encourage new growth and a second flush of flowers by cutting the stems back to ground level after flowering.

Propagation Divide and replant at any time in fall or early spring. Alternatively, sow seeds in early fall, and overwinter in a cold frame or other protected spot. Set out in nursery rows for the summer and transplant in fall.

Pests/diseases Slugs may eat young plants. Mildew and rust cause stunting and discoloration.

GERMANDER — see *Teucrium*

Geum

avens

Geum reptans

❏ Height 6-12 in (15-30 cm)
❏ Spread 9-15 in (23-38 cm)
❏ Flowers late spring to midsummer
❏ Rich, neutral to acid soil
❏ Sunny or partially shaded site
❏ Perennial
❏ Hardy to zone 6

Avens *(Geum)* is a plant with long-lasting appeal. Its neat rosettes of bright green leaves are attractive by themselves; they are enhanced from late spring to midsummer, when large, saucer-shaped and roselike, golden-yellow or bright orange flowers rise above the foliage on slender stems. The flowers are followed by attractive, fluffy, silver-pink seed heads.

Popular species
Geum montanum grows 6-12 in (15-30 cm) high, with a spread of up to 1 ft (30 cm). Its medium green leaves are deeply lobed and carried in pairs along the stems, with a larger terminal lobe at the tip. The golden-yellow flowers are 1 in (2.5 cm) wide. The cultivar 'Lamb's Variety,' an evergreen plant, produces extra-large flowers on 4-6 in (10-15 cm) stems from spring to frost.
Geum reptans is very similar to *G. montanum* but is the larger of the two species, with a height of 9-12 in (23-30 cm) and a spread up to 15 in (38 cm). This species develops conspicuous red runners, but it can be difficult to establish. It is best grown in a sunny scree bed with acid soil.

Geum montanum, seed heads

Cultivation
Plant avens in fall or early spring in sun or partial shade in soil that is enriched with organic matter. *G. reptans* needs acid soil.
Propagation Divide plants in early to mid spring and replant at once. *G. reptans* produces small plantlets on runners; you can detach the plantlets in summer and treat them like seedlings. Or sow seeds in 3 in (7.5 cm) pots of compost and place in a cold frame. Plunge the seedlings in an outdoor bed in spring (with the lips of the pots at soil level) and plant out in fall.
Pests/diseases Generally trouble free.

GLOBE DAISY — see *Globularia*

Globularia

globe daisy

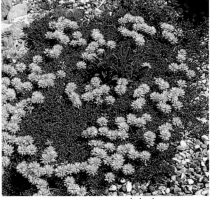

Globularia repens

❏ Height 1-12 in (2.5-30 cm)
❏ Spread up to 1½ ft (45 cm)
❏ Flowers late spring to early summer
❏ Well-drained soil
❏ Sunny site
❏ Evergreen subshrubby perennial
❏ Hardy to zone 5

Globe daisy *(Globularia)* is a delightful plant that bears puffs of lavender-blue flowers in early summer. Some species grow in rosettes of leathery, paddle-shaped leaves; others grow as tangled stems covered with minute spear-shaped leaves. When well established, the plants form useful ground-covering mats.

Popular species
Globularia cordifolia is hardy to zone 6. It grows 2 in (5 cm) high, spreading its woody stems to 8 in (20 cm). This is an evergreen, shrubby species with small, dark green, oval leaves notched at the tips. Round, fluffy lavender-blue flowers appear on short stems during early summer.
Globularia meridionalis, syn. *G. bellidifolia,* is hardy to zone 5. It grows 9 in (23 cm) high and wide in tangled mats of woody stems with glossy dark green leaves. The flowers are blue to lavender-purple and carried on short stems in early summer.
Globularia nudicaulis, an herbaceous species, has tufts of leathery green leaves. It is almost leafless, and 6-9 in (15-23 cm) high stems rise from the center of the leaf rosettes, carrying round heads of clear blue flowers in early summer. This species is hardy to zone 5.
Globularia punctata, hardy to zone 5, forms rosettes of rounded, leathery leaves. The pale blue

Gypsophila
baby's breath

Globularia nudicaulis

bell-shaped flowers are borne on
9-12 in (23-30 cm) high stems in
early summer.

Globularia repens, syn. *G. nana,*
is similar to *G. cordifolia* but even
smaller. It is hardy to zone 6 and
spreads to a dense mat of tangled
stems covered with minute, dark
green, leathery leaves. It creeps
attractively, forming an evergreen carpet over rocks, walls,
and ledges. The flower heads,
which are almost stemless, are
pale blue fading to lilac.

Globularia trichosantha grows
about 9 in (23 cm) high and is
hardy to zone 6. It is herbaceous
and very similar to *G. nudicaulis,*
with leafless stems and fairly
large, medium blue flower heads.
It is somewhat coarser in growth.

Cultivation
In early to mid fall or in early to
mid spring, plant globe daisies in
any well-drained soil in full sun.
They thrive in alkaline soil and
will do well in scree beds and in
soil pockets.

Propagation Divide clumps in
fall or spring. Alternatively, take
stem cuttings in summer and root
in a cold frame.

Pests/diseases Trouble free.

GLORY-OF-THE-SNOW — see
Chionodoxa
GOLDEN DROP — see *Onosma*
GOLDENROD — see *Solidago*
GRAPE HYACINTH — see
Muscari
GROUND BOX — see *Polygala*
GROUND MORNING GLORY
— see *Convolvulus*

Gypsophila aretioides

- Height 2-6 in (5-15 cm)
- Spread 6-24 in (15-60 cm)
- Flowers late spring to late summer
- Any well-drained soil
- Sunny site
- Perennial
- Hardy zones 3-10

Dwarf species of *Gypsophila* (baby's breath), with their semievergreen foliage and delicate pink or
white flowers, are perfect for rock
gardens, walls, and sunny banks.

Popular species
Gypsophila aretioides is hardy to
zone 5. It grows 2 in (5 cm) high
but spreads to a 9 in (23 cm) wide
cushion of tiny, oval gray-green
leaves. It bears white or pale pink
flowers in early summer.

Gypsophila cerastioides, hardy to
zone 5, grows 3 in (7.5 cm) high
and wide, with clumps of oval,
gray leaves. It produces saucer-
shaped white flowers marked
with purple veins in late spring
and early summer.

Gypsophila repens is hardy in
zones 3-10. It grows 6 in (15 cm)
high and forms a 2 ft (60 cm) wide
mat of many-branched, wiry stems
and narrow gray-green leaves.

Gypsophila cerastioides

Sprays of white to deep pink flowers appear from early to late summer. The cultivar 'Rosea' is pink.

Cultivation
In early spring or early fall, plant
baby's breath in well-drained soil
in a sunny site. *G. repens* is best
planted where it can trail over
rocks or walls.

Propagation Root young shoots
of *G. aretioides* in a cold frame or
other protected spot in spring. Divide and replant *G. cerastioides* in
spring or fall. Take basal-shoot
cuttings of *G. repens* in spring
and root in a cold frame.

Pests/diseases Trouble free.

Haberlea
haberlea

Haplopappus
haplopappus

Haberlea rhodopensis

Haplopappus acaulis

- ❑ Height 6-12 in (15-30 cm)
- ❑ Spread 1 ft (30 cm)
- ❑ Flowers early to late summer
- ❑ Any well-drained soil
- ❑ Sunny site
- ❑ Evergreen perennial
- ❑ Hardy to zone 3

- ❑ Height 3-6 in (7.5-15 cm)
- ❑ Spread 6-9 in (15-23 cm)
- ❑ Flowers late spring
- ❑ Enriched, well-drained soil
- ❑ Shaded site
- ❑ Perennial
- ❑ Hardy to zone 6

Haberlea is a useful rock garden plant because it is one of the few that prefer a shady site. It thrives in crevices in north-facing rocks or walls. The plant has proportionally large leaves, with prominent veins and toothed edges. They contrast well with the delicate frilled petals of the flowers.

Popular species
Haberlea ferdinandi-coburgii grows 4-6 in (10-15 cm) high and spreads 6-9 in (15-23 cm). It forms a rosette of thick, dark green oval leaves. The lilac-pink flowers have frilled lobes and are about 1 in (2.5 cm) wide; the long throats are white inside, spotted with gold. The flowers are produced three or four to a spray on 4-6 in (10-15 cm) high stems during late spring.
Haberlea rhodopensis reaches a height of only 3 in (7.5 cm) but spreads 6-9 in (15-23 cm). It is similar to *H. ferdinandi-coburgii* but is smaller and its flowers are

lavender-pink. 'Virginalis' is a pure white cultivar.

Cultivation
Plant haberleas in early fall or early spring in well-drained soil, preferably enriched with organic matter. They flourish in cool, shady sites. Ideally, plant them in vertical rock crevices so that rain is prevented from accumulating in the rosettes, causing the plants to rot. If necessary, wedge small pieces of turf around the plants, with the grass side in, to keep the plants in place.
Propagation Mature plants can be divided in spring, but the most rapid method of obtaining new plants is by taking leaf cuttings in early to mid summer. Gently remove whole, mature leaves from the plants and insert up to one-third of their length in potting soil in a cold frame or other protected spot. Pot up in early spring and keep in the cold frame. Plant out in early fall.
Alternatively, sow seeds in spring in a cold frame or other protected spot.
Pests/diseases Slugs may eat leaves and flower stems.

Haplopappus is a member of the daisy family and bears typical rayed flowers with a central boss of a delightful golden color. This 1 ft high, subshrubby perennial is somewhat large for the rock garden, but it is compact and neat-looking. Because the plants are evergreen where hardy, they are useful for winter interest as well as for summer color.

Popular species
Haplopappus acaulis, syn. *Stenotus acaulis,* is hardy to zone 3. It grows into a mat, 6 in (15 cm) tall and 12 in (30 cm) wide, of glossy leaves on green or red-brown stems. The yellow flower heads measure 1 in (2.5 cm) wide.
Haplopappus glutinosus, syn. *H. coronopifolius,* is hardy to zone 8. It grows 1 ft (30 cm) high, forming a mound of dark green, leathery toothed leaves. A profusion of golden-yellow daisies, carried on upright, wiry stalks, is produced in early to late summer.

Cultivation
In early to mid fall or mid to late spring, plant haplopappus in any fast-draining soil in a sunny site.
Propagation Divide and replant mature plants in spring. Alternatively, take stem cuttings in summer and root in a cold frame.
Pests/diseases Trouble free.

HAWKWEED — see *Crepis, Hieracium*

Hebe
hebe

Hebe buxifolia 'Patty's Purple'

Hebe 'Youngii'

- ❏ Height 2-48 in (5-120 cm)
- ❏ Spread 6-36 in (15-90 cm)
- ❏ Flowers late spring to fall
- ❏ Any well-drained soil
- ❏ Sunny site
- ❏ Evergreen shrub
- ❏ Hardy zones 7-9

Dwarf hebes are ideal for sunny rock gardens, brightening them throughout summer with lilac, purple, or white spikes and clusters and throughout the year with their neat foliage. Most hebes are natives of New Zealand, and as such they are not reliably cold hardy in the northern states. They flourish, however, in such temperate regions as the Pacific Coast; when planted inland, they should be protected from the hot afternoon sun. Because hebes are tolerant of salt, they make excellent seaside plantings.

Popular species and hybrids
Hebe 'Autumn Glory' forms a compact mound 2 ft (60 cm) high and wide. The leaves are oval and 1½ in (3.75 cm) long. Spikes of dark lavender-blue flowers, 2 in (5 cm) long, are borne in late summer and fall.
Hebe buchananii grows only 2 in (5 cm) high and 6 in (15 cm) wide. It is a cushion-forming species that consists of dense, wiry twigs with tiny, round, green leaves. The white flowers, which are borne in summer, are small, stemless, and sparse.
Hebe buxifolia reaches up to 4 ft (1.2 m) high, but it may be kept more compact through pruning. The lustrous dark green leaves

are ½ in (1.25 cm) long; they resemble those of boxwood. The flowers appear in midsummer and consist of 1 in (2.5 cm) long white spikes. 'Patty's Purple' has pink-purple flowers. This species is most tolerant of heat and cold.
Hebe chathamica is another ground-cover shrub. This species reaches a height of 1½ ft (45 cm) and spreads to 3 ft (90 cm). The leaves are ½ in (1.25 cm) long and deep green; the lavender flowers appear in summer.
Hebe pinguifolia 'Pagei' is 6-9 in (15-23 cm) high and 2 ft (60 cm) wide or more. It is a hardy plant that carries gray-green leaves and produces white blossoms.
Hebe 'Youngii,' syn. H. 'Carl Teschner,' grows 1 ft (30 cm) high and 2 ft (60 cm) wide. It carries gray-green leaves and purple flowers. This plant is suitable for ground cover.

Cultivation
Plant hebes in early to mid fall or mid to late spring. They thrive in most well-drained soils, including alkaline ones. Set in full sun where temperatures do not rise too high; in hot inland areas, provide the plants with some shade. In zone 7 they will benefit from being planted against a warm, south-facing boulder or outcrop. Deadhead all species immediately after flowering. If a plant becomes leggy, cut it back hard in midspring; new shoots usually break freely from the base.

Hebe pinguifolia 'Pagei'

Propagation Take tip cuttings of nonflowering shoots in summer and root in a cold frame.
Pests/diseases Downy mildew and leaf spot may discolor leaves. Fusarium wilt, a fungal disease, is a common problem in Southern California; it may cause the wilting of leaves, the death of branches, or the demise of whole plants. When shopping for hebes, reject any unhealthy-looking plants; dying leaves and a brownish discoloration inside the stems are signs of fusarium wilt.

HEDGEHOG BROOM — see Erinacea
HEDYOTIS — see Houstonia

Helianthemum
rockrose, sunrose

Helianthemum 'Wisley Pink'

Helianthemum 'Raspberry Ripple'

❑ Height 3-8 in (7.5-20 cm)
❑ Spread 1-3 ft (30-90 cm)
❑ Flowers midspring to midsummer
❑ Any well-drained soil
❑ Sunny site
❑ Evergreen shrub
❑ Hardy zones 5-10

The hardy, free-flowering rockroses, or sunroses *(Helianthemum),* are not planted as often as

Helianthemum 'Fire Dragon'

they should be in American rock gardens. They are dwarf, twiggy bushes, up to 8 in (20 cm) high, that produce a delightful display of colorful flowers from midspring to midsummer (depending on the local climate), with an occasional blossom opening thereafter. The flower colors range from pure white through pink and yellow to dark red.

Because the plants can spread to 3 ft (90 cm) wide, give rockroses plenty of room; otherwise they can overrun other, less aggressive plants. Rockroses are useful for growing in large rock gardens, on sunny banks, and on retaining walls. They also make fine container plantings for a sunny terrace or patio.

Popular species and hybrids
Helianthemum nummularium, the most widely grown species, is hardy in zones 5-10. It reaches a height of 4-6 in (10-15 cm), with a

spread of about 2 ft (60 cm). The oval leaves are deep green above, paler underneath. The flowers appear in profusion in early and mid summer.

The species has been superseded by numerous hybrids, in which *H. nummularium* has been mated with another species. These include the 'Ben' series, such as 'Ben Heckla' (coppergold) and 'Ben Nevis' (tawny orange-gold). Other hybrids are 'Fire Dragon' (vermilion), 'Henfield Brilliant' (orange-red), 'Jubilee' (yellow double flowers), 'Raspberry Ripple' (pink-and-white-striped blossoms; silver leaves), 'St. Mary's' (white), 'Wisley Pink' (pink), and 'Wisley Primrose' (soft yellow flowers). *Helianthemum oelandicum* ssp. *alpestre* is only 3-4 in (7.5-10 cm) high, but it spreads to about 1 ft (30 cm). This species produces oval, medium green leaves and displays bright yellow flowers in abundance. It is hardy to zone 6.

Cultivation
Plant rockroses in any well-drained soil in a sunny spot in fall or spring. Once the plants are established, they will tolerate considerable drought; take care not to overwater them. Cut *H. nummularium* back hard after flowering to maintain a neat shape. Trim all rockroses after flowering to encourage fresh blooms.
Propagation Take heel cuttings of nonflowering lateral shoots in summer and root them in a cold frame. Set the plants out in their permanent positions the following spring.
Pests/diseases Powdery mildew and leaf spot may occur on the leaves.

Helichrysum
strawflower

Helichrysum arenarium

❑ Height 6-20 in (15-50 cm)
❑ Spread 6-20 in (15-50 cm)
❑ Flowers spring to fall
❑ Any very well drained soil
❑ Sunny, sheltered site
❑ Evergreen perennial subshrub or annual
❑ Hardy zones 4-9

The alpine species of strawflower (*Helichrysum*) are grown for their handsome gray-green, or woolly white, evergreen foliage, though some also bear attractive flowers.

Popular species
Helichrysum arenarium, a shrubby species, is hardy to zone 4. It is 1 ft (30 cm) high and wide, with woolly whitish-gray foliage and loose clusters of 2 in (5 cm) yellow to orange-red flowers in summer. *Helichrysum scorpioides*, a frost-sensitive plant, is hardy to zone 9. It is shrubby and reaches 16 in (40 cm) high. Its woolly leaves are whitish above, gray-green beneath. Solitary flower heads appear in fall; they are brown with a yellow center and woolly.
Helichrysum selago, hardy to zone 8, is a compact, wiry shrublet, 6-9 in (15-23 cm) high and wide. It has closely overlapping, scalelike, silver-gray leaves; buff-white flowers appear in summer.
Helichrysum subulifolium, an annual, grows 20 in (50 cm) high. Erect stems bear pointed, glossy green leaves. Solitary brownish flower heads, ½ in (1.25 cm) wide, appear in spring and summer.

Cultivation
In early fall or late spring, plant in any very well drained soil in a sunny, sheltered site. Protect the perennial species in winter.
Propagation Take heel cuttings of side shoots in early summer.
Pests/diseases Downy mildew may occur.

Helichrysum selago

HEMLOCK, CANADIAN — see *Tsuga*

Hepatica
hepatica

Hepatica nobilis

❑ Height 4-10 in (10-25 cm)
❑ Spread 6-12 in (15-30 cm)
❑ Flowers late winter to early spring
❑ Rich, moist soil
❑ Partial shade
❑ Semievergreen perennial
❑ Hardy to zones 4 and 5

Hepatica was formerly classified as *Anemone*, and it resembles that genus closely. It thrives in shady woodland conditions and flowers in late winter or early spring, before the trilobed, medium green leaves have fully developed.

Popular species
Hepatica acutiloba resembles *H. americana*, though it reaches a height of 10 in (25 cm) and has somewhat larger leaves. The pale pink flowers measure up to 1 in (2.5 cm) wide. The species is hardy to zone 4.
Hepatica americana is hardy to zone 4. It carries trilobed, rounded leaves and reaches up to 6 in (15 cm) in height. The ¾ in (2 cm) wide flowers are generally pale blue-purple but may also be pink or white.
Hepatica nobilis, syn. *Anemone hepatica*, grows 4 in (10 cm) high and is hardy to zone 5. The flowers range from white to red or purple; some are double-flowered.

Cultivation
Plant hepaticas in early to mid fall. They thrive in any deep, moist soil that contains plenty of organic matter, and they do best in partial shade.
Propagation Divide plants in early fall and replant at once in their permanent positions.
Pests/diseases Trouble free.

Hieracium

hawkweed

Hieracium aurantiacum

❏ Height 4-18 in (10-45 cm)
❏ Spread 1 ft (30 cm)
❏ Flowers early to mid summer
❏ Any well-drained soil
❏ Sunny or partially shaded site
❏ Perennial
❏ Hardy zones 3-10

Hawkweeds *(Hieracium)* resemble dandelions and, like them, are weeds that inhabit grassy and rocky areas. A few species are suitable for garden borders and rock gardens. They thrive even in poor, dry soil and are good where little else will grow.

The plants are grown for their rosettes of silver-gray foliage. In summer they bear dandelionlike orange or yellow flowers with strap-shaped petals.

Hieracium villosum

Popular species

Hieracium aurantiacum is hardy in zones 3-9. It reaches 9-12 in (23-30 cm) high and bears medium green leaves and rich orange-red flowers. These plants are invasive and spread freely by means of runners; they also self-seed from fluffy airborne seeds.
Hieracium lanatum, syn. *H. tomentosum,* is hardy in zones 3-10. It grows 4-18 in (10-45 cm) high, with ground-hugging rosettes of leaves covered in snow-white hairs. Attractive woolly bracts surround the flower buds, but these should be removed to allow the leaves to give their best show.
Hieracium mixtum, syn. *H. bombycinum,* is hardy to zone 6. It grows 6 in (15 cm) high and produces silvery, hairy leaves and yellow flowers.
Hieracium villosum (shaggy hawkweed), hardy in zones 3-9, forms rosettes of grayish, white-felted leaves 6 in (15 cm) wide. Wiry 1 ft (30 cm) high stems rise from the centers of the rosettes, bearing orange-yellow, slightly cup-shaped flowers in summer.

Cultivation

In fall or spring plant hawkweed in any well-drained soil, including poor and shallow types, in sun or partial shade.
Propagation Divide plants in fall or spring and replant in their permanent positions.
Pests/diseases Trouble free.

Horminum

horminum

Horminum pyrenaicum

❏ Height 6-9 in (15-23 cm)
❏ Spread up to 1 ft (30 cm)
❏ Flowers in summer
❏ Any well-drained soil
❏ Sunny, open site
❏ Perennial
❏ Hardy to zone 7

Horminum is a modest but hardy plant that is related to sage. It is worth growing for its spikes of rich purple tubular flowers, and it is a good ground-cover plant. There is only one species, *Horminum pyrenaicum,* which grows wild in Europe from the Pyrenées to the Tyrol. It produces basal rosettes of rough toothed leaves with puckered surfaces. During early to late summer the plant produces sturdy 6-9 in (15-23 cm) high stems that carry numerous clusters of blooms with slightly protruding stamens. The cultivar 'Roseum' displays pink flowers.

Cultivation

In fall or early spring, plant horminum in any well-drained soil in a sunny, open position.
Propagation Divide and replant established clumps in spring, or sow seeds in fall.
Pests/diseases Trouble free.

HORNED RAMPION — see
Phyteuma
HOUSELEEK — see
Sempervivum

Houstonia
bluet

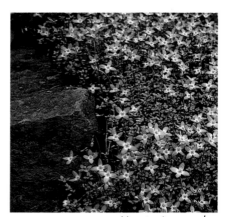

Houstonia caerulea

Houstonia purpurea

Hylomecon
hylomecon

Hylomecon japonicum

❏ Height 3-18 in (7.5-45 cm)
❏ Spread 1-1½ ft (30-45 cm)
❏ Flowers midspring to midsummer
❏ Moist, neutral to acid soil
❏ Partial shade
❏ Perennial
❏ Hardy to zone 3, depending on the species

Houstonia — or *Hedyotis,* as it has recently been reclassified by botanists — is a genus of North American wildflowers commonly known as bluets. These are undemanding plants that flourish in poor and dry soils and produce a host of exquisite blue, white, or purple flowers, usually in springtime. Though they are not often seen in rock gardens, these plants deserve more widespread use.

Popular species
Houstonia caerulea, syn. *Hedyotis caerulea,* is more widely known under its common name, Quakerladies. Hardy to zone 3, it grows to a height of 3 in (7.5 cm), with a spread of 1-1½ ft (30-45 cm). Its foliage resembles that of chickweed, and it forms bright green carpets of tiny spoon-shaped leaves. An abundance of cross-shaped four-petaled flowers appears from mid to late spring — these blooms are porcelain-blue with yellow centers. The cultivar 'Alba' is white.
Houstonia michauxii, syn. *H. serpyllifolia* (creeping bluet), is a prostrate species that forms a mat up to 3 in (7.5 cm) high and 1-1½ ft (30-45 cm) wide. It is similar to *H. caerulea* but has darker flowers and rounded leaves. It is hardy to zone 6.
Houstonia purpurea, which is hardy to zone 6, is considerably

larger than the other species are. It forms a cluster of stems that grow up to 18 in (45 cm) tall, and carries 2 in (5 cm) long ovate leaves. The funnel-shaped flowers are ⅜ in (10 mm) long, purple or lilac-colored, and they are borne in bunches on the stem tips in mid to late spring.
The variety *longifolia* is sometimes treated as a separate species, *Houstonia longifolia.* It grows 5-10 in (13-25 cm) high and bears white or lilac-colored flowers that are purple while in bud. It is hardy to zone 4.
Houstonia purpurea montana is hardy to zone 7. It reaches up to 12 in (30 cm) high, bearing clusters of ½ in (1.25 cm) wide dark purple flowers in midsummer.

Cultivation
Plant bluets in early to mid spring in a semishaded site. These plants require a moist soil in spring but can withstand considerable drought thereafter. They also seem indifferent to soil pH and thrive in nutrient-poor soils.
Propagation Divide mature plants in early to mid spring, or immediately after flowering, and replant right away. Alternatively, sow seeds every year — or let the plants self-seed. Bluets are not long-lived plants, but they set seed freely, and "volunteers" — self-sown seedlings — will appear around the garden, replacing their parents.
Pests/diseases Trouble free.

❏ Height 8-12 in (20-30 cm)
❏ Spread up to 1 ft (30 cm)
❏ Flowers early spring
❏ Rich, well-drained soil
❏ Partial shade
❏ Perennial
❏ Hardy to zone 7

Hylomecon japonicum, syn. *Stylophoron japonicum,* is a Japanese woodland plant grown for its poppylike, bowl-shaped, bright yellow flowers that are borne on slender stems early in the spring.
The elegant foliage is a lush bright green, and each leaf is divided into two or three pairs of leaflets. The plants become dormant by late summer.

Cultivation
In early to mid spring plant hylomecon in rich, moist soil enriched with plenty of organic matter. These plants require a shady or woodland site. Lift and divide the plants every few years; hylomecon has fleshy roots that soon become congested, reducing the flowering vigor of the plant.
Propagation Take root cuttings or divide the plants in spring. Replant strong-growing sections right away.
Pests/diseases Generally trouble free.

Hypericum
St.-John's-wort

Hypericum cerastoides

- ❏ Height 3-12 in (7.5-30 cm)
- ❏ Spread 9-18 in (23-45 cm)
- ❏ Flowers early summer to fall
- ❏ Any well-drained soil
- ❏ Sunny site
- ❏ Evergreen and deciduous shrubs
- ❏ Hardy zones 6-10

Dwarf species of St.-John's-wort *(Hypericum)* are good ground-cover shrubs for sunny banks and large rock gardens. They bear bright golden flowers and have distinctive tufts of long stamens. The species described here are hardy and, unless stated otherwise, evergreen.

Popular species
Hypericum aegypticum grows 6 in (15 cm) high and 9 in (23 cm) wide, with a spreading habit. It has tiny gray leaves and, in summer, yellow, goblet-shaped flowers. It is hardy in zones 7-10.
Hypericum balearicum, hardy to zone 7, is 1 ft (30 cm) or more tall. It is covered in small, puckered leaves and bears fragrant flowers from early summer onward.

Hypericum cerastoides, syn. *H. rhodopeum,* is hardy to zone 6. It is semiprostrate, 6 in (15 cm) high and 12 in (30 cm) wide, and has hairy oval gray-green leaves. Flowers appear in midsummer.
Hypericum coris, hardy to zone 7, is 6 in (15 cm) high and thrives in poor and alkaline soils. It bears heatherlike gray-green leaves and golden blooms in midsummer.
Hypericum olympicum, a deciduous shrub, is hardy to zone 6. It grows as a 9-12 in (23-30 cm) high hummock. It has gray-green, oval leaves and bears golden flowers at its tips in summer. 'Citrinum' has pale lemon-yellow flowers.
Hypericum pallens is a shrublet, hardy in zones 6-9. It grows 8 in (20 cm) high and 12 in (30 cm) wide, with thick, rounded gray leaves. The flowers are red while in bud, yellow when open.
Hypericum reptans is hardy to zone 7. A mat-forming species, it grows only 3 in (7.5 cm) high but spreads 1-1½ ft (30-45 cm). Its rounded light green leaves turn red-brown in fall. Scarlet buds

open to orange-yellow flowers from midsummer to early fall.

Cultivation
Plant St.-John's-worts in mid-spring in any well-drained soil, even a poor one, in a sunny site.
Propagation In late spring take cuttings of soft basal shoots; root in a cold frame or protected spot. Plant out the following spring.
Pests/diseases Rust disease may damage the leaves.

Hypericum olympicum 'Citrinum'

Hypsela
hypsela

Hypsela reniformis

❑ Height 1 in (2.5 cm)
❑ Spread 9 in (23 cm) or more
❑ Flowers in summer
❑ Moist soil
❑ Semishaded site
❑ Perennial
❑ Hardy to zone 8

Hypsela is a useful creeping plant that provides good ground cover in shady rock gardens. While it flourishes in peaty, organic soils, it can become invasive. Hypsela is more manageable in ordinary soil, provided it is moisture-retentive.

Only one species is in general cultivation, *Hypsela reniformis,* syn. *H. longiflora,* a native of South America. This plant grows 1 in (2.5 cm) high and spreads 9 in (23 cm) or more. The bright green, somewhat fleshy leaves are round or heart-shaped. During summer small, starry, pale pink flowers appear on very short stems that grow from the axils of the leaves.

Cultivation
Plant hypsela in a cool, sheltered, semishaded spot in moist soil in fall or early spring.
Propagation Divide mature plants in early spring and replant in their permanent positions.
Pests/diseases Trouble free.

Iberis
candytuft

Iberis sempervirens

❑ Height 3-12 in (7.5-30 cm)
❑ Spread 1-2 ft (30-60 cm)
❑ Flowers midspring and midsummer
❑ Any well-drained soil
❑ Sunny site
❑ Perennial and subshrub
❑ Hardy zones 4-10

The perennial species of candytufts *(Iberis)* are ideal rock garden plants. They form neat mounds of dark green foliage smothered by dense clusters of snow-white or pink flowers in midspring and midsummer. The plants thrive in most areas and tolerate air pollution. *Iberis sempervirens* spreads widely and is often planted into banks or walls, where it cascades down.

Popular species
Iberis gibraltarica grows to 1 ft (30 cm) high and spreads 1-1½ ft (30-45 cm). It is an evergreen subshrub, hardy in zones 7-10. It self-seeds freely; the seeds often replace the parent plant where it cannot survive cold winters. The dark green, narrowly oblong leaves are thick. Pink flowers are borne in dense, flattened clusters in mid and late spring.
Iberis saxatilis, a herbaceous perennial, is hardy to zone 6. It grows 3 in (7.5 cm) high and 1 ft (30 cm) wide, with slender, fleshy dark green leaves. It bears white flowers in flat-topped clusters from late spring to midsummer.
Iberis sempervirens, a perennial evergreen, is hardy to zone 4. It grows up to 9 in (23 cm) tall and 2 ft (60 cm) or more wide. The leaves are narrowly oblong and dark green. Dense heads of snow-white flowers appear from late spring to early summer. 'Little Gem' is a compact cultivar, only 4 in (10 cm) high; 'Snowflake' is larger and more vigorous, growing 12 in (30 cm) high and wide.

Cultivation
Plant candytufts in fall or early spring in ordinary soil in a sunny site. Deadhead after flowering.
Propagation Take cuttings of nonflowering shoots in early to late summer and root in a cold frame or other protected spot.
Pests/diseases Flea beetles may make small holes in the leaves.

Iberis gibraltarica

Inula

inula

Inula ensifolia 'Compacta'

- ❑ Height 2-18 in (5-45 cm)
- ❑ Spread up to 18 in (45 cm)
- ❑ Flowers mid to late spring and late summer
- ❑ Moist, fertile soil
- ❑ Sunny site
- ❑ Perennial
- ❑ Hardy zones 3-9

The golden, finely rayed, daisy-like flowers of inula are a familiar sight in borders, and two compact species are suitable for growing in the rock garden.

Popular species

Inula ensifolia is generally available only as the cultivar 'Compacta,' which grows 10 in (25 cm) high and spreads to 12 in (30 cm). This plant is clump-forming, with slender lance-shaped leaves, and bears a profusion of yellow flowers in late summer. The species is hardy in zones 3-9.

Inula hirta is hardy to zone 4 and reaches a height of 18 in (45 cm). It has rough, hairy leaves and yellow flowers.

Cultivation

Plant inula in fall or early spring in any moisture-retentive, fertile soil in a sunny position.

Propagation Divide and replant mature plants in spring or early to mid fall.

Pests/diseases Generally trouble free.

Ipheion

ipheion

Ipheion uniflorum 'Wisley Blue'

- ❑ Height 4-6 in (10-15 cm)
- ❑ Spread 2-3 in (5-7.5 cm)
- ❑ Flowers mid to late spring
- ❑ Any well-drained soil
- ❑ Sheltered site in sun or partial shade
- ❑ Bulb
- ❑ Hardy to zone 6

Ipheion is a genus of approximately 20 species of bulbs that are native to Mexico and southward as far as Chile. Only one species, *Ipheion uniflorum,* syn. *Triteleia uniflora,* is in cultivation in the United States. This plant is ideal for growing in sheltered pockets in a rock garden. The leaves and bulbs smell faintly of garlic.

Ipheion carries grasslike pale green leaves and reaches 4-6 in (10-15 cm) high. The starlike flowers are white to violet-blue; they are sweetly scented and appear in mid to late spring. The only available cultivar, 'Wisley Blue,' displays deep blue flowers.

Cultivation

Plant ipheion bulbs about 2-3 in (5-7.5 cm) deep in early or mid fall. Choose a sheltered spot in sun or partial shade, with good, well-drained soil. Keep free of weeds and remove dead leaves and flower stems in late summer.

Divide and replant regularly to maintain a show of flowers.

Ipheion uniflorum

Propagation Offsets are freely produced, and the plants spread of their own accord. Every two or three years, lift the bulbs as the leaves die down, separate the bulblets, and replant them at once. If the bulbs must be kept until the fall before replanting, keep them cool and do not allow them to dry out or get wet.

Pests/diseases Trouble free.

Iris
iris

Iris reticulata 'Clairette'

❑ Height 4-18 in (10-45 cm)
❑ Spread up to 15 in (38 cm)
❑ Flowers early winter to early summer
❑ Well-drained soil
❑ Sunny site
❑ Rhizomatous or bulbous perennial
❑ Hardy zones 3-10

The beauty and variety of the flowers of the iris family can be enjoyed as much in a rock garden as in other garden settings — there are many charming dwarf species and hybrids. Their dainty flowers have the typical iris shape, with upright inner petals (standards) and lower petals (falls) that curve downward. So-called bearded irises have a small tuft of hair on each of the falls.

Iris leaves are sword-shaped or grassy and provide interest after the bloom is past. In some species the leaves are tiny or nonexistent at flowering time.

Iris innominata

Iris danfordiae

Iris tectorum

Popular species and cultivars

Iris chamaeiris, syn. *I. lutescens,* is a variable species of dwarf bearded iris. It is hardy to zone 6, thrives in alkaline soil, and grows 6-10 in (15-25 cm) high. Although similar to *I. pumila,* it has a real stem and sometimes more than one flower to a stem. The flowers appear in spring and may be white, yellow, or purple.

Iris cristata, a crested iris, grows 6 in (15 cm) high. It produces its main flush of flowers in mid to late spring, usually in pairs. They are a striking lilac and orange, with a white, orange-tipped crest. Cultivars include 'Abbey's Violet' (deep violet-blue) and 'Alba' (pure white with yellow on the falls). It is hardy in zones 6-9.

Iris danfordiae is a bulbous iris, hardy to zone 6. It is 4 in (10 cm) high and blooms in mid to late winter before the leaves develop. The flowers are lemon-yellow, with a honeylike scent; the falls are dusted with black spots.

Iris graminea belongs to the Spuria group of beardless irises and is hardy to zone 6. It reaches 8 in (20 cm) high and has dense tufts of grassy leaves that can obscure the fragrant flowers. Produced in early summer, the flowers are red-purple with white falls veined with blue-purple.

Iris histrioides 'Major' is a bulbous iris only 4 in (10 cm) high. It is hardy to zone 6 and is among the earliest irises to flower, often budding in early winter. It survives all weather — even snow.

The leaves are just 1 in (2.5 cm) high at flowering time but eventually reach 1½ ft (45 cm). The flowers are bright royal blue with a yellow ridge on the falls.

Iris innominata, one of the beardless Pacific Coast irises, is hardy to zone 8. It forms small clumps of grassy leaves 6 in (15 cm) high. Flowers appear singly or in pairs in spring and early summer. They are usually cream, beige, yellow, or orange, with tawny brown veins; there are also deep pink and blue-purple forms.

Iris pumila is a bearded dwarf iris that is hardy in zones 3-10. It grows up to 4 in (10 cm) high. Most forms are stemless. The flowers, which appear in midspring, have recurved falls in shades of purple, white, yellow, and brown-tinted yellow.

Iris reticulata, a bulbous iris, grows 6 in (15 cm) tall. It is hardy to zone 6. The flowers are purple with golden patches on the falls. They appear in late winter to early spring, accompanied by leaves. Popular cultivars include 'Cantab' (pale blue, orange-marked falls), 'Clairette' (sky-blue, deep royal blue and white falls), 'Harmony' (sky-blue, falls marked yellow), 'Joyce' (sky-blue, falls marked light red), 'J. S. Dijt' (red-purple, marked orange), 'Pauline' (red-violet, marked white), and 'Violet Beauty' (deep violet).

Iris ruthenica is a beardless iris that flowers in spring. While it is hardy to zone 6, it is unreliable. In some years it is smothered in

flowers; in others, it bears none. The upper petals are purple; the falls, white veined with blue. It has deciduous grasslike leaves and grows 6-9 in (15-23 cm) high.

Iris tectorum is a crested species that is hardy in zones 4-10. It reaches 1 ft (30 cm) in height and flowers in late spring and early summer. The flowers are lavender, the falls are mottled with darker spots, and the crest is white. 'Alba' has white flowers.

Popular hybrids

Dwarf irises include a number of hybrids that are 4-6 in (10-15 cm) high and are ideal for rock gardens. *Iris* 'Frank Elder' is a hybrid of *Iris winogradowii* and *Iris histrioides* 'Major'; it is bulbous and grows 5 in (13 cm) high. In early spring it has soft blue flowers touched with yellow and distinctively veined with dark blue.

Other hybrids include 'Bee Wings' (yellow, brown-spotted falls), 'Buckeye Baby' (yellow with brown spots), 'Egret Snow' (pure white), 'Natasha' (blue and white, orange markings), 'Ritz' (yellow, falls marked maroon), 'Sleepy Time' (light blue, white beard), and 'Zipper' (golden-yellow with a blue beard).

Cultivation

Position iris rhizomes (with the exception of crested and Spuria types) with the tops showing just above ground and all facing the same way to receive the most sunshine. Plant species iris bulbs

Jasione
jasione

Jasione perennis

Iris chamaeiris

Iris histrioides 'Major'

❑ Height 4-9 in (10-23 cm)
❑ Spread up to 9 in (23 cm)
❑ Flowers in summer
❑ Any well-drained soil
❑ Sunny site
❑ Perennial
❑ Hardy zones 5-9

The small, neat species of jasione are grown in the rock garden for their fluffy blue globular flowers, which somewhat resemble those of scabious. These plants are cold hardy and easy to grow.

Popular species
Jasione humilis forms neat basal rosettes of narrow leaves. Bright blue flower heads are displayed on 4 in (10 cm) stems in summer. *Jasione perennis,* syn. *J. laevis,* is a tufted plant that grows to 9 in (23 cm) high and 8 in (20 cm) wide. The narrowly oblong gray-green leaves are covered with rough hairs. In summer deep blue flowers are borne on wiry branching stems.

Cultivation
In fall or early spring, plant jasione in any well-drained soil, including alkaline ones, in an open, sunny position.
Propagation Divide established clumps in spring and replant in their permanent positions.
Pests/diseases Trouble free.

2-3 in (5-7.5 cm) deep and hybrid bulbs 4-6 in (10-15 cm) deep.
❑ Dwarf bearded irises: plant from early to late summer in rich, well-drained soil in full sun. Replant every two to three years.
❑ Dwarf beardless Pacific Coast irises: plant in late fall in sun or partial shade. *I. innominata* benefits from neutral or acid soil enriched with leaf mold.
❑ Beardless Spuria irises: plant rhizomes 2 in (5 cm) deep in any fertile soil in a sunny spot in mid to late fall. Avoid lifting, as they do not tolerate disturbance.
❑ Crested irises: plant rhizomes just below soil level in late spring to early summer in slightly moist soil enriched with plenty of leaf

mold in a sheltered spot. *I. tectorum* tolerates alkaline soil.
❑ Bulbous irises: plant bulbs in early and mid fall in light, well-drained, alkaline soil in sun.
Propagation To increase bearded irises, dig up the rhizomes after flowering, cut into pieces (each with a strong fan of foliage), and replant. Divide and replant rhizomes of beardless irises in early to mid fall. To increase bulbous irises, lift bulbs after the leaves die down, grade according to size, and store until planting time in fall.
Pests/diseases Trouble free.

JACOB'S LADDER — see
Polemonium

Jasminum
dwarf jasmine

Jasminum parkeri

- ❑ Height 8-12 in (20-30 cm)
- ❑ Spread up to 2 ft (60 cm)
- ❑ Flowers early summer
- ❑ Any well-drained soil
- ❑ Sunny, sheltered site
- ❑ Evergreen shrub
- ❑ Hardy to zone 7

Jasminum parkeri is the only species of jasmine suitable for the rock garden. Dwarf and almost prostrate, it forms a dome of crowded, woody stems. It grows 8-12 in (20-30 cm) high and has small dark green leaves. Fragrant pale yellow, tubular flowers are borne in early summer.

Cultivation
Plant dwarf jasmine in midfall or midspring in any well-drained but moist soil in a sheltered and sunny position.
Propagation Take heel cuttings in late summer to early fall.
Pests/diseases Generally trouble free.

JONQUIL — see *Narcissus*
JOVIBARBA — see *Sempervivum*
KNAPWEED — see *Centaurea*
KNOTWEED — see *Polygonum*
LADYBELLS — see *Adenophora*
LADY'S-MANTLE — see *Alchemilla*
LAMB'S TAIL — see *Chiastophyllum*

Leontopodium
edelweiss

Leontopodium alpinum

- ❑ Height up to 9 in (23 cm)
- ❑ Spread up to 9 in (23 cm)
- ❑ Flowers early and mid summer
- ❑ Good, well-drained soil
- ❑ Sunny site
- ❑ Perennial
- ❑ Hardy zones 4-9

Edelweiss, one of the best-known alpine plants, forms clumps of lance-shaped, woolly-haired foliage. Its short stems bear flower heads composed of white bracts densely covered with hairs. The bracts form a star shape and surround the true, silvery flower. It is easy to grow but short-lived.

Edelweiss *(Leontopodium alpinum)* grows 8-9 in (20-23 cm) high and wide, and it thrives in rock crevices. It withstands cold well, but not when combined with wet soil. To ensure rapid drainage, mulch around the plants with a deep collar of grit.

Cultivation
Plant edelweiss in early spring in an open, sunny site in good, very well drained soil.
Propagation Divide and replant mature clumps in spring, before they flower. Alternatively, sow seeds in spring in a cold frame or other protected spot; plant out the following spring.
Pests/diseases Trouble free.

LEPTINELLA — see *Cotula*

Leptospermum
dwarf tea tree

Leptospermum scoparium 'Nanum'

❑ Height 6-12 in (15-30 cm)
❑ Spread up to 3 ft (90 cm)
❑ Flowers late spring to early summer
❑ Acid to neutral, very well drained soil
❑ Sunny, sheltered site
❑ Evergreen shrub
❑ Hardy zones 9-10

Dwarf tea trees (*Leptospermum*) are handsome shrubs, but they are reliably hardy only in virtually frost-free areas. They do not thrive in regions of high humidity but are tolerant of salt, making them good seaside plantings on the Pacific Coast.

Popular species
Leptospermum rupestre, syn. *L. humifusum,* is a mat-forming species, 6 in (15 cm) high and spreading to 3 ft (90 cm). The dark green leaves are narrowly oblong and pointed. Saucer-shaped white flowers appear in great profusion in early summer.
Leptospermum scoparium grows up to 10 ft (3 m) high, making the species too tall for a rock garden. However, the cultivar 'Nanum,' a compact dwarf shrub that is only 10-12 in (25-30 cm) high, is a suitable candidate for the rock garden. It has tiny deep green leaves and deep pink flowers.

Cultivation
Plant container-grown tea trees in good, very well drained, acid to neutral soil in sunny, sheltered sites in mid to late spring.
Propagation Take cuttings of semimature wood in summer and root in a heated propagation unit.
Pests/diseases Trouble free.

LEUCANTHEMOSIS ALPINA
— see *Chrysanthemum alpinum*

Leucojum
snowflake

Leucojum vernum

❑ Height 8-10 in (20-25 cm)
❑ Spread 3-4 in (7.5-10 cm)
❑ Flowers spring or fall
❑ Good, moist soil
❑ Sun or partial shade
❑ Bulb
❑ Hardy to zone 6

Snowflakes (*Leucojum*) produce their graceful, bell-shaped white flowers in different seasons, according to the species. It is the spring- and fall-flowering species that are small enough for the rock garden. They are hardy, bulbous plants with narrow, strap-shaped leaves. The flowers are similar to those of the snowdrop (*Galanthus*) but more rounded, with all six petals the same size and carried on taller stems.

Popular species
Leucojum autumnale (fall snowflake) grows 8-10 in (20-25 cm) high. It has slender, almost grass-like medium green leaves and bears white flowers flushed with pink from midsummer to early fall. It does best in a sunny site.
Leucojum vernum (spring snowflake) grows 8 in (20 cm) high and has strap-shaped medium green leaves. Green-tipped white flowers appear from late winter to early spring. The species naturalizes freely in moist, shady places.

Cultivation
Plant the bulbs as soon as they are available in late summer or early fall. Set *L. autumnale* bulbs 2 in (5 cm) deep in free-draining soil; plant *L. vernum* bulbs in moisture-retentive soil about 4 in (10 cm) deep. Space both types 6-8 in (15-20 cm) apart and leave undisturbed for several years.
When the clumps become overcrowded and produce more leaves than flowers, lift, divide, and replant the bulbs as soon as the leaves die down.
Propagation The bulbs produce offsets; you can detach them when the clumps are lifted. Grow the offsets in a nursery bed; they reach flowering size quickly.
Pests/diseases Trouble free.

Leucojum autumnale

Lewisia

lewisia

Lewisia cotyledon var. *heckneri*

Lewisia rediviva

Lewisia cotyledon, seedling mixture

❑ Height 3-12 in (7.5-30 cm)
❑ Spread 3-10 in (7.5-25 cm)
❑ Flowers midspring to late summer
❑ Rich, well-drained soil
❑ Sunny site
❑ Semisucculent perennial
❑ Hardy zones 3-9

Lewisias are ideal for rock crevices and trough gardens. Many of these plants are evergreen.

Popular species

Lewisia cotyledon is hardy in zones 3-9. It forms a dense rosette of evergreen leaves and grows 1 ft (30 cm) high. The saucer-shaped pink flowers have white veins. 'Alba' bears white flowers; the variety *heckneri* displays rose-pink flowers. Some nurseries offer seedling mixtures that bloom in a range of colors.
Lewisia rediviva (bitterroot) is 3 in (7.5 cm) high and hardy to zone 4. Its red-green leaf rosettes die down in summer as stemless rose-pink or white flowers appear. *Lewisia tweedyi,* hardy to zone 5, grows 6 in (15 cm) high, forming evergreen leaf rosettes. The flowers are borne in spring, and they vary in color from pale pink to soft apricot.

Cultivation

Plant in humus-rich, neutral to acid, well-drained soil in a sunny site in early to mid spring. Lewisias do not tolerate a combination of cold and wet and need a period of drought after flowering. They may be short-lived in the East.
Propagation Detach and pot offsets in early summer.
Pests/diseases Excessive moisture may cause plants to rot.

Linaria

toadflax

Linum 'Gemmell's Hybrid'

Linum

flax

- ❏ Height 2-16 in (5-40 cm)
- ❏ Spread 9-16 in (23-40 cm)
- ❏ Flowers summer to fall
- ❏ Any well-drained soil
- ❏ Open, sunny site
- ❏ Herbaceous or shrubby perennial
- ❏ Hardy zones 5-10

Linaria alpina

- ❏ Height 3-6 in (7.5-15 cm)
- ❏ Spread up to 10 in (25 cm)
- ❏ Flowers throughout summer
- ❏ Any well-drained soil
- ❏ Sunny site
- ❏ Perennial
- ❏ Hardy to zone 4

Toadflaxes *(Linaria)* are easily grown plants — too easily in the case of the species *Linaria vulgaris,* commonly called butter-and-eggs. This pretty wildflower with yellow-and-orange blossoms can become a troublesome weed.

There are, however, other less invasive toadflaxes that make a welcome addition to the rock garden. All summer long they bear colorful spikes of flowers that most closely resemble spurred snapdragons. These plants are ideal for trailing over rocky ledges or for planting into drystone walls and between paving. While toadflaxes are often short-lived, they seed themselves freely.

Popular species and cultivars
Linaria aeruginea 'Elfin Delight' is hardy to zone 6, grows to a height of 6 in (15 cm), and carries narrow grayish leaves. It bears flowers that are bicolored, in shades of yellow and pink or violet; they appear over a long period during summer.

Linaria alpina is hardy to zone 4. It grows 3-6 in (7.5-15 cm) high, forming compact mats of trailing stems with slender blue-gray leaves. Its violet flowers with orange-striped lower lips are displayed in numerous sprays.

Linaria supina is hardy to zone 7. It grows to a height of about 6 in (15 cm). The narrow leaves grow in whorls and the pale yellow flowers are borne in bunches.

Cultivation

Plant toadflaxes in midfall or early spring in any well-drained soil in a sunny site.

Propagation Sow seeds directly in the flowering site.

Pests/diseases Generally trouble free.

Linum (flax) is a large genus and includes several dwarf species that are suitable for the rock garden. The golden yellow, white, or blue funnel-shaped flowers are borne in profusion throughout summer and fall. Dwarf flaxes are short-lived but easily started anew from seeds or cuttings.

Popular species and hybrids
Linum flavum reaches 12-16 in (30-40 cm) high and has a similar spread. It is hardy in zones 5-9. The foliage is dark green, and the stems are woody at the base. Bright yellow, 1 in (2.5 cm) wide flowers are borne in loose clusters. A dwarf cultivar, 'Compactum,' is only 8 in (20 cm) tall.

Linum 'Gemmell's Hybrid' is a semievergreen plant with a woody rootstock. It reaches about 6 in (15 cm) high and forms a dome of fleshy gray-green leaves. The short stems display clusters of large golden yellow flowers in early summer. This plant is hardy to zone 6.

Linum perenne grows 1 ft (30 cm) or more high and is hardy in zones 5-10. It has gray-green grasslike leaves and produces an

Lithospermum
lithospermum

Linum perenne alpinum

Lithospermum diffusum 'Heavenly Blue'

abundance of sky-blue flowers throughout summer. *L. perenne alpinum* is a dwarf form that grows only 6 in (15 cm) high. *Linum suffruticosum* ssp. *salsoloides,* is a semiprostrate shrub, growing 2 in (5 cm) high and spreading to 9 in (23 cm). It is hardy to zone 5 and has tiny needlelike leaves on woody stems. This species produces sprays of pearly-white flowers flushed blue or pink. 'Nanum' is a more widely grown cultivar that reaches a height of about 3 in (7.5 cm).

Cultivation
Plant dwarf flaxes in mid to late fall or early to mid spring. Set the plants in any fertile, well-drained soil in an open, sunny site. Trim them back in mid to late fall.
Propagation Dwarf flaxes are easy to grow from seeds, but the cultivars will not breed true to type — that is, the seeds of the cultivars produce plants that differ from the parent. Sow seeds of the species in early to mid spring in a cold frame or other protected spot. Alternatively, take cuttings of basal shoots in mid to late spring and root them in a cold frame. Transfer the cuttings to a nursery bed. In fall or the following spring, plant them out in their permanent positions.
Pests/diseases Trouble free.

LITHODORA — see
Lithospermum

❏ Height 4-6 in (10-15 cm)
❏ Spread up to 2 ft (60 cm)
❏ Flowers late spring to midfall
❏ Good, well-drained soil
❏ Sunny site
❏ Evergreen subshrub
❏ Hardy to zone 7

The mat-forming evergreen *Lithospermum,* which has been reclassified as *Lithodora,* makes an excellent ground cover and bears an abundance of funnel-shaped flowers in shades of blue.

Popular species
Lithospermum diffusum, syn. *Lithodora diffusa,* is 4 in (10 cm) high and 2 ft (60 cm) wide. The prostrate stems bear oval dark green leaves. Deep blue flowers, with five rounded, spreading lobes, are borne from early summer to midfall. 'Grace Ward' is an outstanding cultivar, more vigorous than the species and bearing larger blooms of a more intense shade of blue. 'Heavenly Blue' is the most common form and bears deep blue flowers in profusion. *Lithospermum oleifolium,* syn. *Lithodora oleifolia,* grows to 6 in (15 cm) high. It carries rounded, silver-haired leaves; from late spring to late summer, nodding clusters of pink buds turn sky-blue as they open.

Cultivation
Plant lithospermum in midspring in any fertile, well-drained soil in a sunny site. *L. diffusum* and its cultivars need acid to neutral soil; other species will tolerate alkaline soil.
Propagation Take cuttings of lateral shoots, preferably with a heel, in midsummer. Root them in a cold frame or other protected spot. Water *L. diffusum* liberally and other species moderately until the cuttings have rooted. Overwinter the cuttings in a cool but frost-free, sunny spot; plant out in midspring.
Pests/diseases Trouble free.

LIVINGSTONE DAISY — see
Mesembryanthemum

Lithospermum oleifolium

Lotus

lotus, alpine pea

Lotus berthelotii

❑ Trails or scrambles to 1 ft (30 cm)
❑ Spread up to 3 ft (90 cm)
❑ Flowers early summer to early fall
❑ Any well-drained soil
❑ Sunny site
❑ Perennial
❑ Hardy zones 5-9

A member of the pea family, lotus, or alpine pea, can be grown as ground cover or trailing from baskets. Of the two species described, one is cold hardy and the other thrives only in the South.

Popular species

Lotus berthelotii (parrot's-beak) is 1 ft (30 cm) high, with woody trailing stems and intensely silver hairy leaves. It bears clusters of scarlet, beaklike flowers in early summer. It is hardy to zone 9.
Lotus corniculatus (bird's-foot trefoil), hardy to zone 5, grows wild in much of North America. The best cultivar for the garden is 'Plenus,' a form with double flowers. It is a prostrate and spreading plant with heads of bright yellow flowers that bloom from early summer to early fall.

Cultivation

Grow lotus in any well-drained soil in a sunny spot; *L. berthelotii* needs a warm, sheltered site.
Propagation Take softwood cuttings in early summer and root in a propagation unit.
Pests/diseases Trouble free.

Lychnis

campion

Lychnis flos-jovis

❑ Height 4-24 in (10-60 cm)
❑ Spread 2-12 in (5-30 cm)
❑ Flowers late spring to late summer
❑ Any well-drained soil
❑ Sun or light shade
❑ Perennial
❑ Hardy zones 3-9

The species of *Lychnis* (campion) offer a range of flower colors, from white to pink, red and orange to purple. They are easily cultivated. Low-growing types are best for edgings and rock gardens; taller species, for borders.

Popular species

Lychnis alpina, syn. *Viscaria alpina,* grows up to 4 in (10 cm) high and 2 in (5 cm) wide, forming a tuft of dark green strapshaped leaves. Short stems bear dense flower clusters, usually deep rose-pink, from late spring onward. This is ideal as a trough plant. It is hardy to zone 5.
Lychnis flos-jovis (flower of Jove) is large — up to 2 ft (60 cm) high. It has thick, silvery or gray, spearshaped leaves and rich red or purple flowers. The species is hardy to zone 5. 'Hort's Variety,' which produces pink flowers, reaches only 12 in (30 cm) high.
Lychnis viscaria (German catchfly), syn. *Viscaria vulgaris* and *V. viscosa,* grows 1 ft (30 cm) high and is hardy in zones 3-9. It has tufts of grassy leaves and bears tight clusters of carmine-pink

Lychnis alpina

flowers in early summer. 'Splendens Plena,' a showier form, has double, carnationlike flowers.

Cultivation

Plant campions in any welldrained soil in full sun or light shade in midfall or early spring. Deadhead to prevent self-seeding.
Propagation Sow seeds in a cold frame or other cool but protected spot in late spring or early summer. Propagate cultivars from cuttings taken in late spring and rooted in a cold frame.
Pests/diseases Aphids and spittlebugs may attack and stunt flowering shoots.

Lysimachia
creeping Jenny, moneywort

Lysimachia nummularia

❏ Height 1-2 in (2.5-5 cm)
❏ Spread 1½ ft (45 cm) or more
❏ Flowers early to mid summer
❏ Moist soil
❏ Sun or partial shade
❏ Perennial
❏ Hardy to zone 4

Lysimachia nummularia (creeping Jenny, moneywort) is, like other species of *Lysimachia*, highly invasive. However, it makes admirable ground cover in moist soil and creeps easily over stones in the rock garden. Creeping Jenny forms a dense carpet of medium green rounded evergreen leaves. In early to mid summer it bears bright yellow, cup-shaped flowers. The cultivar 'Aurea' has golden-yellow leaves.

Cultivation
Plant creeping Jenny in moist soil in sun or partial shade in midfall or early to mid spring. In the wild it is a waterside plant and will grow in as little as 2 in (5 cm) of soil. However, it adapts easily to dry soil — even alkaline soil is acceptable provided it does not dry out in hot weather.
Propagation Divide and replant at any time between midfall and early spring. Alternatively, in midspring or early fall take 3-4 in (7.5-10 cm) long stem cuttings and plant directly in their growing positions.
Pests/diseases Trouble free.

Mazus
mazus

Mazus reptans

❏ Height 1-2 in (2.5-5 cm)
❏ Spread 1 ft (30 cm) or more
❏ Flowers late spring to late summer
❏ Any moist soil
❏ Sunny site
❏ Perennial
❏ Hardy to zone 3

Mazus has tiny flowers that resemble flattened snapdragons. This little-known but hardy plant makes a useful ground cover and does well between paving stones.

Popular species
Mazus pumilio, the most compact species, forms neat mats only 1 in (2.5 cm) high but 12 in (30 cm) wide. Its blooms are lavender-blue and white. It is hardy to zone 7.
Mazus reptans, hardy to zone 3, grows 2 in (5 cm) high. The creeping mat of spear-shaped, toothed leaves spreads 12 in (30 cm). The lilac-colored flowers have lips speckled with gold and white. 'Albus' has completely white flowers.

Cultivation
In early spring plant mazus in a sunny site; any soil that does not dry out is suitable.
Propagation Divide and replant in spring or fall.
Pests/diseases Trouble free.

MEADOW RUE — see *Thalictrum*

Mesembryanthemum
Livingstone daisy

Mesembryanthemum 'Lunette'

❏ Height up to 6 in (15 cm)
❏ Spread 6-12 in (15-30 cm)
❏ Flowers early to late summer
❏ Any well-drained soil
❏ Sunny site
❏ Succulent, half-hardy annual
❏ Hardy to zone 10

Although Livingstone daisies have traditionally been assigned to the genus *Mesembryanthemum*, botanists have reclassified the plants as *Dorotheanthus bellidiformis*. Whatever the plant is called, it is an ideal annual for a warm, dry climate, such as that of Southern California, and it makes a fine container planting elsewhere. It bears a profusion of large, brilliantly colored daisylike flowers that open wide in full sun. They make good fillers in the rock garden. Tuck the flowers between newly planted dwarf or alpine (high-mountain) plants, then remove them as the choicer plants expand to occupy the space. Because the Livingstone daisy comes from the desert of South Africa, it thrives in the gritty, well-drained soil of a rock garden.

Popular species and cultivars
Mesembryanthemum criniflorum, syn. *Dorotheanthus bellidiformis* (Livingstone daisy), grows 6 in (15 cm) high, with a spread of up to 1 ft (30 cm). The narrow, almost cylindrical, succulent, pale green leaves have a glistening, almost sugar-coated appearance.

Mimulus
monkey flower

Mesembryanthemum criniflorum

Mimulus x hybridus, flowers

Given bright sun, the plant produces a succession of daisylike flowers from early to late summer. The range of vivid colors includes white, crimson to pink, and orange-gold to buff.

Among the popular cultivars are 'Lunette,' also known as 'Yellow Ice,' which has lemon-yellow petals and a rust-red central disk, and 'Magic Carpet Mixed,' which has yellow, orange, pink, red, and lavender flowers. The darker colors show a white band around the central disk.

Cultivation
Plant Livingstone daisies in full sun in any well-drained soil; they thrive in sandy soil. In the North plant in containers of sandy soil and move to a protected spot if there is a danger of frost.

Propagation Start seeds indoors in late winter or early spring — February or March. Sow seeds in flats filled with sterilized seed-starting mix and keep at a temperature of 59°F (15°C). Prick out into pots or cell packs and harden off seedlings before planting out in late spring, after all danger of frost is past. In regions with a warm climate, you may sow the seeds directly into the flowering sites in early spring and thin out the seedlings as necessary.

Pests/diseases Plants may collapse at ground level because of fungal rot.

MILKWORT — see *Polygala*

- ❑ Height 3-12 in (7.5-30 cm)
- ❑ Spread 9-12 in (23-30 cm)
- ❑ Flowers late spring to early fall
- ❑ Any moist soil
- ❑ Sun or light shade
- ❑ Annual or perennial
- ❑ Hardy zones 6-10

In the wild, monkey flowers *(Mimulus)* are wetland plants; they adapt well to any moist soil. Low-growing types are suitable for the rock garden and for edging. They thrive in sun or shade but are short-lived. The flowers, which resemble open-mouthed snapdragons, are brightly colored and blotched in contrasting hues.

Popular species and hybrids
Mimulus cupreus, an annual, grows 9-12 in (23-30 cm) high and 9 in (23 cm) wide. The leaves are medium green and oblong. The flowers, which bloom from early summer to early fall, are yellow when they open and change to coppery-orange, spotted brown.

Mimulus × hybridus, a group of hybrids derived in part from *M. cupreus,* are sometimes treated as annuals but can be grown as perennials in zones 6-10. They include 'Andean Nymph' (pink-and-yellow) and the 'Malibu' series (red, orange, or yellow).

Mimulus luteus is a perennial hardy in zones 6-9. It grows 12 in (30 cm) high and wide, with creeping stems that root where the leaf nodes touch the ground. The 1-2 in (2.5-5 cm) long oval leaves are toothed; the yellow flowers are 1-2 in (2.5-5 cm) wide and have red or purple spots.

Cultivation
In early to late spring plant monkey flowers in sun or light shade in any moisture-retentive soil. In cold areas protect the plants on cool spring nights with hot caps.

Propagation Increase by dividing, taking stem cuttings, or sowing seeds in early to mid spring.

Pests/diseases Trouble free.

Mimulus x hybridus 'Andean Nymph'

Minuartia
minuartia

Minuartia verna

- Height ½-4 in (1.25-10 cm)
- Spread up to 1 ft (30 cm)
- Flowers late spring to early summer
- Well-drained soil
- Sunny site
- Evergreen perennial
- Hardy to zone 2

Minuartias are tiny, almost mosslike plants ideal for growing in troughs, rock crevices, or between paving stones. They are covered with starry white flowers from late spring to early summer. Minuartias may be listed as *Arenaria,* a closely related genus.

Popular species
Minuartia laricifolia, syn. *Arenaria laricifolia,* forms loose, grassy mats of slender, gray-green leaves, up to 4 in (10 cm) high. The flowers are milky white and are borne in loose clusters. It is hardy to zone 5.
Minuartia sedoides forms a cushion of densely packed, fleshy leaves to ⅔ in (17 mm) high. It bears solitary, stemless yellow flowers and is hardy to zone 5.
Minuartia verna, syn. *Arenaria verna,* forms a neat, rounded dome of tiny, narrow, emerald-green leaves. In spring it is smothered with white flowers on threadlike 1 in (2.5 cm) high stems. This species is hardy to zone 2.

Cultivation
Plant minuartia in early to mid fall in an open, sunny position in well-drained soil.
Propagation Divide established plants after flowering. Or take cuttings of semimature shoots in midsummer and root in a cold frame or other protected spot.
Pests/diseases Trouble free.

Moltkia
moltkia

Moltkia petraea

- Height 1 ft (30 cm)
- Spread up to 1 ft (30 cm)
- Flowers early to late summer
- Any well-drained soil
- Sunny site
- Evergreen subshrub
- Hardy to zone 6

Moltkia is closely related to *Lithospermum* and was formerly included in that genus. The species are hardy, low-growing shrubs of compact habit. They produce attractive, narrow, lance-shaped grayish-green foliage. The leaves are similar in appearance to those of lavender, and when not in bloom, the plant may be mistaken for lavender by the novice gardener. Drooping clusters of funnel-shaped, blue or purple flowers are borne from early to late summer. There is only one species that is suitable for the rock garden.

Popular species
Moltkia petraea grows up to 1 ft (30 cm) high and spreads as much or more across, with narrow, hairy grayish-green leaves. It produces an abundance of flowers that are pinkish-purple when they open and gradually deepen to violet-blue. These flowers are 1-1½ in (2.5-3.75 cm) wide and are displayed in small clusters at the ends of the branches.

Cultivation
Plant moltkias in spring or fall in any well-drained, acid or alkaline soil in a site with full sun. These shrubs will flourish in sunny, dry climates, such as that of Southern California.
Propagation Take cuttings of semimature wood in midsummer and root in a cold frame or other protected spot.
Pests/diseases Generally trouble free.

MONEYWORT — see *Lysimachia*
MONKEY FLOWER — see *Mimulus*
MOUNT ATLAS DAISY — see *Anacyclus*
MOUNTAIN AVENS — see *Dryas*
MOUSE-EAR CHICKWEED — see *Cerastium*
MULLEIN — see *Verbascum*

Muscari
grape hyacinth

Muscari botryoides 'Album'

❏ Height 6-12 in (15-30 cm)
❏ Spread 3-4 in (7.5-10 cm)
❏ Flowers early spring to early summer
❏ Any well-drained soil
❏ Sunny site
❏ Bulb
❏ Hardy to zone 4

Muscari armeniacum

Common grape hyacinth *(Muscari)* is a familiar springtime sight. This plant produces attractive heads of tightly packed flowers that resemble small blue grapes. More unusual species have purple-and-green or yellow-and-brown flower spikes. All bring welcome color to rock gardens and window boxes. The species described here have medium green, strap-shaped leaves with a channeled inner surface. The upper flowers are sterile and do not open; except for those of *Muscari comosum,* they are paler than the lower, urn-shaped ones.

Grape hyacinths are easy to grow and return a lot of color for a very small investment of labor. When planted in sunny areas in deep and sandy but rich soil, they multiply freely, each bulb surrounding itself with smaller offsets that develop into flowering plants in just a couple of seasons. Along with narcissus, grape hyacinth provides some of the best bulbs for naturalizing in a rock garden, at the front of a flower border, or even in the lawn.

Popular species
Muscari armeniacum reaches 8-10 in (20-25 cm) high and carries densely packed, cobalt blue flowers with white rims. It is hardy to zone 5. Cultivars include 'Blue Spike' (scented, medium blue double flowers in densely packed spikes), 'Cantab' (bright blue), 'Early Giant' (strongly scented, cobalt blue), and 'Heavenly Blue' (bright sky-blue).

Muscari aucheri, syn. *M. tubergenianum* (Oxford and Cambridge grape hyacinth), grows about 9 in (23 cm) high. The almost-round flower clusters are dark blue at the top, fading to paler blue at the base of the spike. The species is hardy to zone 6.

Muscari azureum grows to 8 in (20 cm) tall. It has bluish-green leaves and bears blue flowers in dense, short clusters in early spring. The flowers are fragrant. This species is hardy to zone 4.

Muscari botryoides reaches a height of 6-12 in (15-30 cm) and is hardy to zone 4. The upright leaves are narrow and grasslike. The fragrant sky-blue flowers are borne in tight spikes in early spring. The cultivar 'Album' produces white flowers.

Muscari comosum (tassel hyacinth), hardy to zone 5, grows 1 ft (30 cm) or more high. The lower flowers are olive-green; the sterile upper flowers are purple. *M. c.* 'Plumosum,' syn. 'Monstrosum' (feather hyacinth), produces only sterile flowers that are violet-blue or reddish purple, with petals cut into a tangle of fine filaments.

Muscari latifolium is hardy to zone 5. It grows to a height of 1 ft (30 cm). Each bulb produces just one leaf — a long, flat one that measures nearly 1 in (2.5 cm) wide. In early spring ¼ in (6 mm) long flowers are borne in clusters of 10 to 20 blooms; the lower

Muscari blossom

Myosotis

alpine forget-me-not

Narcissus

dwarf daffodil

Myosotis alpestris 'Indigo Blue'

- ❏ Height 4-6 in (10-15 cm)
- ❏ Spread 4-6 in (10-15 cm)
- ❏ Flowers late spring to early summer
- ❏ Any well-drained soil
- ❏ Sunny site
- ❏ Perennial
- ❏ Hardy to zone 2

Unlike the forget-me-nots *(Myosotis)* grown in borders, the alpine (or high-mountain) types are true, hardy perennials. They may be short-lived, but they seed themselves almost as readily as the biennial species do. More compact in habit, alpine forget-me-nots are ideal for rock gardens of any size and for trough plantings.

Myosotis alpestris, syn. *M. sylvatica alpestris,* is a compact plant. It grows up to 6 in (15 cm) high and wide, forming clumps of hairy green spear-shaped leaves. The fragrant flowers, which are produced in dense clusters, are azure-blue, with a distinctive yellow eye. The cultivar 'Indigo Blue' has deep blue flowers; 'Rosea' bears pink ones.

Cultivation

Alpine forget-me-nots grow in any soil and position, but for best results plant them in a sunny site in well-drained, gritty soil during early or mid fall.
Propagation Sow seeds in mid to late spring in a cold frame or an outdoor seedbed.
Pests/diseases Generally trouble free, but in cold, wet conditions botrytis may cause flowers to rot and become covered in a furry grayish mold.

Narcissus triandrus 'Hawera'

- ❏ Height 2-12 in (5-30 cm)
- ❏ Spread up to 8 in (20 cm)
- ❏ Flowers late winter to midspring
- ❏ Good, well-drained soil
- ❏ Sun or partial shade
- ❏ Bulb
- ❏ Hardy to zone 4

Dwarf narcissi have all the charm of their larger cousins, the trumpet daffodils, and are easy to grow. They are ideal in rock gardens, troughs, and raised beds.

Popular species

Narcissus asturiensis, syn. *N. minimus,* is hardy to zone 4 and grows 3 in (7.5 cm) high. The 1 in (2.5 cm) long flowers are borne on weak stems in late winter.
Narcissus bulbocodium (hooppetticoat daffodil) reaches 2-6 in (5-15 cm) high. Wide-open 1 in (2.5 cm) long yellow trumpets appear in late winter, dominating the very narrow yellow petals. This species is hardy to zone 6.
Narcissus jonquilla (wild jonquil) is hardy to zone 4 and grows 1 ft (30 cm) high. The scented, 1½-2 in (4-5 cm) wide, deep yellow flowers have a small central cup; they appear in midspring.
Narcissus minor, hardy to zone 4, is 8 in (20 cm) high. It has pale yellow flowers with slightly deeper yellow trumpets in early spring.
Narcissus triandrus is hardy to zone 4. Its cultivars bear pendent flowers with funnel-shaped cups and backswept petals. Cultivars

---

Muscari comosum

flowers in each cluster are dark violet-blue, and the upper ones are pale blue.
Muscari neglectum, syn. *Muscari racemosum,* is hardy to zone 4 and reaches up to 9 in (23 cm) high. It bears dark blue, white-edged flowers that fade to yellowish green.

Cultivation

Because grape hyacinths flower so early in the spring, plant them very early in the fall — August or September in the North — to give the bulbs time to root into the soil. Plant the bulbs in any well-drained soil in full sun. If planted in shade, they will produce plenty of leaves but few flowers. Set the bulbs 3 in (7.5 cm) deep, in small groups. Lift and divide the plants every three years.
Propagation Many species spread readily on their own by producing offsets (bulblets) or self-sown seeds. Divide congested clumps after three years. Wait until the flowers have passed and the leaves are yellow (in preparation for summer dormancy) before lifting the plants. Separate the bulbs and replant immediately, setting one bulb in each of the new locations.
Pests/diseases Generally trouble free, although the flowers can be affected by smut fungus.

Narcissus bulbocodium

include 'Albus' (3-4 in/7.5-10 cm tall; creamy-white flowers), 'Hawera' (8 in/20 cm high; lemon-yellow flowers), and 'Ice Wings' (10 in/25 cm high; pure white).

Cultivation
Plant dwarf narcissi in fertile soil in sun or partial shade as soon as bulbs are available in early fall. Plant in small groups, spacing the bulbs 2-3 in (5-7.5 cm) apart, in flat-bottomed holes three times the depth of the bulbs. Leave undisturbed; let the leaves turn brown before removing them.
Propagation Lift overcrowded bulbs in early fall, remove any offsets, and plant in a nursery bed. They will reach flowering size in two to three years.
Pests/diseases Root-rot fungi or basal rot may stunt growth.

NAVELWORT — see *Omphalodes*
NEW ZEALAND BUR — see *Acaena*
NEW ZEALAND DAPHNE — see *Pimelea*

Narcissus minor

Nierembergia
nierembergia

Nierembergia repens

- Height 2-8 in (5-20 cm)
- Spread up to 2 ft (60 cm)
- Flowers early to late summer
- Moist, well-drained soil
- Sunny, sheltered site
- Perennial
- Hardy zones 7-10

The small nierembergias, whose funnel- or cup-shaped flowers bloom in summer, are suitable for edgings and rock gardens.

Popular species
Nierembergia hippomanica var. *violacea,* syn. *N. caerulea* (cupflower), is usually grown as an annual, but it can be grown as a perennial in hardy zones 7-10. The species reaches a height and spread of 6-8 in (15-20 cm). Slender branching stems form a hummock of linear medium green leaves. The flowers are pale lavender with a yellow throat. The cultivar 'Purple Robe' has deep purple flowers.
Nierembergia repens, syn. *N. rivularis* (white cup), grows only 2 in (5 cm) high but spreads 1½-2 ft (45-60 cm). It forms a low mat of rooting stems set with light green spoon-shaped leaves. The flowers are white with a yellow center. It is hardy to zone 7.

Cultivation
Plant nierembergias in spring in moist but well-drained soil in a sunny, sheltered position.
Propagation Divide and replant *N. repens* in early to mid spring. Sow seeds of *N. hippomanica* indoors in late winter or take cuttings in summer.
Pests/diseases Trouble free.

Oenothera
evening primrose, sundrops

Oenothera macrocarpa

- Height 3-12 in (7.5-30 cm)
- Spread up to 1½ ft (45 cm)
- Flowers late spring to midfall
- Any well-drained soil
- Sunny, sheltered site
- Perennial
- Hardy zones 4-10

Most evening primroses *(Oenothera)* open short-lived scented flowers in the evening. The shorter species are ideal for a rock garden.

Popular species
Oenothera acaulis, syn. *O. taraxacifolia,* is hardy to zone 5. It is 6 in (15 cm) high and 8 in (20 cm) wide, forming rosettes of prostrate zigzag branches with dandelionlike, toothed green leaves. Stemless off-white flowers that turn rose-pink open in the evening from late spring onward.
Oenothera caespitosa is hardy to zone 4. It grows 3-4 in (7.5-10 cm) high and spreads to 8 in (20 cm) by means of underground runners. It has narrow, oval, sometimes toothed green leaves. The fragrant white flowers open on summer evenings.
Oenothera macrocarpa, syn. *O. missouriensis* (Ozark sundrops), is 4-6 in (10-15 cm) high, with spear-shaped green foliage. The near-prostrate stems spread 1½ ft (45 cm). In summer the buds, often red-spotted on the outside, open in the evening to yellow flowers. It is hardy in zones 4-10.
Oenothera perennis, syn. *O. pumila* (dwarf sundrops), is hardy to

zone 5. It is 1 ft (30 cm) or more high and wide but has a floppy growth habit. The green leaves are lance-shaped. Loose, leafy spikes of yellow flowers open at night in early summer to early fall.

Cultivation
Plant in midfall or midspring in any well-drained soil in a sunny, sheltered site. Protect *O. caespitosa* from wet soil in wintertime.
Propagation Take cuttings of semimature lateral shoots in late summer; root in a cold frame or other protected spot. Or divide and replant mature clumps in spring.
Pests/diseases Trouble free.

Oenothera perennis

Omphalodes
navelwort

Omphalodes verna

❏ Height 4-9 in (10-23 cm)
❏ Spread up to 2 ft (60 cm)
❏ Flowers late winter to early spring
❏ Acid soil
❏ Partial shade or sun
❏ Perennial
❏ Hardy zones 5-10

Navelworts *(Omphalodes)* produce five-petaled blue flowers that resemble large forget-me-nots. They are hardy rock-garden plants. Though not commonly grown in the United States, they are valuable because of their early season of bloom.

Popular species
Omphalodes cappadocica is hardy in zones 6-10. It reaches 6-9 in (15-23 cm) high and 2 ft (60 cm) wide, forming clumps of bright green hairy leaves. Sprays of azure-blue flowers appear in late winter or early spring.
Omphalodes verna (blue-eyed Mary) grows 6 in (15 cm) high and spreads up to 1 ft (30 cm). It is hardy in zones 5-9. Sprays of bright blue white-eyed flowers are borne freely from late winter through early spring.

Cultivation
Plant in midspring in acid soil in a partially shaded or sunny site.
Propagation Divide and replant in midspring or after flowering.
Pests/diseases Trouble free.

ONION, ORNAMENTAL — see
Allium

Onosma
Onosma

Onosma alboroseum

❏ Height 6-10 in (15-25 cm)
❏ Spread up to 10 in (25 cm)
❏ Flowers late spring to late summer
❏ Any well-drained soil
❏ Full sun
❏ Evergreen subshrub
❏ Hardy to zone 6

Onosmas have pendent tubular flowers that are often golden yellow and fragrant. The leaves are rough-textured and hairy. These tenacious plants thrive in rock gardens and in crevices of walls.

Popular species
Onosma alboroseum is hardy to zone 7 and grows 6 in (15 cm) or more high and 10 in (25 cm) wide. It bears tufts of silver-haired leaves and clusters of white flowers that age to pink in summer.
Onosma stellulatum is hardy to zone 6 and grows 10 in (25 cm) tall. The stems and leaves are covered with white, bristly hairs. It bears clusters of pale yellow flowers from late spring to summer.

Cultivation
Plant in midspring in any well-drained soil in full sun.
Propagation Take softwood cuttings in summer; root in a cold frame or other protected spot.
Pests/diseases Trouble free.

Onosma stellulatum

Origanum
origanum, dittany

Origanum amanum

Origanum rotundifolium

- ❏ Height 2-12 in (5-30 cm)
- ❏ Spread 6-12 in (15-30 cm)
- ❏ Flowers early summer to early fall
- ❏ Any well-drained soil
- ❏ Sheltered, sunny site
- ❏ Perennial and subshrub
- ❏ Hardy zones 8-10

Some species of *Origanum*, or dittany, are used as culinary herbs (marjoram and oregano), while others are grown for their ornamental value in borders and rock gardens or as ground covers. Those described here thrive in sunny and sheltered sites, and they are notably drought-tolerant plants. These species are deciduous subshrubs or woody-stemmed perennials suitable for trailing over rock ledges and walls and for carpeting sunny banks.

Popular species
Origanum amanum grows 2-4 in (5-10 cm) high and spreads to 6 in (15 cm), forming a mat of slender stems closely set with pale green, heart-shaped leaves. It produces tubular, rose-pink flowers that are surrounded by showy purple bracts from midsummer to early fall. This species does not flourish in climates of prolonged humidity and wet.

Origanum dictamnus, syn. *Amaracus dictamnus* (Cretan dittany), reaches 1 ft (30 cm) high and wide and is of rounded habit. Its arching stems die back in winter. The rounded aromatic leaves are covered in dense, white, woolly hairs. The pale pink flowers, which are borne from early to late summer, are almost hidden by purple-pink bracts.

Origanum laevigatum reaches 10-12 in (25-30 cm) high and spreads to 8 in (20 cm) or more. It forms a neat, shrubby mat of aromatic gray-green leaves that contrast with the maroon stems.

Throughout summer the plant displays a profusion of small pink flowers that are surrounded by red-purple bracts.

Origanum rotundifolium reaches a height of 8-9 in (20-23 cm), with a spread of 1 ft (30 cm). It is a woody-stemmed rhizomatous perennial that spreads by means of underground runners. The small, rounded leaves are medium green with a bluish tinge. Nodding whorls of tiny, pale pink flowers are surrounded by conspicuous yellow-green bracts; they are borne freely in summer.

Cultivation
Plant origanums in early to mid spring in a sunny, sheltered site in any well-drained soil. These plants thrive in a warm, arid climate, such as that of Southern California. In areas of hot, very humid summers, such as the Gulf South, origanums are disease-prone and must be provided with a very well drained, airy position.

Propagation Take cuttings of nonflowering basal shoots between midsummer and early fall and root in a cold frame or other protected spot. Plant out the following early to mid spring.

Pests/diseases Generally trouble free.

Ornithogalum
star-of-Bethlehem

Ornithogalum nutans

❑ Height 4-15 in (10-38 cm)
❑ Spread 4-8 in (10-20 cm)
❑ Flowers late winter to late spring
❑ Good, well-drained soil
❑ Sun or partial shade
❑ Bulb
❑ Hardy zones 5-9

The species of *Ornithogalum* described here are excellent for rock gardens. Their starry white flowers have broad green stripes on the back, which are visible when they are in bud or half open; the flowers close nightly. Medium to dark green strap-shaped, slender leaves are produced at the base of the plants.

Ornithogalum umbellatum

Popular species
Ornithogalum dubium is hardy only to zone 9 and grows 10-15 in (25-38 cm) tall. It bears spikes of orange to yellow flowers from late winter into spring.
Ornithogalum nutans is hardy to zone 6 and grows to 15 in (38 cm) high. It produces stems of nodding bell-shaped flowers in mid to late spring. The species thrives in semishaded sites.
Ornithogalum umbellatum (star-of-Bethlehem) reaches a height of 1 ft (30 cm). The sturdy stems carry clusters of glistening white flowers in mid to late spring. It is hardy to zone 5.

Cultivation
Plant ornithogalums in fertile, well-drained soil in fall. Set the bulbs in irregular groups about 2 in (5 cm) deep. The plants will thrive in partial shade; in a hospitable spot, they will flourish without care for years.
Propagation The plants self-seed readily. Alternatively, lift established clumps when the leaves die down and detach the bulblets.
Pests/diseases Trouble free.

Ourisia
ourisia

Ourisia macrophylla

❑ Height 6-24 in (15-60 cm)
❑ Spread 1½-2 ft (45-60 cm)
❑ Flowers late spring to early fall
❑ Moist, preferably acid soil
❑ Partial shade
❑ Evergreen perennial
❑ Hardy to zone 7

Ourisias are low-growing woodland evergreens that flourish in partial shade. These plants will spread widely from creeping rootstocks and do best in loose, acid soil rich in leaf mold.

Popular species
Ourisia macrocarpa grows to a height of 2 ft (60 cm). It is a robust plant, carrying erect stems and leathery dark green leaves. This species displays whorls of yellow-throated white flowers in spring and summer.
Ourisia macrophylla is 8-12 in (20-30 cm) high and spreads to about 1½ ft (45 cm). This is a sturdy plant. It has rounded, toothed medium green leaves and produces dense clusters of tubular white flowers with yellow centers in midsummer.

Cultivation
Plant ourisias in early to mid spring in a partially shaded site in moist, acid soil.
Propagation Divide established clumps in midspring and replant immediately.
Pests/diseases Generally trouble free.

Oxalis
wood sorrel

Oxalis bowiei

Oxalis tetraphylla

- ❏ Height 3-16 in (7.5-40 cm)
- ❏ Spread 4-16 in (10-40 cm)
- ❏ Flowers spring to late fall
- ❏ Rich, well-drained soil
- ❏ Sun or partial shade
- ❏ Perennial
- ❏ Hardy zones 5-9

Wood sorrel *(Oxalis)* is a large and diverse genus that includes some aggressive weeds as well as plants of delicate charm. All are characterized by shamrocklike leaves. Those described here have attractive leaves and flowers and are ideal for the rock garden. The

funnel-shaped flowers open in sun and close up at night.

Popular species
Oxalis adenophylla is hardy to zone 5. It is 3 in (7.5 cm) high and 4 in (10 cm) wide and has rosettes of elaborately folded gray-green foliage. The flowers are satin-pink with maroon eyes; they bloom from late spring onward.
Oxalis bowiei, a bulbous species, is hardy to zone 8. It is 8-12 in (20-30 cm) tall and bears thick, leathery green leaves on erect stems. Bright rose to pink flowers

with yellow throats appear from summer to fall.
Oxalis corymbosa has three-lobed leaves rising from a scaly bulb. It is hardy to zone 9 and is 6-16 in (15-40 cm) tall. White-eyed red to purple flowers appear in spring to early summer. 'Aureo-reticulata' has yellow-veined leaves.
Oxalis depressa, syn. *O. inops*, is hardy to zone 5. It forms a 4 in (10 cm) tall mat of light green three-lobed leaves and bears pink flowers in summer.
Oxalis regnellii, hardy to zone 8, is 4-10 in (10-25 cm) high, with large triangular leaves. From spring to summer it bears an abundance of white flowers. 'Atropurpurea' has bright pink foliage and pale lavender flowers.
Oxalis tetraphylla, syn. *O. deppei*, is hardy to zone 8. It grows 10 in (25 cm) high and 6 in (15 cm) wide. The four-lobed leaves are marked with brown blotches; the flowers are carmine-pink to purplish red and are borne in loose sprays in late spring and summer.

Cultivation
Plant oxalis in early spring or early fall in sun or partial shade in any well-drained soil enriched with organic matter. *O. corymbosa* needs a sheltered site; at the northern edge of its range, plant it where the roots can spread under a rock and survive if top growth dies.
Propagation Divide and replant in early spring.
Pests/diseases Trouble free.

Oxalis adenophylla

Papaver

alpine poppy

Papaver pyrenaicum

❑ Height 4-10 in (10-25 cm)
❑ Spread 4-10 in (10-25 cm)
❑ Flowers early summer
❑ Well-drained soil
❑ Sunny site
❑ Perennial
❑ Hardy zones 5-10

Alpine poppies *(Papaver)* are miniature relations of the glamorous Oriental poppy grown in herbaceous borders. They have broad-petaled and bowl-shaped flowers in glowing colors; they open from attractive furry buds and are followed by shapely seed heads.

Popular species

Papaver alpinum grows 4-10 in (10-25 cm) high and wide. This perennial is short-lived and often raised annually from seeds. It forms a low mound of deeply dissected gray-green leaves, from which slender, leafless flower stems rise. The 1-2 in (2.5-5 cm) wide flowers range from white and yellow to red and orange in color. It is hardy in zones 5-10. *Papaver pyrenaicum* is a similar plant but is slightly taller and sturdier and has greener leaves. It is hardy to zone 5.

Cultivation

Plant alpine poppies in any well-drained soil in full sun in rock gardens, between paving stones, or on retaining walls.
Propagation The plants self-seed freely. Or sow seeds in the flowering site in early spring.
Pests/diseases Yellow blotches on the leaves are caused by downy mildew; the undersurfaces develop a gray fungal growth.

Parahebe

parahebe

Parahebe catarractae

❑ Height 2-8 in (5-20 cm)
❑ Spread up to 12 in (30 cm)
❑ Flowers early summer
❑ Any well-drained soil
❑ Sunny site
❑ Evergreen perennial
❑ Hardy to zone 8

Parahebes are related to the *Hebe* and *Veronica* species. The plants' small size makes them suitable for the rock garden.

Popular species and hybrids

Parahebe × bidwillii is a mat-forming hybrid that grows just 2 in (5 cm) high but 1 ft (30 cm) wide. It has tiny rounded leaves and bears an abundance of small, pale lavender flowers in summer. *Parahebe catarractae* is a shrubby plant 8 in (20 cm) high and 12 in (30 cm) wide, with toothed oval leaves. It bears funnel-shaped, crimson-veined white flowers. *Parahebe decora,* syn. *Veronica bidwillii,* is 8 in (20 cm) high and 12 in (30 cm) wide and has semi-prostrate stems and tiny rounded leaves. The white or pale lilac flowers are veined with pink.

Cultivation

Plant parahebes in any good, well-drained soil in a sunny site.
Propagation Take softwood cuttings in early summer and root in a cold frame.
Pests/diseases Trouble free.

PASQUEFLOWER — see *Pulsatilla*
PEARLWORT — see *Sagina*

Penstemon

alpine penstemon

Penstemon pinifolius

❑ Height 3-18 in (7.5-45 cm)
❑ Spread 6-18 in (15-45 cm)
❑ Flowers late spring to early fall
❑ Any well-drained but moist soil
❑ Sunny site
❑ Perennial or subshrub
❑ Hardy zones 3-10

This large, varied group consists mostly of North American flowers native to the Midwest and the West. Penstemons tolerate heat, cold, and drought. They are ideal for the rock garden, where their long-lasting spikes of tubular flowers provide a colorful show.

Popular species

Penstemon alpinus is hardy to zone 4. It forms a 10 in (25 cm) high and 6 in (15 cm) wide clump with broad leaves. Blue or purplish flowers with white throats appear in early summer.
Penstemon confertus is a prostrate semievergreen species, hardy to zone 3. It is 6 in (15 cm) high and 18 in (45 cm) wide, with lance-shaped medium green foliage. Cream-white or pale yellow flowers appear in midsummer.
Penstemon davidsonii is a low subshrub, 3 in (7.5 cm) high and 9 in (23 cm) wide; it is hardy to zone 6. It has broadly oval gray-green leaves and bears ruby-red flowers on short spikes in late spring and early summer.
Penstemon eriantherus, syn. *P. cristatus,* is a bushy species, 10 in (25 cm) high and hardy to zone 3. The leaves are lance-shaped to oval; red-purple flower spikes are borne in midsummer.
Penstemon heterophyllus flourishes in zones 5-10. This is a

Petrophytum
rock spiraea

Petrophytum caespitosum, flower buds

❑ Height 3 in (7.5 cm)
❑ Spread to 12 in (30 cm) or more
❑ Flowers in midsummer
❑ Very well drained, alkaline soil
❑ Sunny site
❑ Evergreen shrub
❑ Hardy to zone 3

Petrophytum is a small genus of subshrubs closely related to *Spiraea* and known as rock spiraea. It is ideal for growing in the crevices of rocks or in a scree bed.

Petrophytum caespitosum, syn. *Spiraea caespitosa,* is the only species commonly available from commercial sources. This shrub grows in the wild from South Dakota to California and southward to New Mexico; it is hardy to zone 3. It grows to 3 in (7.5 cm) high, forming dense mats that spread 1 ft (30 cm) wide or more. The leaves are small, silky-hairy, and gray-green. Numerous spikes of tightly packed, fluffy white flowers are borne in midsummer.

Cultivation
In fall or spring plant in very well drained, gritty, preferably alkaline soil in full sun. In the Northeast a north-facing slope is best.
Propagation Take softwood cuttings in early summer and root them in a cold frame or other protected spot.
Pests/diseases Aphids and spider mites may attack the foliage.

Penstemon scouleri

semievergreen shrubby species that grows 1 ft (30 cm) high and wide. In early to mid summer, blue, sometimes pink-flushed, flowers are borne. 'Blue Spring' has azure-blue flowers.
Penstemon laetus ssp. *roezlii* is hardy to zone 5. This subshrub is 4-9 in (10-23 cm) high and 12 in (30 cm) wide. The medium green leaves are narrowly spear-shaped. Sprays of lavender to violet-blue flowers appear in midsummer.
Penstemon menziesii grows 9 in (23 cm) high and 15 in (38 cm) wide and is hardy to zone 7. It is a semierect evergreen subshrub with green oblong to oval leaves. Clusters of violet-purple flowers appear in early summer.

Penstemon newberryi

Penstemon newberryi is similar to *P. menziesii* but is shorter and has pink or rose-purple flowers. It is hardy only through zone 8.
Penstemon pinifolius grows in neat clumps, 6-9 in (15-23 cm) high and 6 in (15 cm) wide, with narrow gray-green leaves. In early summer to early fall, it bears loose spikes of orange-red flowers. It is hardy to zone 8.
Penstemon rupicola, a subshrub hardy to zone 7, reaches 3-4 in (7.5-10 cm) tall and 9 in (23 cm) wide. It has oval leaves and, in late spring, rose-carmine flowers.
Penstemon scouleri is 1 ft (30 cm) high and wide, with leathery spear-shaped leaves. Clusters of lilac flowers appear in early and mid summer. It is hardy to zone 5.

Cultivation
In mid to late fall or early spring, plant penstemons in good, well-drained but moist soil in full sun.
Propagation Take cuttings of nonflowering side shoots in mid to late summer and root in a cold frame or other protected spot. Overwinter in the cold frame before planting out in late spring.
Pests/diseases Trouble free.

PERIWINKLE — see *Vinca*

PHEASANT'S EYE— see *Adonis*

Phlox
phlox

Phlox subulata 'Scarlet Flame'

Phlox douglasii

- ❑ Height 2-12 in (5-30 cm)
- ❑ Spread up to 1½ ft (45 cm)
- ❑ Flowers spring to fall
- ❑ Fertile, well-drained or moist soil
- ❑ Sun or partial shade
- ❑ Evergreen perennial
- ❑ Hardy zones 2-9

Phlox is a large genus of plants that is, for the most part, native to North America. These flowers grow wild in nearly every region of the United States, and as a result they are easily cultivated in American gardens. Although the familiar summer phlox *(Phlox paniculata)* do not adapt well to rock garden conditions, there are a number of fine species that will flourish there.

While summer phlox are tall, upright plants, most of the rock garden types are mat-forming and carry medium green lance-shaped evergreen leaves. They will root in crevices between rocks and do equally well in cracks in a wall and in cracks between paving stones. Phlox produces five-petaled flowers in shades of pink, red, purple, and blue as well as white.

Popular species and cultivars
Phlox bifida (sand phlox) is hardy to zone 5 and forms a mound up to 8 in (20 cm) high, with lilac or lavender flowers.
Phlox 'Chattahoochee' grows 8 in (20 cm) high and displays violet purple-eyed flowers through summer and into fall. It is hardy in zones 5-9.
Phlox divaricata (wild sweet William) is hardy in zones 4-9. This woodland plant grows 1 ft (30 cm) tall and wide, forming a loose mat of ovate semievergreen leaves that are 2 in (5 cm) long. In late spring the stems are topped with light blue or lavender flowers. This species requires a moist soil enriched with organic matter and a site in partial shade. The cultivar 'Fuller's White' displays white flowers.
Phlox douglasii is a subshrubby species that forms a dense, prostrate mat, 2-4 in (5-10 cm) high and 1½ ft (45 cm) wide. Hardy in zones 2-9, it bears pale lavender flowers from summer through fall. Among the popular cultivars are 'Crackerjack' (crimson red), 'Crater Lake' (lavender), 'McDaniel's Cushion' (rose-pink),

Phlox bifida

Phyteuma
horned rampion

Phyteuma scheuchzeri

❏ Height 2-8 in (5-20 cm)
❏ Spread 6-8 in (15-20 cm)
❏ Flowers early to mid summer
❏ Very well drained, neutral soil
❏ Sun or partial shade
❏ Perennial
❏ Hardy zones 6-9

Horned rampion *(Phyteuma)* produces unusual claw-shaped, tubular flowers that are densely packed into globular or oval heads. The species can be grown in rock gardens, scree beds, raised beds, or stone walls.

Popular species
Phyteuma hemisphaericum grows to a height of 4 in (10 cm), forming a dense clump of grasslike leaves. In summer it displays oval or rounded compact heads of clear blue flowers on 3 in (7.5 cm) long stems.
Phyteuma scheuchzeri grows to a height of 6-8 in (15-20 cm). It has grasslike medium green leaves, and its spiky, globular flower heads are deep blue.

Cultivation
Plant phyteumas in a scree bed, rock garden, or drystone wall in sun or partial shade in very well drained, preferably neutral soil in early spring. Sun or light shade is equally acceptable, although a certain amount of protection from afternoon sun is helpful in areas of intense sunshine. Protect from waterlogging in winter.
Propagation Divide and replant after flowering or in spring.
Pests/diseases Stems and leaves may be eaten by slugs.

Phlox nana

'Red Admiral' (crimson), 'Snow White' (white), and 'Waterloo' (dark purple).
Phlox nana, syn. *Phlox mesoleuca* (Chihuahuan phlox), is native to the Southwest and is hardy in zones 7-9. It forms a sprawling mound of 3 in (7.5 cm) long leaves and reaches 6-12 in (15-30 cm) high and 18 in (45 cm) wide. This species requires a deep but well-drained soil and dry conditions in winter. It is admirably adapted to conditions in the scree bed of a western rock garden. Popular cultivars include 'Arroyo' (carmine rose), 'Mary Maslin' (vermilion with a yellow eye), and 'Tangelo' (bright orange).
Phlox stolonifera forms a mat of foliage up to 10 in (25 cm) high and 1 ft (30 cm) or more wide; it is hardy in zones 3-9. Deep rose-purple flowers borne in loose clusters emerge on upright stalks in spring. This species will tolerate a sunny position in cool climates but elsewhere it should be planted in dappled shade. The cultivar 'Blue Ridge' has clear, pale blue flowers; 'Bruce's White' has pure white flowers with yellow stamens. 'Pink Ridge' has

pink flowers, and 'Sherwood Purple' has purple flowers.
Phlox subulata forms a mat of needlelike medium green leaves. It grows 2-4 in (5-10 cm) high and up to 1½ ft (45 cm) wide and bears purple or pink flowers. The species is hardy in zones 2-9. Among the popular cultivars are 'Blue Emerald' (lavender blue), 'Crimson Beauty' (crimson red), 'Millstream Coral Eye' (white with a coral eye), 'Millstream Daphne' (deep pink), 'Oakington Blue' (sky-blue), 'Scarlet Flame' (magenta with a red eye), and 'Schneewitchen' (snow-white).

Cultivation
Plant phlox in fall or early spring. Most of these plants will flourish in rich, well-drained soil in full sun; however, *P. divaricata* and *P.* 'Chattahoochee' prefer a moist, acid soil and partial shade, and *P. stolonifera* prefers dappled shade in areas with hot summers. No matter the type of phlox, trim back all plants after flowering.
Propagation Take cuttings of nonflowering side shoots in early summer and root in a cold frame.
Pests/diseases Trouble free.

Picea
dwarf spruce

Picea abies 'Reflexa'

❏ Height 3-48 in (7.5-120 cm)
❏ Spread up to 3 ft (90 cm) or more
❏ Foliage plant
❏ Moist, acid soil
❏ Sunny, sheltered site
❏ Dwarf evergreen conifer
❏ Hardy zones 2-7

Dwarf spruces *(Picea)* are attractive in the rock garden. These plants have short, needlelike, usually medium green leaves and are mainly conical in shape.

Popular species and cultivars
Picea abies is hardy in zones 2-7. The cultivar 'Gregoryana' grows 8 in (20 cm) high and has dense sea-green foliage on a rounded, flat-topped shrub. 'Little Gem' grows 1 ft (30 cm) high in a dense

Picea mariana 'Nana'

cushion shape. 'Nidiformis' has a flat-topped form, 1 ft (30 cm) high and 3 ft (90 cm) wide. 'Pygmaea' is a very slow-growing, globular to dome-shaped plant, about 8 in (20 cm) high. 'Reflexa,' a prostrate cultivar, forms a low, wide-spreading dome of rigid stems with upward-swept tips.
Picea glauca is a species that is hardy in zones 2-6. The cultivar 'Conica' grows slowly, forming a cone-shaped shrub 4 ft (1.2 m) high. 'Echiniformis,' a dense, miniature globe, has gray-green leaves. 'Pixie' is an extremely dwarf form that makes a pyramid 3-6 in (7.5-15 cm) tall.
Picea mariana is a parent of 'Nana,' a slow-growing cultivar that reaches 1 ft (30 cm) high. It forms a neat rounded shrub with fine gray-green foliage. The species is hardy in zones 2-6.
Picea pungens is a species hardy in zones 2-7. 'Glauca Globosa' is a dense, flat-topped, silvery-blue rounded shrub, 2 ft (60 cm) high.

Cultivation
Plant dwarf spruces in moist, preferably acid soil in a sheltered, sunny site in fall or early spring. Plant in spring if the soil is heavy.
Propagation Home propagation is inadvisable; buy new stock.
Pests/diseases Adelgids (aphids) produce galls on young shoots.

Pimelea
New Zealand daphne

Pimelea prostrata

❏ Height 4-6 in (10-15 cm)
❏ Spread up to 1 ft (30 cm)
❏ Flowers in summer
❏ Well-drained, acid soil
❏ Sunny, sheltered site
❏ Evergreen subshrub
❏ Hardy zones 9-10

New Zealand daphnes are frost-sensitive plants that thrive in the moist and temperate climate of the Pacific Coast regions, where they suffer neither cold winters nor torrid summers. The shrubs are related to the true daphnes and they do best in scree beds.
Pimelea prostrata forms a prostrate, spreading mat of tangled stems bearing tiny gray-green leaves. The fragrant flowers that bloom in summer are waxy-white and are followed by white berries.

Cultivation
Plant pimeleas in acid soil in mid to late spring. Well-drained soil and a sheltered position are essential to protect against winter winds and waterlogging.
Propagation Take semimature cuttings with a heel in midsummer; root in a propagation unit.
Pests/diseases Generally trouble free, but the plants are occasionally subject to sudden dieback.

PINE, MOUNTAIN — see *Pinus*
PINK — see *Dianthus*

Pinus
mountain pine

Pinus mugo 'Mops'

❑ Height 4-20 in (10-50 cm)
❑ Spread up to 4 ft (1.2 m)
❑ Foliage plant
❑ Any well-drained soil
❑ Sunny site
❑ Dwarf evergreen conifer
❑ Hardy zones 2-7

The only species of pine with dwarf forms suitable for the rock or scree garden is *Pinus mugo*, the ultrahardy mountain pine. Like all pines, it has a gnarled, rugged appearance, with bottle-brushlike sprays of stiff, dark green needlelike foliage.

The species, which forms a medium to large shrub of dense, bushy habit, is too large for the rock garden, but the cultivars described here are slow-growing, naturally dwarf, and maintain their neat shape without pruning.

Popular cultivars
'Gnome,' one of the most widely grown dwarf mountain pines, is of compact habit and has dark green foliage. It eventually grows 20 in (50 cm) high.
'Mops' is a compact, globular type that grows 16 in (40 cm) high.
'Valley Cushion' makes a dense, low cushion of deep green needles 4-8 in (10-20 cm) high.
'Winter Gold' has a spreading habit and yellow foliage in winter.

Cultivation
Plant dwarf mountain pines during fall or spring in any well-drained soil in a sunny site; they tolerate alkaline soil.
Propagation Buy new plants.
Pests/diseases Trouble free.

Plantago
plantain

Plantago major 'Atropurpurea'

❑ Height 1-5 in (2.5-13 cm)
❑ Spread up to 1 ft (30 cm)
❑ Foliage plant
❑ Very well drained soil
❑ Sunny site
❑ Evergreen perennial
❑ Hardy zones 3-10

The genus *Plantago* includes that curse of the perfect lawn, the common plantain, as well as several species that are grown for their attractive rosettes of silver and gray-haired, sometimes rich beet-red leaves. They are suitable for sunny scree beds.

Popular species
Plantago argentea is hardy to zone 6 and forms rosettes of long, narrow, densely felted leaves covered with long silvery hairs. It grows 5 in (13 cm) high and spreads to 9 in (23 cm).
Plantago major is a pernicious weed in its wild form, and only cultivated forms of this species should be planted; it is hardy in zones 3-10. The cultivar 'Atropurpurea' forms a rosette of ribbed leaves that are bronze-purple on top, bronze-green underneath. 'Rosularis' (rose plantain) forms a silvery leaf rosette; instead of flower spikes, it bears a central rosette of curly bracts (much like a small posy). 'Rosularis Rubrifolia' has reddish-purple foliage.

Cultivation
Plant plantains in spring or fall in any very well drained soil in full sun. If the plants are not given the fast drainage they require, cold, wet winter weather may cause rot to set in.
Propagation Divide and replant established plantains during fall or spring.
Pests/diseases Trouble free.

Pleione
pleione

Pleione bulbocodioides, white form

❑ Height 6-10 in (15-25 cm)
❑ Spread 4 in (10 cm)
❑ Flowers midwinter or spring
❑ Rich, well-drained soil
❑ Sheltered, partially shaded site
❑ Orchid
❑ Hardy to zone 7 with winter protection

Pleiones are beautiful orchids, deciduous and terrestrial and almost hardy. A few species can be grown in the open, but they do better in shallow pots in a cool but frost-free greenhouse; such container-grown plants can be moved outside to a shady site for the summer months. Like many other orchids, pleiones grow from pseudobulbs, each of which produces, usually after the flowers, one or two long-stalked, narrowly lance-shaped leaves.

The large blooms, which have narrow, spreading petals surrounding a frilled trumpet or lip, are white, yellow, pink, or lilac, usually with attractive markings in contrasting colors. In a greenhouse the flowers bloom from late winter onward; outdoors they blossom in mid and late spring. The foliage begins to turn yellow in early fall as the pseudobulbs become dormant.

Popular species
Pleione bulbocodioides, syn. *P. limprichtii*, is the hardiest species and can be grown in a sheltered rock garden even in southern zone 7. It grows 8 in (20 cm) high and bears flowers to 4 in (10 cm) wide, either singly or in pairs, on short stalks. They are variable, but the flowers typically have long, narrow petals and sepals that are white to pale or deep lilac in color; the trumpet-shaped fringed lips are usually spotted

Pleione bulbocodioides 'Versailles'

Polemonium
Jacob's ladder

Polemonium carneum

- ❑ Height 6-15 in (15-38 cm)
- ❑ Spread up to 1 ft (30 cm)
- ❑ Flowers late spring to summer
- ❑ Rich, well-drained soil
- ❑ Sun or partial shade
- ❑ Perennial
- ❑ Hardy zones 3-9

with red or yellow. Very large spear-shaped, heavily ribbed leaves develop after the flowers are finished. Among the popular cultivars are 'Etna' (rose-purple flowers with a freckled lip), 'Tolima' (large mauve-pink flowers), and 'Versailles' (lilac petals with an orange-spotted lip).

Pleione formosana is hardy to zone 7 if it is given a sheltered spot and the protection of a blanket of evergreen boughs in winter. It grows 10 in (25 cm) high and has round to oval pseudobulbs. The flower stalks produce one to two white, lilac, or magenta blossoms with white lips that are often stained with yellow. Popular cultivars include 'Blush of Dawn' (pale lilac petals with a pale mauve-tinted white lip), 'Oriental Grace' (purple-red to violet petals with a yellow-lined white lip), and 'Polar Sun' (pure white, with a lip marked with lemon-yellow).

Pleione speciosa, hardy to zone 8, grows to a height of 9 in (23 cm). It produces one to two bright magenta flowers per stem, with lips that are blotched with red and yellow. This species will usually grow vigorously.

Cultivation
Plant pleiones outdoors in mid to late spring in well-drained soil enriched with plenty of organic matter. Choose a sheltered site in partial shade. In winter protect dormant plants with a blanket of evergreen boughs.

In the greenhouse, pot pleiones in late winter or early spring in a humus-rich soil mix containing plenty of fine grit. Set three to five pseudobulbs in a 6 in (15 cm) pot, covering the bottom third of each bulb with the soil mixture. Water carefully until growth is well advanced, then water more generously with a fine spray until the foliage dies down. Thereafter, withhold water and store the bulbs in their pots in a cool but frost-free cold frame or greenhouse. In early spring start the growth cycle again with renewed watering; repot every other year.

Shade the greenhouse from hot sun and ventilate freely throughout the year, unless there is freezing weather.

Propagation Detach offsets when repotting and pot separately; repot the offsets as necessary until they reach flowering size. Or pot the bulblets that form on top of the mature bulbs; treat them as offsets.

Pests/diseases Slugs feed on shoots and flowers of plants grown outdoors; spider mites may attack plants grown indoors. Brown blotches on the foliage usually result from overwatering.

POCKETBOOK FLOWER — see *Calceolaria*

Dwarf Jacob's ladders *(Polemonium),* with their bowl-shaped blue or purple flowers and delicate feathery foliage, thrive in sunny rock gardens. These are hardy but short-lived plants.

Popular species
Polemonium carneum is a clump-forming species, 15 in (38 cm) high. Its many-branched stems bear finely divided medium green leaves and pinkish flowers. It is hardy in zones 5-9.

Polemonium reptans is hardy in zones 3-9. It grows 6 in (15 cm) high, forming matted clumps of deep green leaves, and it displays sprays of bright blue flowers in late spring to midsummer.

Polemonium viscosum, syn. *P. confertum,* is hardy to zone 5. It grows 6-8 in (15-20 cm) high and wide. The woody stems carry sticky leaves that are divided into fine leaflets. Dense heads of clear blue flowers are borne in summer.

Cultivation
In fall or early spring plant dwarf Jacob's ladders in rich, well-drained soil in sun or partial shade. Cut flowering stems back to basal shoots after flowering.

Propagation Divide and replant in midfall or early spring.

Pests/diseases Trouble free.

Polygala
milkwort

Polygala chamaebuxus

❑ Height 2-6 in (5-15 cm)
❑ Spread 9-12 in (23-30 cm)
❑ Flowers midspring to late summer
❑ Well-drained, fertile soil
❑ Sun or partial shade
❑ Evergreen perennial
❑ Hardy to zone 6

Milkworts *(Polygala)* have glossy leaves and attractive pealike flowers. They are ideal for rock and trough gardens, for scree beds, and as ground-cover plants.

Popular species
Polygala calcarea (milkwort), an evergreen prostrate plant, grows only 2-3 in (5-7.5 cm) high but 1 ft (30 cm) wide. It forms a mat of medium to dark green branches covered with small oval leaves. Sprays of lilac-blue flowers appear in profusion from late spring onward. It is hardy to zone 7.
Polygala chamaebuxus (ground box) has woody 6 in (15 cm) high stems with hard, boxlike evergreen leaves. It is hardy to zone 6. The yellow-and-cream flowers have a purple base. The variety *P. c. grandiflora,* syn. *P. c. rhodoptera,* has striking magenta-and-gold flowers.

Cultivation
Plant milkwort in fall or early spring. Both species will grow in ordinary, well-drained soil but do better in fertile soil enriched with organic matter. *P. chamaebuxus* prefers partial shade.
Propagation Take softwood cuttings of lateral or basal shoots, preferably with a heel, in early and late summer and root them in a cold frame or other protected spot. For *P. chamaebuxus* you can also divide the plants and replant them in early spring.
Pests/diseases Trouble free.

Polygala calcarea

Polygonum
knotweed

Polygonum tenuicaule

❑ Height 4-24 in (10-60 cm)
❑ Spread 1-2 ft (30-60 cm)
❑ Flowers early spring to midfall
❑ Well-drained soil
❑ Sun or partial shade
❑ Perennial
❑ Hardy zones 3-9

Knotweeds belong to a diverse genus, *Polygonum*. It includes common weeds, rampant climbers, and decorative garden plants. Several ground-hugging, mat-forming species are suitable for the rock garden.

Popular species
Polygonum affine grows 6-9 in (15-23 cm) high and spreads up to 1½ ft (45 cm). It is good ground cover for large rock gardens. Two cultivars are commonly grown. 'Darjeeling Red' forms a dense mat of narrow, lance-shaped dark green leaves that turn russet-brown in winter. It produces deep pink flowers on 6 in (15 cm) long spikes from midsummer to early fall. 'Donald Lowndes' is more compact and has larger leaves. The rose-red flower spikes are 6-8 in (15-20 cm) long and appear in early summer; young plants flower for a longer period. The species is hardy in zones 3-9.
Polygonum miletti is hardy to zone 5. It is 18-24 in (45-60 cm) tall and produces dense, broad spikes of rich crimson flowers from summer to early fall.
Polygonum tenuicaule is hardy to zone 6 and grows 4 in (10 cm) high and 1-1½ ft (30-45 cm) wide. It has ovate medium green leaves

Polygonum affine 'Darjeeling Red'

and white flower spikes borne in early to mid spring, before the leaves expand.

Cultivation

Plant knotweeds in fall or early spring in any well-drained soil. *P. affine* prefers a sunny position, but *P. miletti* and *P. tenuicaule* require partial shade and moist soil. Choose the site carefully, since the plants are invasive.

Propagation Divide and replant in early spring or fall.

Pests/diseases Trouble free.

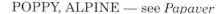

POPPY, ALPINE — see *Papaver*

Polygonum affine, fall foliage

Potentilla
cinquefoil

Potentilla cinerea

- ❑ Height 2-4 in (5-10 cm)
- ❑ Spread up to 1½ ft (45 cm)
- ❑ Flowers in summer
- ❑ Any well-drained soil
- ❑ Sunny site
- ❑ Perennial
- ❑ Hardy zones 3-10

Cinquefoils *(Potentilla)* bear lovely saucer-shaped flowers. There are several mat-forming species.

Popular species

Potentilla cinerea, syn. *P. tommasiniana,* is hardy to zone 3. It forms a mat 3 in (7.5 cm) high and 1½ ft (45 cm) wide, with hairy gray leaves and yellow flowers.
Potentilla crantzii is hardy to zone 5. It forms 4 in (10 cm) tufts of palmate leaves and bears loose clusters of yellow flowers marked with orange blotches.
Potentilla nitida, hardy to zone 5, is 3 in (7.5 cm) tall and 1 ft (30 cm) wide. It has silvery leaves and pink, crimson-centered flowers.
Potentilla × tonguei, hardy in zones 5-10, grows 2 in (5 cm) high and 10 in (25 cm) wide. It bears dark green leaves and soft apricot flowers with crimson centers.

Cultivation

Plant in fall or early spring in any well-drained soil in a sunny site. *P. nitida* thrives in poor soil.

Propagation Divide and replant in fall or spring. Or take basal cuttings in spring; root in a cold frame or other protected spot.

Pests/diseases Trouble free.

Primula

primula

Primula x polyantha

- ❑ Height 2-24 in (5-60 cm)
- ❑ Spread 3-12 in (7.5-30 cm)
- ❑ Flowers midwinter to early summer
- ❑ Well-drained or moist, fertile soil
- ❑ Sun or partial shade
- ❑ Herbaceous and evergreen perennials
- ❑ Hardy zones 3-10

Primula sieboldii, white form

Primula auricula

Primulas come in a bewildering range of shapes, sizes, and colors, with diverse growing needs. The alpine (high-mountain) types, which are suitable for edgings, raised beds, and rock gardens, are less exacting and relatively cold hardy. The problem for gardeners in the South will be the plants' intolerance of summer heat.

Primulas are often grouped according to botanical affinities:
Auricula (A) Rounded flower clusters; fleshy leaves usually covered with a mealy powder.
Cortusoid (C) Clustered flowers; lobed, crinkled, hairy leaves.
Denticulate (D) Clustered flowers; toothed leaves, mealy buds and stems.
Farinose (F) Clustered flowers; usually mealy leaves.
Muscarioid (M) Flower spikes held like those of grape hyacinth.
Nivalis (N) Flower clusters on tall stems; strap-shaped leaves.
Petiolaris (P) Clustered short-stemmed flowers; dense rosettes.
Soldanelloid (S) Clustered bell-shaped flowers, usually pendent; soft, hairy leaves.
Vernalis (V) Single primrose flowers; crinkled, hairy leaves.

Popular species and hybrids

Primula allionii (A), hardy to zone 7, grows 2 in (5 cm) tall. It forms a 6 in (15 cm) wide sticky-leaved hummock hidden by purple or rose-red to white flowers in early and mid spring. It is best adapted to climates with mild winters and cool summers, such as those along the coastal regions of the Pacific Northwest.

Primula alpicola (F), hardy to zone 6, forms a rosette of basal leaves 4 in (10 cm) long and 3 in (7.5 cm) wide. Flower stems 1-2 ft (30-60 cm) high bear one to two umbels each of large, nodding white, yellow, or purple blossoms.

Primula auricula (A) is hardy in zones 3-9. It has scented yellow flowers on 6 in (15 cm) tall stems in spring. Cultivars include 'Argus' (rusty-red with cream at the center), 'Rhemus' (blue with a white eye), and 'Sundancer' (red and yellow with a golden center).

Primula daonensis (A), hardy in zones 5-7, grows 4 in (10 cm) tall and 6 in (15 cm) wide. Its rosette of leaves is edged with rusty hairs; rose-pink flowers bloom in spring in clusters of two to eight.

Primula darialica (F), hardy to zone 5, forms a rosette of toothed leaves to 3 in (7.5 cm) long. Rose or carmine-red flowers are borne in clusters on 4 in (10 cm) stems.

Primula denticulata (D) is hardy in zones 3-8. It grows 10-15 in (25-38 cm) tall and 9 in (23 cm) wide. Its crinkled leaves are 3-4 in (7.5-10 cm) long before it blooms and 1 ft (30 cm) long afterward; the foliage is finely toothed along the margins. The flowers may be white, lavender, lilac, or pale purple, with a yellow eye at the center. The cultivar 'Snowball' is all white; 'Ruby' has red flowers.

Primula marginata (A), a woody-based species, is hardy to zone 7. It is 4 in (10 cm) tall, has silver-edged toothed leaves, and bears fragrant, pale lavender to violet flowers in spring.

Primula nutans (S) carries spikes of nodding lavender-violet flowers on 1 ft (30 cm) tall stems in early summer. The velvety leaves form 1 ft (30 cm) wide rosettes. It is hardy to zone 6.

Primula × polyantha (V) is hardy in zones 3-9 and blooms early in spring in northern gardens. This group of hybrids has rosettes of round-toothed dark green leaves 4-6 in (10-15 cm) long. The plants carry flat-topped clusters of fragrant flowers on stems 10-15 in (25-38 cm) tall. The colors of the flowers range from white to red, maroon, lavender, purple, and purplish-blue; all have a yellow eye. The 'Regal' strain of hybrids is the best-adapted to a wide range of garden conditions.

Primula reidii (S) is 4 in (10 cm) tall. It has rosettes of soft, hairy

Primula nutans

Primula 'Wanda'

leaves and bears clusters of semi-pendent, bell-shaped, ivory-white flowers in late spring. It is hardy to zone 6.

Primula rosea (F) is 6 in (15 cm) tall and wide; clusters of carmine-rose flowers bud in early spring. It is hardy to zone 6.

Primula sieboldii (C) is hardy to zone 5 and grows to 9 in (23 cm) high, with a similar or greater spread. Umbels of rose-purple flowers appear in late spring.

Primula vialii (M) is hardy in zones 5-9. It has erect rosettes of leaves and bears dense spikes of pinkish to lavender-blue flowers, which are crimson in bud, on 1 ft (30 cm) tall stems.

Primula vulgaris (V), or common primrose, is hardy in zones 5-9. Its wrinkled leaves form rosettes, on top of which nearly stalkless blossoms, yellow marked with darker blotches at the center, appear in early spring.

Some fine hybrids, most commonly the Juliana strain, are available. They bear white, pink, and red flowers from midwinter to spring on 3-6 in (7.5-15 cm) high plants. Outstanding among the Juliana hybrids is 'Wanda,' which bears wine-purple flowers amid purple-green foliage.

Cultivation
Plant in fall or early spring. Conditions vary according to section:
❑ Auricula: well-drained soil; semishade in warm areas, full sun in cool gardens.

Primula sieboldii

Primula vialii

❑ Cortusoid: moist, fertile soil; semishade.

❑ Denticulate: well-drained, moist soil; semishade.

❑ Farinose: moist, cool soil; sun or partial shade.

❑ Muscarioid: alkaline, well-drained soil; partial shade.

❑ Nivalis: moist but well-drained soil; semishade.

❑ Petiolaris: humus-rich, well-drained soil; cool, humid shade; protect in winter from waterlog.

❑ Soldanelloid: moist, acid, gritty soil; cool semishade.

❑ Vernalis: cool, humus-rich soil; light shade; divide regularly.

Propagation Divide primulas after flowering. Take cuttings in summer and root in a cold frame or other protected spot. Or sow seeds from late spring onward.

Pests/diseases Aphids, caterpillars, and cutworms may damage top growth. Various rots, botrytis, leaf spot, rust, and several viral diseases may disfigure plants.

Primula rosea

Prunella

self-heal

Prunella x webbiana 'Pink Loveliness'

- ❑ Height 6-12 in (15-30 cm)
- ❑ Spread up to 1½ ft (45 cm)
- ❑ Flowers late spring to early fall
- ❑ Any moist, well-drained soil
- ❑ Sun or partial shade
- ❑ Perennial
- ❑ Hardy zones 3-9

Although self-heals *(Prunella)* are not dramatic specimens, they have their place in the rock garden. Self-heals are hardy plants and easy to grow. They provide good ground cover and a long season of color with their dense spikes of lipped flowers. Because they are vigorous spreaders, confine self-heals to the wilder parts of the rock garden.

Popular species and hybrids

Prunella grandiflora spreads up to 1½ ft (45 cm), producing dense spikes, 6 in (15 cm) tall, of hooded tubular flowers and oval, slightly diamond-shaped medium green leaves. The flowers, which appear in summer and early fall, are purple or violet-blue. The species is hardy in zones 4-9.
Prunella vulgaris is a native of North America that is hardy to zone 3 and often grows as a weed in lawns. Its spikes of violet flowers reach a height of 9 in (23 cm). In its natural form this plant is too aggressive for rock garden planting; however, the less invasive (and more decorative) white, pink, and rose-red cultivars are suitable choices. 'Rubra,' which is sometimes listed as *P. incisa,*

rarely spreads more than 15 in (38 cm) and produces rich violet-purple flower spikes.
Prunella × webbiana comprises a range of hybrids, of which *P. grandiflora* is a parent (the hybrids closely resemble *P. grandiflora*). Hardy in zones 4-9, these plants generally reach a height of 1 ft (30 cm) when in bloom. Among the available cultivars are 'Loveliness,' which bears pale violet flowers, and 'Pink Loveliness,' 'Purple Loveliness,' and 'White Loveliness,' each of which displays flowers of the color indicated by its name.

Cultivation

Self-heals will grow in any ordinary, moist but well-drained soil in a sunny or partially shaded site. Plant them in early spring and, because of their self-seeding nature, deadhead frequently to prevent the growth of unwanted seedlings. It is advisable to keep these spreading plants away from slower-growing, more delicate neighbors.
Propagation The spreading habit makes division easy; this can be done at any time in fall or early spring. Alternatively, sow seeds in spring; these cultivars will come true to type — the offspring resemble their parents.
Pests/diseases Generally trouble free.

Pterocephalus

pterocephalus

Pterocephalus perennis

- ❑ Height up to 4 in (10 cm)
- ❑ Spread up to 1 ft (30 cm)
- ❑ Flowers in summer
- ❑ Any well-drained soil
- ❑ Sunny site
- ❑ Evergreen perennial
- ❑ Hardy to zone 6

Pterocephalus perennis, syn. *P. parnassii* and *Scabiosa pterocephala,* is a low, cushion-forming plant with gray-green, usually toothed leaves covered with dense, soft hairs. During most of the summer it bears 1 in (2.5 cm) wide, scabiouslike flower heads of purplish pink held on short stems just above the foliage; they are followed by fluffy seed heads.

Cultivation

Plant in early fall or midspring in a sunny site. These small plants flower best in poor, well-drained, and alkaline soil; in rich soil they produce an excessive amount of leaves and few flowers. Rock crevices, drystone walls, the cracks between paving stones, and sunny scree beds are ideal sites.
Propagation Divide and replant in early spring or midfall. Or take 2 in (5 cm) cuttings of soft basal shoots in midspring and root in a propagation unit. Alternatively, sow seeds in late summer; overwinter in a cold frame or other protected spot.
Pests/diseases Trouble free.

Pulsatilla vulgaris

Pulsatilla
pasqueflower

Pulsatilla vulgaris 'Rubra'

❑ Height 6-12 in (15-30 cm)
❑ Spread 6-10 in (15-25 cm)
❑ Flowers midspring to early summer
❑ Rich, well-drained soil
❑ Sunny, open site
❑ Perennial
❑ Hardy to zone 4

The long-lived, hardy, and reliable pasqueflowers *(Pulsatilla)* are ideal for an open rock garden. They display cup-shaped nodding flowers, each with a boss of golden stamens, ferny leaves, soft, hairy buds, and silky seed heads.

Popular species
Pulsatilla alpina is the tallest species, up to 12 in (30 cm) high, and 6 in (15 cm) wide. It is hardy to zone 5. The white flowers, to 2½ in (6.25 cm) wide, open in late spring and early summer; they are sometimes flushed bluish purple on the outside. A subspecies, *P. alpina apiifolia,* syn. *P. alpina sulphurea,* bears attractive pale yellow flowers.
Pulsatilla vernalis, syn. *Anemone vernalis,* is small and almost prostrate, with a height and spread of 6 in (15 cm). Hairy buds open in midspring to reveal pearl-white flowers, some 2 in (5 cm) wide, flushed with pink or purple-blue on the outside. This species is hardy to zone 4.
Pulsatilla vulgaris, syn. *Anemone pulsatilla* (true pasqueflower), is the best-known species and is hardy to zone 5. It reaches up to 9 in (23 cm) tall, and its purple

flowers can grow as wide as 3 in (7.5 cm). Several fine cultivars with flowers of different colors are available. They include 'Alba' (white), 'Red Bells' (bright red), and 'Rubra' (red).

Cultivation
Pasqueflowers do not tolerate root disturbance. Set out young container-grown plants in early fall in a sunny, open position in rich, well-drained soil. Almost all thrive in alkaline soil; *P. alpina apiifolia* prefers acid soil.
Propagation Sow seeds in midsummer in shallow pots or boxes of seed-starting mix in a cold frame or other protected spot. When the seedlings are large enough to handle, prick them off and overwinter in a cool but frost-free spot. Pot up when the new leaves make their appearance, and plant out in their permanent positions in early fall.
Pests/diseases Trouble free.

Pulsatilla alpina apiifolia

Puschkinia
striped squill

Puschkinia scilloides

❑ Height 4-6 in (10-15 cm)
❑ Spread up to 3 in (7.5 cm)
❑ Flowers early to late spring
❑ Moist, well-drained, fertile soil
❑ Sun or light shade
❑ Bulb
❑ Hardy to zone 5

The small striped squill *(Puschkinia scilloides,* syn. *P. libanotica)* is the only species generally available. It is a delightful, hardy, bulbous plant, excellent for trough gardens and for small pockets near the front of a rock garden.
Striped squill has strap-shaped leaves and slender stems. It bears clusters of icy-blue bell-shaped flowers in spring; each petal has a darker blue central stripe. The cultivar 'Album' is white.

Cultivation
Plant the bulbs in fall in an open or lightly shaded site in well-drained, moisture-retentive, fertile soil. You can leave the bulbs undisturbed for several years.
Propagation The bulbs readily produce offsets. Lift overcrowded plants when the foliage dies down in late summer. Remove the offsets and grow them on separately. Plant larger bulbs right away.
Pests/diseases Trouble free, but slugs eat bulbs, stems, and leaves.

PUSSY-TOES — see *Antennaria*
PYRETHROPSIS
HOSMARIENSE — see
Chrysanthemum hosmariense

Ramonda

ramonda

Ramonda myconi

❑ Height 4-6 in (10-15 cm)
❑ Spread up to 9 in (23 cm)
❑ Flowers mid to late spring
❑ Moist, rich soil
❑ Shade
❑ Evergreen perennial
❑ Hardy to zone 6

Ramondas are long-lived plants ideal for north-facing sites. They bear African-violetlike flowers in mid and late spring. The attractive evergreen leaf rosettes are deep green and deeply toothed.

Popular species
Ramonda myconi, syn. *R. pyrenaica,* to 6 in (15 cm) high, has mauve or blue-violet flowers with yellow stamens. Cultivars may have white, blue, or pink flowers.
Ramonda nathaliae grows 4 in (10 cm) high. It bears pale green leaves and, in late spring, clusters of white or lavender flowers.
Ramonda serbica resembles *R. nathaliae,* but its flowers are cup-shaped and lilac-blue.

Cultivation
In early spring plant ramondas in well-drained soil enriched with organic matter. Plant in north-facing rock crevices or walls.
Propagation Divide and replant rosettes in early spring. Or take leaf cuttings in mid to late summer; root in a cold frame or other protected spot. Or sow seeds in early spring or fall in a cold frame.
Pests/diseases Slugs may feed on the foliage.

Ranunculus

alpine buttercup

Ranunculus gramineus

❑ Height 4-18 in (10-45 cm)
❑ Spread 4-12 in (10-30 cm)
❑ Flowers early spring to midsummer
❑ Well-drained, moisture-retentive soil
❑ Sunny site
❑ Perennial
❑ Hardy zones 4-9

Alpine buttercups *(Ranunculus)* are hardy clump-forming plants. They are easy to grow, lack the invasive habit of other buttercups, and are ideal for the rock garden.

Popular species
Ranunculus amplexicaulis, hardy to zone 6, grows to 8 in (20 cm) tall and has lance-shaped blue-gray leaves. White flowers appear in late spring. By late summer the whole plant dies down.
Ranunculus asiaticus is hardy only to zone 8. It grows to 18 in (45 cm) high, forming a clump of lobed, divided leaves. The single or double flowers reach 1-4 in (2.5-10 cm) in diameter and may be red, pink, yellow, or white. The cultivar 'Alba' has white flowers; the hybrid strain 'Pot Dwarf' has red, orange, and yellow flowers.
Ranunculus ficaria (lesser celandine) is a native of Europe that has naturalized in the northeastern United States; it is hardy to zone 6. This species may reach a height of 1 ft (30 cm) and is a vigorous spreader, forming a ground-covering mat. It has glossy heart-shaped leaves and displays 2 in (5 cm) wide golden-yellow flowers from early to late spring.

Ranunculus glacialis is hardy to zone 4 and grows to 6 in (15 cm) high. Its fleshy green leaves are lobed. The white flowers, which may measure 1 in (2.5 cm) or more wide, are borne in spring and summer.
Ranunculus gouanii is a hairy perennial that reaches a height of 1 ft (30 cm). The flowers may grow 1½ in (3.75 cm) in diameter; they are a rich yellow and are displayed in clusters of up to five blossoms per stem.
Ranunculus gramineus is hardy to zone 6. It grows 1 ft (30 cm) tall and has grasslike leaves. This species produces bright yellow flowers from late spring to midsummer.
Ranunculus montanus, hardy to zone 6, has round, lobed dark green leaves and grows about 6 in (15 cm) tall. Shiny, bright yellow flowers bloom from late spring to summer. 'Molten Gold' is a free-flowering cultivar.
Ranunculus parnassifolius forms 4 in (10 cm) tufts of leathery heart-shaped leaves and produces 1 in (2.5 cm) wide flowers that are white on the inside and reddish on the outside. This species is hardy to zone 5.

Cultivation
Plant in a sunny site in any well-drained but moisture-retentive soil in fall or early to mid spring.
Propagation Divide and replant in fall or spring.
Pests/diseases Trouble free.

Raoulia
raoulia

Raoulia australis

- ❏ Height ¼-3 in (6-75 mm)
- ❏ Spread 6-12 in (15-45 cm)
- ❏ Foliage plant
- ❏ Well-drained, gritty soil
- ❏ Full sun
- ❏ Evergreen perennial
- ❏ Hardy to zone 8

The slowly spreading, carpeting or cushion-forming raoulias are good ground covers and are ideal between paving stones and for softening rocky outlines. Its tiny, hairy evergreen leaves often form rosettes and may bear stemless flower heads in spring or summer. They prefer the temperate climate of the Pacific Coast.

Popular species
Raoulia australis, syn. *R. lutescens,* forms a film of tiny gray-green leaves and yellow flowers from late spring to early summer. *Raoulia glabra* forms a mat, 6 in (15 cm) wide, of pale green leaves. It has fluffy white flowers. *Raoulia hookeri* is ½ in (1.25 cm) high and 12 in (30 cm) wide. It forms a carpet of tight silver rosettes and sometimes displays pale yellow, fluffy flower heads.

Cultivation
In midspring plant raoulias in gritty, well-drained soil in full sun. Waterlogging during the winter months is usually fatal. In the North these plants are fine for a cool greenhouse; plant them in early spring in shallow pots of standard potting soil mixed with an equal amount of grit. Repot every second or third year in midspring. Water from the bottom.
Propagation Divide and replant between midsummer and early fall. Or detach small portions from the edges of mature plants in spring and pot up.
Pests/diseases Trouble free.

Raoulia glabra

Rhododendron
rhododendron

Rhododendron polycladum

- ❏ Height 2-48 in (5-120 cm)
- ❏ Spread 1-5 ft (30-150 cm)
- ❏ Flowers late winter to early summer
- ❏ Moist, rich, acid soil
- ❏ Partial shade
- ❏ Evergreen shrub
- ❏ Hardy zones 4-8

Dwarf, compact, and creeping forms of rhododendron are perfect specimen shrubs for large rock gardens with acid soil. They add vibrant color for several months, and the neat evergreen foliage is attractive year-round.

Popular species and hybrids
Rhododendron calostrotum keleticum, hardy to zone 6, forms hummocks up to 1 ft (30 cm) high and 1½ ft (45 cm) wide. In late spring and early summer, it carries wide-open flowers of crimson-purple with darker markings.
Rhododendron campylogynum is hardy to zone 7. It reaches 1½ ft (45 cm) or more high and wide. In late spring and early summer, it bears bell-shaped waxy flowers in shades of purple, rose, and pink. *R. c. myrtilloides* is 6 in (15 cm) tall and has plum-purple flowers.
Rhododendron 'Chikor' is 1-2 ft (30-60 cm) high and wide and produces clusters of yellow flowers in late spring.
Rhododendron ferrugineum (alpine rose) is hardy to zone 4. It forms a dome-shaped shrub 3-4 ft (90-120 cm) high and wide. The

Rhodohypoxis
rhodohypoxis

Rhododendron campylogynum myrtilloides

Rhodohypoxis baurii

- ❏ Height up to 3 in (7.5 cm)
- ❏ Spread 4-6 in (10-15 cm)
- ❏ Flowers late spring to early fall
- ❏ Well-drained, acid soil
- ❏ Sunny site
- ❏ Perennial
- ❏ Hardy to zone 8

leaves are red on the undersides. Trusses of rose-red flowers are borne in early summer.

Rhododendron forrestii, syn. *R. repens,* is hardy to zone 8 and has a creeping habit. It is 1 ft (30 cm) high and 5 ft (1.5 m) wide, with rounded leaves. Large crimson bell-shaped flowers bloom in mid and late spring.

Rhododendron leucaspis is 2 ft (60 cm) tall and 4 ft (120 cm) wide. Its saucer-shaped white flowers have brown anthers and appear from late winter to early spring. It is hardy to zone 7 and is best grown in a sheltered site.

Rhododendron forrestii

Rhododendron pemakoense is a true alpine, or high-mountain, species of suckering habit. It reaches just 2 in (5 cm) high but spreads to 3 ft (90 cm). The leaves are small and rounded, and the flowers, which open in early and mid spring, are large, pink-mauve, and funnel-shaped. Avoid sites where early-morning sun will strike buds frozen in a spring frost. It is hardy to zone 6.

Rhododendron polycladum, syn. *R. scintillans,* is hardy to zone 7. It makes a twiggy little shrub, 2 ft (60 cm) high and wide, with small clusters of funnel-shaped lavender to violet flowers in midspring.

Cultivation

In fall or midspring plant dwarf rhododendrons in a moist but well-drained, rich, acid soil in partial shade, or in full sun in areas with cool summers. Be sure that the roots do not dry out.

Propagation Take cuttings from young growths in mid to late summer. Root in a cold frame or other protected spot.

Pests/diseases Weevils and caterpillars may damage flowers and leaves.

The rhizomatous *Rhodohypoxis baurii* is the only species generally available. Hardy except in severe winters, it grows only 3 in (7.5 cm) high, producing tufts of narrow, pale green, hairy leaves. Rose-pink six-petaled flowers are borne from late spring to early fall. Cultivars with flowers in shades of red, pink, and white are available but are not usually listed by name.

Cultivation

Plant in early fall in acid, well-drained soil in a sunny site. Do not let the plants dry out during hot summers, and make sure they are not waterlogged in winter.

Propagation Divide and replant the rhizomes in spring.

Pests/diseases Trouble free.

ROCK CRESS — see *Arabis*
ROCK JASMINE — see *Androsace*
ROCKROSE — see *Helianthemum*
ROCK SPIRAEA — see *Petrophytum*

Roscoea
roscoea

Roscoea cautleoides

Roscoea purpurea

❑ Height 6-12 in (15-30 cm)
❑ Spread 4-8 in (10-20 cm)
❑ Flowers early and mid summer
❑ Rich, moisture-retentive soil
❑ Sheltered site in sun or partial shade
❑ Perennial
❑ Hardy zones 6-9

The tuberous-rooted roscoeas produce spikes of orchidlike flowers in summer, and they carry leaves that are lance-shaped and erect. Roscoeas grow naturally in woodland conditions and flourish in regions with cool summers and mild winters. In general, these plants will perform best in cool pockets in the rock garden and at the front of borders.

Popular species
Roscoea alpina is a miniature species no more than 6 in (15 cm) high and wide. Soft pink-purple flowers are borne among the leaves. It is hardy to zone 6.
Roscoea cautleoides is a robust plant that is hardy in zones 8-9. It grows 1 ft (30 cm) high and 6 in (15 cm) wide. The species has long, sheathlike leaves and, in summer, displays handsome soft yellow flowers.
Roscoea purpurea reaches a height of 1 ft (30 cm) and a spread of 8 in (20 cm). It produces spikes of long, tubular, rich violet-purple flowers with prominent lower lips. It is hardy in zones 8-9.

Cultivation
Plant roscoeas in good, moisture-retentive, cool soil in early spring. Choose a sheltered site in sun or partial shade. Set the tuberous roots 3-4 in (7.5-10 cm) deep. Mark the site so that you do not inadvertently dig up the dormant roots — growth does not begin until late spring. The plants die down in early fall.
Propagation Divide and replant the crowns in early spring. Alternatively, sow mature seeds in a cold frame or other protected spot in late summer or early fall.
Pests/diseases Generally trouble free.

Sagina
pearlwort

Sagina subulata 'Aurea'

❑ Height ½-1 in (1.25-2.5 cm)
❑ Spread to 10 in (25 cm)
❑ Foliage plant
❑ Well-drained, moist soil
❑ Sun or partial shade
❑ Evergreen perennial
❑ Hardy to zone 4

Pearlworts *(Sagina)* are generally weedy plants, but a few species are well behaved enough for a place in the rock garden. While their greenish or white summer flowers are fairly insignificant, their mat- or hummock-forming habit makes them suitable as ground cover, for filling the cracks between paving stones, and for softening rocky outlines.

Popular species
Sagina subulata, syn. *Sagina glabra,* is the only species generally available from commercial sources in the United States. It spreads into a pale green carpet with tiny white flowers. The cultivar 'Aurea' is more decorative and carries golden leaves.

Cultivation
Plant pearlworts in fall or spring in well-drained but moist soil in sun or semishade.
Propagation Divide and replant clumps in fall or spring.
Pests/diseases Generally trouble free, but spider mites and aphids can be troublesome.

ST.-JOHN'S-WORT — see *Hypericum*

Salix
dwarf willow

Salix arctica

- ❏ Height 4-36 in (10-90 cm)
- ❏ Spread 1-3 ft (30-90 cm)
- ❏ Catkins in spring
- ❏ Moist, loamy soil
- ❏ Sun or partial shade
- ❏ Deciduous shrub
- ❏ Hardy zones 1-8

Most willows *(Salix)* are fast-growing trees that are simply too large for the rock garden. There are, however, a number of dwarf and compact species that will fit into such a setting. These smaller species offer colorful bark that provides winter interest, and they produce some of the earliest-blooming flowers in the spring. The foliage is often outstandingly handsome as well.

When ordering willows, specify male plants, if possible; they will produce the largest and showiest pussies, or flower catkins.

Popular species
Salix arctica (arctic willow) is as cold hardy as its name suggests, flourishing as far north as zone 1. This species forms a prostrate mat of branches and elliptical leaves that reaches no more than 4 in (10 cm) high but spreads up to 2 ft (60 cm) wide.
Salix elaeagnos, syn. *S. rosmarinifolia,* is a low-growing shrub that reaches a height and spread of 3 ft (90 cm). It is similar to the creeping willow but has thin leaves that give it the appearance of an outsize rosemary plant. It is hardy in zones 4-7.
Salix repens (creeping willow) is hardy to zone 5 and, as its name suggests, is another procumbent species whose branches typically spread along the ground, carrying a mat of leaves that are grayish-green above and silvery underneath. The catkins are small, but they crowd the naked stems in early spring. 'Voorthuizen' is a dwarf cultivar that may not spread more than 1 ft (30 cm), making it especially suitable for the rock garden.

Cultivation
Plant willows in fall or early spring in good, moist soil in sun or light shade. Prune away any deadwood in winter.
Propagation Take hardwood cuttings in fall and root in a nursery bed of moist soil. Plant out rooted cuttings after one year.
Pests/diseases Caterpillars, beetles, aphids, and scale insects may damage leaves. Galls may also be a problem.

SANDWORT — see *Arenaria*

Sanguinaria
bloodroot

Sanguinaria canadensis 'Flora Plena'

- ❏ Height 6-8 in (15-20 cm)
- ❏ Spread 1 ft (30 cm)
- ❏ Flowers mid to late spring
- ❏ Rich, moist, acid soil
- ❏ Partial shade
- ❏ Perennial
- ❏ Hardy zones 3-9

Bloodroot *(Sanguinaria canadensis),* the only species in its genus, gets its common name from the red color of its sap. Palmate, gray-green leaves, which push up through the soil in early spring, unfurl to reveal the flower buds, which open in midspring. The leaves continue to develop, but by late summer they die down. Each cup-shaped flower, 1½ in (3.75 cm) wide, is carried on a single stem and consists of eight to ten waxy white petals and a central boss of golden stamens. The cultivar 'Flora Plena' is a beautiful double-flowered plant and produces long-lasting blossoms.

Bloodroot prefers acid soil rich in organic matter and is a good plant for a shady woodland area.

Cultivation
Plant bloodroots in dappled shade in rich, moisture-retentive, acid soil in fall.
Propagation Divide and replant after flowering; take care not to damage the brittle rhizomes.
Pests/diseases Trouble free.

Saponaria
soapwort

Saponaria x lambergii 'Max Frei'

- ❏ Height 4-6 in (10-15 cm)
- ❏ Spread 4-6 in (10-15 cm)
- ❏ Flowers late spring to early fall
- ❏ Well-drained, fertile soil
- ❏ Full sun
- ❏ Perennial
- ❏ Hardy zones 5-8

The hardy, low-growing soapworts (Saponaria) are colorful, sun-loving plants that are ideal for planting into the crevices between rocks or for growing in troughs and scree beds.

Popular species and hybrids
Saponaria × lambergii 'Max Frei' is a compact plant that grows no more than 6 in (15 cm) high. It is hardy in zones 5-8. The leaves are oval and blue-green, and masses of carmine-pink flowers appear from spring through midsummer. Saponaria lutea, hardy to zone 6, forms tufts of hairy stems and foliage up to 4 in (10 cm) high. In early summer it produces small yellow flowers with violet-colored filaments at the centers.

Cultivation
Plant soapworts in fall or spring in a sunny site in well-drained, gritty soil. S. lutea requires alkaline soil.
Propagation Divide and replant in fall or spring. Alternatively, take cuttings of nonflowering shoots in early summer.
Pests/diseases Trouble free.

Saxifraga
saxifrage

Saxifraga Mossy Hybrid

- ❏ Height 2-24 in (5-60 cm)
- ❏ Spread 6-18 in (15-45 cm)
- ❏ Flowers winter, spring, and summer
- ❏ Well-drained, alkaline soil
- ❏ Sun or partial shade
- ❏ Evergreen perennial
- ❏ Hardy to zone 2

Saxifrages are neat in habit and come in a wide range of shapes, sizes, and colors. They are ideal in rock gardens, the crevices of walls, and troughs.

This evergreen genus is divided into sections according to growth habit and requirements, plus a miscellaneous section (Misc). The most commonly grown saxifrages belong to just three:
Cushion (C), or Kabschia, saxifrages form cushions of rosettes with silvery, often lime-encrusted leaves; they bloom in spring.
Encrusted (E), Euaizoonia or Aizoon, saxifrages have rosettes of strap-shaped, lime-encrusted leaves of silvery appearance. Sprays of flowers, usually white and often spotted, appear in early summer; the rosettes die after flowering, but more are produced on runners for the next season.
Mossy (M), or Dactyloides, saxifrages form hummocks of divided leaves and bear sprays of starry flowers in mid to late spring.

Popular species and hybrids
Saxifraga × apiculata (C), hardy to zone 6, forms a 16 in (40 cm) wide cushion; 3 in (7.5 cm) stems bear primrose-yellow flowers.

Saxifraga × borisii 'Marianna' (C), a sun-tolerant species, is hardy to zone 6. Gray-green cushions, to 6 in (15 cm) wide, bear yellow flowers on reddish stems.
Saxifraga burserana (C), hardy to zone 6, carries large white flowers above spiny, 6 in (15 cm) wide gray-green cushions. It flowers early, in late winter and spring.
Saxifraga callosa (E) is hardy to zone 7. It bears 15 in (38 cm) tall, arching sprays of white flowers, often spotted red in summer. The leaves form blue-green rosettes with a spread of 1 ft (30 cm).
Saxifraga cochlearis (E) grows to 8 in (20 cm) tall and 1 ft (30 cm) wide, with silvery rosettes and sprays of milky-white flowers in summer. It is hardy to zone 6.
Saxifraga cotyledon (E) is hardy to zone 6. It forms large rosettes of foliage to 9 in (23 cm) wide and 2 ft (60 cm) tall sprays of white flowers; the blooms of 'Southside Seedling' are spotted with red.
Saxifraga × elizabethae (C), hardy to zone 6, forms green cushions 3 in (7.5 cm) tall and 1 ft (30 cm) wide. The hybrid is difficult to obtain, but there are several cultivars available. 'Carmen' bears yellow flowers that are reddish at the base; 'Primrose Dame' has flowers in hues of yellow, ranging from cool to warm, and is more cold tolerant than its parent.
Saxifraga granulata (Misc) is a deciduous plant, hardy to zone 5. It has kidney-shaped gray-green leaves in loose rosettes up to 8 in

Saxifraga oppositifolia

Saxifraga x apiculata

(20 cm) wide; they die down in early summer. In midspring white flowers appear on 10 in (25 cm) stems. Bulblets form around the underground part of the stem.

Saxifraga hostii (C) forms a 1 ft (30 cm) wide mat. It is hardy to zone 6. Narrow leathery leaves turn reddish brown in fall; white flowers are borne in a cluster.

Saxifraga longifolia (E), hardy to zone 6, forms a long-lived rosette 1 ft (30 cm) wide. It eventually bears a 1½ ft (45 cm) long, arching spray of white flowers, then dies; it sets plenty of seeds. 'Tumbling Waters' has white flowers.

Saxifraga moschata (M) forms a bright green hummock to 3 in (7.5 cm) high and 1½ ft (45 cm) wide; yellow or white flowers appear in spring. 'Cloth of Gold' is golden-leaved.

Saxifraga oppositifolia (Misc) is hardy to zone 2. Its 2 in (5 cm) high, 1½ ft (45 cm) wide, dark green mat bears crimson to red-purple flowers in early spring. 'Florissa' is lilac-pink.

Cultivation

Plant saxifrages in early fall or early spring. The encrusted types do best in well-drained, alkaline soil. In regions with hot summers, they need partial shade; they do not thrive where summers are humid and hot. Mossy types do best in moist soil and light shade.

Propagation Divide and replant after flowering. Or detach non-flowering types in late spring and early summer; root as cuttings.

Pests/diseases Trouble free, but not adapted to regions with hot, humid summers.

Saxifraga callosa

Scabiosa
scabious

Scabiosa alpina

❑ Height 6-9 in (15-23 cm)
❑ Spread 8-10 in (20-25 cm)
❑ Flowers midsummer to midfall
❑ Well-drained, alkaline soil
❑ Sunny site
❑ Perennial
❑ Hardy zones 5-10

Dwarf scabious *(Scabiosa)*, with its elegant, finely cut foliage and large flowers, is perfect for pockets in rock gardens.

Popular species
Scabiosa alpina is the name used in catalogs for the dwarf forms of *S. columbaria*. These plants grow up to 6 in (15 cm) high and 9 in (23 cm) wide. Lavender-blue flowers are borne from midsummer to midfall above gray-green leaves.
Scabiosa graminifolia forms a clump, about 9 in (23 cm) tall and 10 in (25 cm) wide, of grassy, silvery leaves that make an attractive setting for the pinkish-purple flower heads displayed in mid and late summer. The foliage is evergreen in all but severe winters.

Cultivation
Plant in fall or spring in a sunny position in well-drained soil. Scabious thrives in alkaline soil; treat acid soil with lime to raise the pH level.
Propagation Divide and replant in early spring or midfall. Or sow seeds in late summer and overwinter in a cold frame or other protected spot.
Pests/diseases Trouble free.

Scilla
squill

Scilla peruviana

❑ Height 3-12 in (7.5-30 cm)
❑ Spread 3-8 in (7.5-20 cm)
❑ Flowers late winter to early summer
❑ Well-drained, moist soil
❑ Sun or partial shade
❑ Bulb
❑ Hardy to zone 5

Glossy strap-shaped leaves and graceful, bell-shaped or starry flowers make dwarf squills *(Scilla)* ideal for pockets in small rock gardens and for naturalizing.

Popular species
Scilla bifolia is hardy to zone 6. It usually has only two leaves per bulb. In early spring it bears star-shaped, gentian-blue flowers on spikes to 8 in (20 cm) high. The cultivar 'Alba' has white flowers; those of 'Rosea' are shell-pink.
Scilla mischtschenkoana, syn. *S. tubergeniana,* is 4 in (10 cm) tall and hardy to zone 6. Open bell-like flowers appear from late winter to early spring. They are pale blue with darker stripes.
Scilla peruviana, hardy to zone 8, grows up to 1 ft (30 cm) high. It carries dense clusters, up to 6 in (15 cm) wide, of about 100 deep blue, starry flowers during late spring and early summer.
Scilla siberica, hardy to zone 5, has 6 in (15 cm) tall stems of brilliant blue, nodding, star-shaped flowers in early spring. 'Alba' is a white cultivar. The deep blue flowers of 'Atrocaerulea' ('Spring

Beauty') are larger and bloom earlier than the species does.

Cultivation
In fall plant the bulbs in any well-drained, moisture-retentive soil in sun or dappled shade; set at a depth of three times their size.
Propagation When the leaves die down, lift crowded clumps and replant. Remove offsets at the same time, and plant them out. Or sow ripe seeds in early summer in a cold frame or other protected spot. Plants will reach flowering size after two or three years.
Pests/diseases Stem and bulb nematodes weaken growth, and rust may infect the leaves.

Scilla siberica 'Atrocaerulea'

Scutellaria
skullcap

Scutellaria alpina

- ❑ Height 6-12 in (15-30 cm)
- ❑ Spread 1-1½ ft (30-45 cm)
- ❑ Flowers summer and early fall
- ❑ Well-drained soil
- ❑ Sunny site
- ❑ Perennial
- ❑ Hardy zones 5-10

Skullcaps *(Scutellaria),* so named for the shape of the upper part of their two-lipped, tubular flowers, are hardy plants suitable for rock gardens and scree beds.

Popular species
Scutellaria alpina is hardy to zone 5. It grows 9 in (23 cm) high, with a spread of 1½ ft (45 cm), and it carries toothed oval leaves. In late summer clusters of purple flowers are borne at the tips of ground-hugging stems.
Scutellaria baicalensis, hardy in zones 5-10, is a bushy plant that reaches a height of 1 ft (30 cm). The flowers, which bloom in summer, have a dark blue upper lip and a light blue lower lip.

Cultivation
Plant in fall or early spring in well-drained soil in a sunny site.
Propagation Sow seeds in early fall. Or take stem cuttings in late spring or early summer.
Pests/diseases Trouble free.

SEA HEATH — see *Frankenia*

Sedum
stonecrop

Sedum acre

- ❑ Height ½-8 in (1.25-20 cm)
- ❑ Spread 4-18 in (10-45 cm)
- ❑ Flowers late spring to midfall
- ❑ Ordinary, well-drained soil
- ❑ Full sun
- ❑ Evergreen and herbaceous perennials
- ❑ Hardy zones 3-10

Stonecrops *(Sedum)* belong to a large genus of easily grown and hardy succulents, many of which are well suited to a rock garden, a raised bed, paving, or a drystone wall. They have attractive fleshy leaves that are often evergreen and small but profuse, starlike flowers in a wide range of colors.

Popular species
Sedum acre is a somewhat invasive plant that bears numerous bright yellow flowers in early to mid summer. It grows no more than 2 in (5 cm) tall but spreads to 1 ft (30 cm) or more and makes a mat of egg-shaped leaves. It is hardy to zone 3. The golden-leaved 'Aureum' is less vigorous.
Sedum album is hardy to zone 3. This plant will grow 6 in (15 cm) high and 15 in (38 cm) wide, forming a mat of evergreen egg-shaped leaves on pink stems. Loose clusters of white flowers are borne freely in midsummer.
Sedum cauticolum, syn. *Hylotelephium cauticolum,* is a woody-based plant 4-6 in (10-15 cm) high and 12 in (30 cm) wide. Floppy purple-red stems are set with ovate gray-green leaves. Flat,

branched heads of crimson-cerise flowers are borne in late summer. It is hardy to zone 3.
Sedum dasyphyllum is only ½ in (1.25 cm) tall but spreads to 1 ft (30 cm). It has small blue-green oval leaves and bears flat clusters of miniature white flowers in early summer. It is hardy to zone 4.
Sedum ewersii, syn. *Hylotelephium ewersii,* is hardy to zone 4. Rounded grayish-blue leaves are borne on trailing stems that grow up to 6 in (15 cm) tall and spread 1-1½ ft (30-45 cm). In late summer to midfall, the plant bears rounded heads of pink or red flowers.
Sedum kamtschaticum, hardy to zone 3, is evergreen and does well in semishade. It grows about 4 in (10 cm) high and 8 in (20 cm) wide. From midsummer to early fall, golden-yellow flowers in flattish clusters are held above tufts of spoon-shaped leaves. The cultivar 'Variegatum' carries white-margined leaves and displays flowers that turn red in fall.
Sedum oreganum is hardy to zone 4. It grows 3 in (7.5 cm) high but spreads to 9 in (23 cm). It forms loose evergreen rosettes of glossy green, rounded leaves suffused with red. Bright yellow flower heads appear on pink stems in summer.
Sedum pilosum, hardy to zone 7, grows 3 in (7.5 cm) tall and 4 in (10 cm) wide. It forms softly hairy rosettes and produces rose-pink flowers in late spring and early

Sempervivum
houseleek

Sedum spurium

Sempervivum montanum

Sedum kamtschaticum

summer. This species flowers after two or three years and then dies, scattering plenty of seeds to start a new generation of plants. *Sedum pulchellum* forms tufts 3 in (7.5 cm) tall and 6 in (15 cm) wide of narrow, lance-shaped, rich green leaves on erect reddish stems. Rosy-purple flowers appear on branched sprays in mid and late summer. This species is hardy to zone 8.
Sedum reflexum (stone orpine), hardy to zone 7, is an evergreen mat-forming plant with gray-green, egg-shaped leaves. It is 8 in (20 cm) tall and 12 in (30 cm) wide. Flat heads of bright yellow flowers are borne in midsummer.

Sedum sieboldii, syn. *Hylotelephium sieboldii,* bears pink flowers in mid to late summer, but its foliage is the chief attraction. The plant, which is 3 in (7.5 cm) tall and 16 in (40 cm) wide, features blue-gray, rounded leaves carried in threes along spreading stems. The species is hardy to zone 7 and the plants die down in winter. The leaves of 'Medio-Variegatum' are splashed with creamy yellow.
Sedum spurium, hardy to zone 3, forms a tangled mat of evergreen, slightly toothed, oval, medium-green leaves on reddish stems. The plant grows 4 in (10 cm) tall and spreads to 16 in (40 cm), and it bears flat heads of rich pink flowers in mid and late summer.

Cultivation
Plant in fall or spring in ordinary, well-drained soil in a sunny, open site. *S. ewersii* tolerates semishade; *S. pulchellum* likes moist soil and semishade. Do not deadhead after flowering. Instead, leave the faded stems intact until the following spring, when you can easily snap them off.
Propagation You can sow seeds in a cold frame or other protected spot in spring. Or simply divide the plants in fall or early spring.
Pests/diseases Generally trouble free, although slugs may attack large-leaved sedums.

SELF-HEAL — see *Prunella*

❑ Height ½-12 in (1.25-30 cm)
❑ Spread 8-12 in (20-30 cm)
❑ Foliage plant
❑ Well-drained soil
❑ Sunny site
❑ Evergreen perennial
❑ Hardy zones 5-10

Houseleeks *(Sempervivum)* have succulent leaves arranged in perfectly symmetrical rosettes. They form low mounds and spread slowly by means of short runners. Houseleeks are evergreen, providing year-round interest in a rock garden, drystone wall, or trough. A stout leafy stem rises from the center of each rosette, carrying star-shaped flowers with 10 or more petals. After flowering the rosette dies, but it is replaced by offsets. A few species have bell-shaped flowers and are often classified in the genus *Jovibarba.*

Popular species
Sempervivum arachnoideum (cobweb houseleek) is covered by silvery, woolly hairs that stretch between the tips of the green, often red-flushed leaves. Bright pink flowers are carried on 6 in (15 cm) tall stems from early summer to early fall. The cultivar 'Laggeri' has deep pink flowers; 'Royal Ruby' produces ruby-red leaves.
Sempervivum arenarium, syn. *Jovibarba hirta* ssp. *arenaria,* grows only ½ in (1.25 cm) high, and produces bicolored rosettes of pale green and red. It is hardy to

Sempervivum tectorum

Shortia

shortia

Shortia galacifolia

- ❑ Height 4-6 in (10-15 cm)
- ❑ Spread 12-15 in (30-38 cm)
- ❑ Flowers early to late spring
- ❑ Neutral or acid, moist soil
- ❑ Partial shade
- ❑ Evergreen perennial
- ❑ Hardy zones 4-8

Suitable for cool, semishaded sites in a rock garden, shortias spread by means of creeping roots and runners. They tolerate both cold and heat and have evergreen leaves and fringed, funnel- or bell-shaped flowers.

Popular species
Shortia galacifolia, 6 in (15 cm) tall and 1 ft (30 cm) wide, has rounded, wavy-edged, pale green leaves that turn bronze in fall and winter. In mid and late spring, it bears white, funnel-shaped flowers that turn pink as they age.
Shortia soldanelloides grows up to 5 in (12.5 cm) high, with dark green, toothed leaves that are reddish in fall. Sprays of deep rose pendent flowers appear in mid and late spring.
Shortia uniflora forms a clump that is 4 in (10 cm) tall and 15 in (38 cm) wide. In early and mid spring, it bears pale pink, funnel-shaped flowers.

Cultivation
In spring or fall plant in rich, well-drained but moist, neutral or acid soil in partial shade. Deadhead after flowering.
Propagation Divide and replant in early summer. Or take softwood cuttings of basal shoots in early summer and root in a cold frame or other protected spot.
Pests/diseases Trouble free.

---

zone 7 and bears yellow flowers from midsummer onward.
Sempervivum grandiflorum is hardy to zone 6. It has rosettes of densely hairy, purple-tipped, dark green leaves that grow up to 4 in (10 cm) high and 8 in (20 cm) wide. Loose clusters of yellow-green flowers with purple bases are borne in summer.
Sempervivum heuffelii, syn. *Jovibarba heuffelii,* is hardy to zone 6. Yellowish flowers on 6 in (15 cm) stems bloom from midsummer to early fall. Instead of having runners, the green or blue-green, sometimes red-flushed rosettes split into two.
Sempervivum montanum has 1 in (2.5 cm) high rosettes of dark green, finely hairy leaves. Pale

red-purple flowers are borne on 6 in (15 cm) stems in summer.
Sempervivum soboliferum, syn. *Jovibarba sobolifera,* takes its common name, hen-and-chickens houseleek, from the many small offset rosettes that surround the main one. They are bright green, often flushed with red. Yellow bell-shaped flowers sometimes appear in summer. This species is hardy to zone 5.
Sempervivum tectorum (common houseleek) is hardy to zone 5. It bears deep pink flowers on stems up to 1 ft (30 cm) tall from midsummer to early fall. The bright green leaf rosettes grow up to 3 in (7.5 cm) tall and 1 ft (30 cm) wide; they are tinged and tipped with maroon. The form *S.t. calcareum* has gray-green rosettes tipped with brownish purple. Among the cultivars with colorful rosettes are 'Red Purple' (deep purple with a reddish center) and 'Tokajense' (light green leaves with red tips that darken in winter).

Cultivation
Plant in well-drained soil in a sunny position in fall or spring. *S. grandiflorum* does not thrive in alkaline soil.
Propagation In fall or spring detach and replant rooted offsets.
Pests/diseases Trouble free.

SHOOTING STAR — see *Dodecatheon*

Sempervivum tectorum calcareum

Silene
dwarf campion

Silene schafta

Silene uniflora

❏ Height 2-8 in (5-20 cm)
❏ Spread 6-18 in (15-45 cm)
❏ Flowers late spring to midfall
❏ Any well-drained soil
❏ Sunny site
❏ Perennial
❏ Hardy to zone 2, depending on
   the species

Dwarf campions *(Silene)* are hardy plants that form tufts or clumps of mats with narrow leaves. The plants bear flowers that are star- or saucer-shaped.

Popular species
Silene acaulis (moss campion) is hardy to zone 2. It has pale green leaves and forms cushions about 2 in (5 cm) tall and 1½ ft (45 cm) wide. Almost stemless, bright pink flowers appear during late spring and early summer.
Silene alpestris, hardy to zone 5, forms tufts up to 6 in (15 cm) tall and wide. Sprays of white flowers with fringed petals are carried on wiry stems in summer. The cultivar 'Plena' (syn. 'Flore Pleno') has double flowers.
Silene schafta grows into a green-leaved clump up to 6 in (15 cm) tall and about 1 ft (30 cm) wide. Magenta-pink flowers are borne from midsummer to midfall. It is hardy to zone 4.
Silene uniflora, syn. *S. maritima* (sea campion) and *S. vulgaris,* has fleshy gray-green leaves and sprawling stems. The plant grows 6 in (15 cm) tall and 1 ft (30 cm)

wide. Numerous white flowers appear from midsummer to early fall. The cultivar 'Plena' ('Flore Pleno') has large double flowers. 'Robin White Breast' displays large white flowers; 'Rosea' produces smaller pink flowers.

Cultivation
Plant in fall or early spring in any good, well-drained soil in a sunny position. Leave undisturbed — campions do not tolerate root disturbance. *S. acaulis* thrives in the gritty conditions of a scree bed.
Propagation Take cuttings of basal shoots in summer; root in a cold frame or other protected spot.
Pests/diseases Trouble free.

Sisyrinchium
sisyrinchium

Sisyrinchium angustifolium

❏ Height 4-12 in (10-30 cm)
❏ Spread 6-12 in (15-30 cm)
❏ Flowers early spring to early fall
❏ Well-drained soil
❏ Sunny site
❏ Herbaceous and evergreen perennials
❏ Hardy to zone 3, depending on
   the species

These usually hardy little plants have a creeping rootstock. Sisyrinchiums produce six-petaled, often starry flowers in clusters amid tufts of irislike leaves. Each flower lasts no more than a day but is quickly replaced by others.

Popular species
Sisyrinchium angustifolium, syn. *S. gramineum* (blue-eyed grass), is hardy to zone 3. It forms a semievergreen clump up to 10 in (25 cm) high and 9 in (23 cm) wide, with tufts of grassy leaves. Irislike blue-violet flowers with a yellow eye open from midsummer to early fall.
Sisyrinchium bermudianum resembles *S. angustifolium,* but it is slightly taller and displays a profusion of pale violet-blue flowers. It is also less hardy, thriving only through zone 8.
Sisyrinchium californicum (golden-eyed grass) is semievergreen and hardy to zone 8. It grows about 1 ft (30 cm) high and wide. Bright yellow flowers with darker veins bloom during the summer.
Sisyrinchium douglasii (grass widow), syn. *Olsynium douglasii,*

Soldanella

soldanella, snowbell

Sisyrinchium bermudianum

Soldanella montana

is hardy to zone 5. This herbaceous species grows 10 in (25 cm) tall in a clump of grassy foliage. Short-stalked, pendent, rich purple bell flowers are borne in early spring. After flowering, the plant dies down completely and rests under the soil until early winter. *Sisyrinchium idahoense,* syn. *S. macounii,* rarely grows more than 4 in (10 cm) high and 6 in (15 cm) wide. It bears narrow gray-green leaf fans and large violet-blue flowers throughout summer. 'Album' is a white-flowered form. The species is hardy to zone 3 and does best in a sunny scree bed.

Cultivation

Plant in fall or early spring in good, well-drained soil. *S. douglasii* dislikes alkaline soil, and because it becomes completely dormant from midspring to early winter, it is best to mark the plant's site to prevent accidental disturbance. *S. californicum* prefers moist soil. All species thrive in sunny, open sites; they resent root disturbance.

Propagation Divide and replant any overgrown clumps in fall or spring. Or sow seeds in a cold frame or other protected spot in fall or early spring. A number of the species are self-sowing.

Pests/diseases Trouble free.

SKULLCAP — see *Scutellaria*
SLIPPER FLOWER — see *Calceolaria*
SNOWBELL — see *Soldanella*
SNOWFLAKE — see *Leucojum*
SOAPWORT — see *Saponaria*

- Height 2-6 in (5-15 cm)
- Spread 4-12 in (10-30 cm)
- Flowers early and mid spring
- Well-drained, acid soil
- Partial shade
- Perennial
- Hardy zones 4-8

Soldanellas have pendent, bluish, bell-shaped, fringed flowers. These well-loved plants flower from early spring onward. The plants are cold hardy, but the flower buds, which form in fall, are often damaged unless they are covered with snow or a blanket of evergreen boughs in winter. Soldanellas thrive in pockets in rock gardens and in troughs.

Popular species

Soldanella alpina (alpine snowbell), hardy to zone 5, grows 3 in (7.5 cm) tall and 9 in (23 cm) wide. The kidney-shaped leaves are green. Lavender-purple flower clusters appear in early spring. *Soldanella carpatica* is hardy in zones 4-8. This vigorous plant grows 5 in (13 cm) high and 6 in (15 cm) wide. Its evergreen leaves are tinged with red beneath; the flowers are fringed with purple. *Soldanella hungarica,* a vigorous dwarf plant, grows 4 in (10 cm)

high and wide and is hardy to zone 6. It has kidney-shaped to rounded leaves and nodding purple flowers on 4 in (10 cm) stems. *Soldanella montana,* hardy to zone 6, resembles *S. alpina,* but it is more robust. This 6 in (15 cm) tall and 1 ft (30 cm) wide plant bears clusters of lavender flowers in early and mid spring. *Soldanella pusilla* is hardy to zone 5 and grows 3 in (7.5 cm) tall and 6 in (15 cm) wide. Pale lavender flowers are carried singly. *Soldanella villosa* is probably a variant of *S. montana.* The flowers are similar, but the leaves are leathery, on hairy stalks. It, too, is hardy to zone 6.

Cultivation

In early and mid fall or in late spring, plant in well-drained, acid soil in partial shade. Surround the plants with a mulch of gravel to ensure perfect drainage, which is very important in wintertime.

Propagation Divide and replant in midsummer. Or take cuttings of basal shoots in late spring or early summer; root in a cold frame or other protected spot.

Pests/diseases Slugs may eat the flower buds and destroy succulent young growth.

Solidago
goldenrod

Solidago virgaurea ssp. *alpestris*

❏ Height 6-9 in (15-23 cm)
❏ Spread up to 6 in (15 cm)
❏ Flowers late summer to early fall
❏ Any well-drained soil
❏ Sun or partial shade
❏ Perennial
❏ Hardy to zone 5

Dwarf goldenrods *(Solidago)* bear golden-yellow, daisylike flower heads in erect, leafy pyramids. They bloom late in the season, at a time when gardens lack color. The plants are usually listed as *Solidago virgaurea* ssp. *alpestris* or *S. v. minuta.*

Cultivation
In fall or spring plant in any well-drained soil in sun or partial shade.
Propagation Divide and replant in spring.
Pests/diseases Powdery mildew may disfigure growth.

SPEEDWELL — see *Veronica*
SPIKE HEATH — see *Bruckenthalia*
SPLEENWORT — see *Asplenium*
SPRING MEADOW SAFFRON — see *Bulbocodium*
SPRUCE, DWARF — see *Picea*
SQUILL — see *Puschkinia, Scilla*
STAR-OF-BETHLEHEM — see *Ornithogalum*
STENOTUS ACAULIS — see *Haplopappus acaulis*
STONECRESS — see *Aethionema*
STONECROP — see *Sedum*
STORKSBILL — see *Erodium*
STRAWFLOWER — see *Helichrysum*
SUNDROPS — see *Oenothera*
SUNROSE — see *Helianthemum*
TEA TREE — see *Leptospermum*

Teucrium
germander

Teucrium pyrenaicum

❏ Height 2-8 in (5-20 cm)
❏ Spread 12-15 in (30-38 cm)
❏ Flowers early summer to early fall
❏ Any well-drained soil
❏ Sunny, sheltered site
❏ Evergreen subshrub
❏ Hardy to zone 5, depending on the species

These small creeping subshrubs bear short terminal spikes or flattened whorls of tubular flowers with a prominent lower lip. The evergreen foliage is often aromatic. Germanders *(Teucrium)* are suitable for ground cover in rock gardens, troughs, and scree beds.

Popular species
Teucrium aroanium is hardy to zone 8. It grows 4 in (10 cm) tall and 1 ft (30 cm) wide. Oval silver-gray leaves on rooting stems contrast with gray-blue flowers in mid and late summer.
Teucrium chamaedrys (wall germander), hardy to zone 5, grows up to 8 in (20 cm) high and 12 in (30 cm) wide. Its oaklike, aromatic leaves are bright green on top and grayish underneath. Spikes of pinkish flowers appear from midsummer to early fall.
Teucrium pyrenaicum is hardy to zone 6. It forms a creeping mat, 2 in (5 cm) high and 15 in (38 cm) wide. The hairy, rounded leaves are silver-green. From early to late summer, it bears dense heads of mauve-and-cream flowers.
Teucrium subspinosum grows up to 4 in (10 cm) high and about 1 ft

(30 cm) wide. It forms a shrubby mat of small gray-backed leaves and long silver spines. In summer it displays an abundance of small crimson blossoms. This species is hardy to zone 6.

Cultivation
Plant in fall or spring in any — even poor — well-drained soil in full sun. A sheltered spot is best in northern gardens. Trim the plants to shape after flowering.
Propagation Take cuttings of basal or lateral shoots in summer and root in a cold frame or other protected spot.
Pests/diseases Trouble free.

Teucrium chamaedrys

Thalictrum
dwarf meadow rue

Thalictrum kiusianum

- ❏ Height 6 in (15 cm)
- ❏ Spread 6 in (15 cm)
- ❏ Flowers early summer to early fall
- ❏ Moist but well-drained soil
- ❏ Sun or partial shade
- ❏ Perennial
- ❏ Hardy to zone 7

Like the tall border forms, dwarf meadow rues *(Thalictrum)* carry elegant fernlike leaves and produce sprays of fluffy flowers.

Popular species
Thalictrum ichangense, syn. *Thalictrum coreanum,* is hardy to zone 7 and grows 6 in (15 cm) tall and wide. It carries bronze-tinted leaves. In midsummer and early fall, this species bears lilac flowers on wiry stems.
Thalictrum kiusianum is a tufted species, 6 in (15 cm) high and wide, with deeply divided, gray to bronzy leaves. Lilac-purple flowers bloom in early and mid summer. It is hardy to zone 8.

Cultivation
Plant in early or mid spring in rich, moist but well-drained soil in a sunny or semishaded site.
Propagation Divide and replant in spring. Or sow seeds in early spring in a cold frame or other protected spot.
Pests/diseases Trouble free.

THISTLE, STEMLESS — see *Carlina*
THRIFT — see *Armeria*
THRIFT, PRICKLY — see *Acantholimon*
THYME — see *Thymus*

Thymus
thyme

Thymus praecox 'Albus'

- ❏ Height 2-8 in (5-20 cm)
- ❏ Spread 6-24 in (15-60 cm)
- ❏ Flowers early to late summer
- ❏ Well-drained soil
- ❏ Sunny site
- ❏ Evergreen subshrub
- ❏ Hardy to zone 3

Thymes are hardy mat formers or bushy subshrubs with evergreen, aromatic leaves. Small, tubular two-lipped flowers are borne in dense spikes or heads. Thymes are ideal for ground cover on banks and in rock gardens and for planting in troughs and in crevices in drystone walls and paving.

Popular species and hybrids
Thymus × citriodorus is hardy to zone 7. It grows 6-8 in (15-20 cm) high and wide. Its green, lemon-scented foliage is often used for culinary purposes. Small clusters of pale lilac flowers are borne throughout summer. The mat-forming cultivar 'Doone Valley' grows 3 in (7.5 cm) high and 1 ft (30 cm) wide; it has variegated green-and-gold leaves and round spikes of lavender flowers. 'Aureus' is a golden-leaved cultivar.
Thymus doerfleri, hardy to zone 5, grows 3 in (7.5 cm) tall and 1½ ft (45 cm) wide and has gray-green, hairy leaves. It bears lilac-pink flowers in early and mid summer.
Thymus herba-barona, hardy to zone 5, forms a caraway-scented dark green mat 2-4 in (5-10 cm) high and 16 in (40 cm) wide. Lilac flowers bloom in early summer.
Thymus praecox was formerly known and is still listed as *T. serpyllum.* It is very hardy, thriving in zone 3, and will form a mat 3 in (7.5 cm) tall and 2 ft (60 cm) wide. This summer-blooming species is represented by the cultivars 'Albus' (white), 'Coccineus' (crimson), 'Elfin' (bright green foliage; pink flowers), and 'Evergold' (pure gold foliage; lilac blooms).

Cultivation
Plant in fall or early spring in well-drained soil in a sunny site. To retain dense, compact shapes, shear the plants after they flower.
Propagation Divide and replant in early spring or late summer. Or take heel cuttings in late spring or early summer and root in a cold frame.
Pests/diseases Trouble free.

TOADFLAX — see *Linaria*

Thymus x citriodorus 'Doone Valley'

Thymus praecox 'Coccineus'

Townsendia
townsendia

Townsendia formosa

❑ Height 2-6 in (5-15 cm)
❑ Spread 4 in (10 cm)
❑ Flowers late spring and early summer
❑ Well-drained soil
❑ Sunny site
❑ Evergreen perennial
❑ Hardy to zone 5, depending on the species

Townsendias are hardy but short-lived plants with asterlike flowers. They are ideal in troughs and pockets in rock gardens where there is no winter waterlogging.

Popular species
Townsendia exscapa is hardy to zone 6. It grows 2 in (5 cm) tall and 4 in (10 cm) wide. White or pink flowers with prominent yellow centers are borne on short stems above narrow gray leaves.
Townsendia formosa is a tufted plant, 4 in (10 cm) tall and wide, and has violet-blue flowers with orange disks; it is hardy to zone 6.
Townsendia parryi will grow 6 in (15 cm) tall and 4 in (10 cm) wide. Lavender-blue flowers with yellow centers appear above a rosette of spatula-shaped leaves. It is often biennial and hardy to zone 5.

Cultivation
Plant in spring in well-drained but moisture-retentive soil in a sunny position.
Propagation Sow seeds in fall in a cold frame or other protected spot. Plant out in midspring.
Pests/diseases Trouble free.

Trifolium
clover

Trifolium repens 'Atropurpureum'

❑ Height 2-4 in (5-10 cm)
❑ Spread 1½-2 ft (45-60 cm)
❑ Foliage plant
❑ Any well-drained soil
❑ Sunny site
❑ Evergreen perennial
❑ Hardy to zone 4

Several unusual alpine clovers are occasionally offered by specialist growers, but the only clover that is generally available is a decorative form of *Trifolium repens*, the common white clover. This cultivar, 'Atropurpureum,' the so-called 'Queen's Clover,' rarely flowers. It is the foliage, which is usually borne in 'lucky' fours, that is the chief attraction. The leaflets are tiny and deep maroon, with a green edge. Because the plant roots at the leaf nodes as it spreads, it can be invasive; it is best to keep it away from more delicate plants. This alpine clover makes a semievergreen ground cover that is suitable for planting over small bulbs.

Cultivation
Plant in fall or midspring in any well-drained soil in a large, sunny rock garden or on a bank.
Propagation Divide and replant in midspring. You can detach rooted runners, pot them up, and grow them on.
Pests/diseases Powdery mildew may disfigure the foliage.

Tsuga
Canadian hemlock

Tsuga canadensis 'Jervis'

❑ Height 6-72 in (15-180 cm)
❑ Spread 10-120 in (25-300 cm)
❑ Foliage plant
❑ Moist, well drained soil
❑ Partially shaded or sunny, sheltered site
❑ Evergreen conifer
❑ Hardy zones 3-7

The Canadian hemlock *(Tsuga canadensis)* is a tall conifer that has sported several dwarf, slow-growing forms suitable as specimens in rock gardens. They reach the sizes given below after about 10 years. The narrow foliage, arranged in two rows along the branches, has twin silver bands underneath.

Popular cultivars
'Brandleyi' is irregularly pyramidal and grows about 3 ft (90 cm) tall. Its dark green foliage contrasts well with the light green new growth of spring.
'Cole' ('Cole's Prostrate') is prostrate. Its ground-hugging branches form a 6 in (15 cm) high and 3 ft (90 cm) wide carpet.
'Everitt's Golden,' syn. 'Aurea,' is a slow-growing, loosely pyramidal form that reaches a height of 6 ft (1.8 m) after 10 years. The foliage is golden and at its brightest when the plant is set in full sun.
'Gracilis Nana' grows as a flat-topped mound, 1½ ft (45 cm) tall and 3 ft (90 cm) wide, with graceful, arching branches.
'Jeddeloh' has light green foliage. It has a weeping, bird's-nest form,

Tulipa
tulip

Tulipa kaufmanniana

❑ Height 4-15 in (10-38 cm)
❑ Spread 3-6 in (7.5-15 cm)
❑ Flowers late winter to late spring
❑ Well-drained soil
❑ Sunny site
❑ Bulb
❑ Hardy to zone 4, depending on species

Tsuga canadensis 'Cole'

with a slight depression in the top center of the needled mound. It is just 20 in (50 cm) high but reaches a width of 3 ft (90 cm).

'Jervis' matures slowly into a small upright tree, reaching only 14 in (36 cm) or so high and wide.

'Minima' is larger than the other dwarfs described here. Still, it makes a fine plant for a large outcrop. Its broadly weeping form gives a mature plant the appearance of a shallow mound of gracefully arched branchlets. It grows to a height of 3 ft (90 cm) with a spread of 10 ft (3 m).

'Minuta' is truly a dwarf, forming a small-leaved, 10 in (25 cm) tall and wide cushion.

'Pendula' has weeping branches that make a dense mound, 3 ft (90 cm) tall and 2 ft (60 cm) wide.

'Rugg's Washington Dwarf' is a dense, globular or mound-shaped cultivar that is about 2 ft (60 cm) high and wide.

'Von Helm's Dwarf' is pyramidal in profile, similar to 'Brandleyi' but of more regular and neater growth. It grows 3 ft (90 cm) tall.

Cultivation
Plant in mid to late fall or early spring in a partially shaded or sunny, sheltered site. Tsugas thrive in deep, well-drained but

moisture-retentive soil; they do not do well in dry or alkaline soil.

Propagation Take heel cuttings of lateral shoots in early fall and root in a cold frame or other protected spot.

Pests/diseases The hemlock woolly adelgid can kill the tree. If small dirty white, cottony masses of insects appear on twigs or at the base of needles, spray with horticultural oil or diazinon in late April to early May and in mid July.

Tsuga canadensis 'Pendula'

The hardy dwarf species of *Tulipa* (tulip) have the charm characteristic of most rock garden plants. The flowers are goblet-shaped, sometimes with slender-pointed petals, sometimes cup- or bowl-shaped. They all open wide in full sunshine and close up at night; most are borne one per stem. The lance-shaped leaves are gray-green to rich green.

Popular species
Tulipa batalinii, hardy to zone 5, has cream-yellow flowers on 6 in (15 cm) stems in mid to late spring.
Tulipa biflora, hardy to zone 5, bears up to five starry flowers on each 6 in (15 cm) stem in early and mid spring. They are white with yellow centers and shaded green and red on the outside.
Tulipa celsiana persica is hardy to zone 4 and is 5 in (13 cm) high, bearing fragrant clear yellow flowers tinged with bronze.
Tulipa clusiana chrysantha (lady tulip) is hardy to zone 6. It grows 6-8 in (15-20 cm) tall. Yellow flowers flushed with red on the outside appear in midspring.
Tulipa kaufmanniana (water-lily tulip) is a variable species. It grows 4-10 in (10-25 cm) high and

Tulipa batalinii

Tulipa linifolia

is hardy to zone 5. Starlike creamy-white flowers with yellow centers open in early spring. The outside of the petals are tinged red and yellow. The cultivar 'Heart's Delight' has flowers that are carmine-red on the outside, pale rose inside. The blossoms of 'Shakespeare' are carmine-red edged with salmon outside and shaded scarlet and gold inside.

Tulipa linifolia, hardy to zone 5, grows 8 in (20 cm) tall, with a rosette of narrow leaves. It produces scarlet flowers with black bases and pointed petals in mid to late spring. *T. maximowiczii* is similar but blooms earlier, and the petal bases are bluish black.

Tulipa pulchella, hardy to zone 5, grows 4-6 in (10-15 cm) high. It has small flowers, often three to a stem, that open flat in late winter or early spring. The flowers are crimson to purplish red with a white-edged bluish base. The narrow leaves are edged with red. 'Violacea' is a deep purple-violet cultivar with a yellow base.

Tulipa sylvestris is 15 in (38 cm) tall and hardy to zone 5. Yellow flowers with reflexed outer petals open in mid and late spring.

Tulipa tarda is hardy to zone 5 and grows to 4 in (10 cm) high. In early spring it bears starry white flowers heavily suffused with yellow in the centers. The flowers are carried in clusters of up to five blooms. The leaves are slender and strap-shaped.

Tulipa turkestanica grows 10 in (25 cm) tall. In midspring it carries up to nine starry, creamy-white flowers with orange-yellow centers on a single stem. The species is hardy to zone 5.

Tulipa undulatifolia, syn. *Tulipa eichleri,* is hardy to zone 5. It reaches a height of 12 in (30 cm), bearing scarlet flowers with a basal black blotch edged with yellow. They open to 4 in (10 cm) wide in early and mid spring.

Tulipa urumiensis is also multi-flowered. It grows 4 in (10 cm) tall and is hardy to zone 5. Star-shaped yellow flowers, with olive-green and red on the outside, open in midspring.

Cultivation

Plant the bulbs 3-4 in (7.5-10 cm) deep and 3 in (7.5 cm) apart (set bulbs of *T. kaufmanniana* 6 in/ 15 cm apart) in late fall in good, well-drained soil in a sunny site; *T. sylvestris* accepts partial shade. Most dwarf tulips can be left to multiply where they grow, but they can also be lifted and stored after the foliage dies down.

Propagation Separate and replant offsets when plants are lifted. They flower after a few years.

Pests/diseases Slugs feed on top growth and bulbs. Tulip fire (botrytis) causes scorched-looking areas on leaves and flowers. Mice dig up and eat the bulbs.

Tulipa pulchella

Vaccinium

blueberry

Vaccinium vitis-idaea

- ❏ Height 3-12 in (7.5-30 cm)
- ❏ Spread 1-1½ ft (30-45 cm)
- ❏ Flowers midspring to midsummer
- ❏ Moist, acid soil
- ❏ Sunny or partially shaded site
- ❏ Evergreen shrub
- ❏ Hardy zones 2-9

Blueberries belong to the heath family and, like most of their relatives, need acid soil. The genus *Vaccinium* includes several large decorative and fruiting shrubs, but those described here are small enough for a rock garden and are hardy evergreens. The bell- or urn-shaped flowers are followed by edible fruits.

Popular species
Vaccinium delavayi grows about 1 ft (30 cm) tall and wide. It is hardy in zones 6-9. The young shoots are hairy, and the leaves, which are tinged with red in winter and spring, are tiny and borne in clusters. In early summer this shrub bears creamy-white or light pink flowers that are followed by carmine or purplish fruits.
Vaccinium oxycoccos (cranberry) is hardy to zone 2. It is a prostrate creeper that grows just 3 in (7.5 cm) high but spreads to 1½ ft (45 cm) wide. The tiny oval leaves are glossy green above and silvery underneath. In late spring and

midsummer, pink flowers with reflexed petals appear. They are followed by red fruits.
Vaccinium vitis-idaea (cowberry) forms a spreading mat 4-10 in (10-25 cm) high and 1½ ft (45 cm) wide. The dark green, boxlike leaves are carried on arching stems. Clusters of white or pinkish urn-shaped flowers are borne in late spring and early summer, followed by red fruits. The species is hardy to zone 2.

Cultivation
In mid to late fall or early spring, plant dwarf blueberries in acid, moisture-retentive, rich soil. Choose a site that is sunny or lightly shaded.
Propagation Layer any long shoots in early fall. Sever and replant rooted portions after one or two years. Alternatively, take cuttings of semimature wood in midsummer and root them in a cold frame or other protected spot. Set out the young plants in a nursery bed in midfall of the following year and grow on for two or three years before transferring to their permanent positions.
Pests/diseases Trouble free.

Valeriana

dwarf valerian

Valeriana montana

- ❏ Height 4-9 in (10-23 cm)
- ❏ Spread 6-9 in (15-23 cm)
- ❏ Flowers late spring to late summer
- ❏ Any well-drained soil
- ❏ Sunny site
- ❏ Perennial
- ❏ Hardy zones 4-9

The dwarf forms of valerian *(Valeriana)* are compact versions of their larger cousins that grow in flower borders. The dwarfs form basal mats of glossy leaves and produce flat heads of small white or pinkish tubular flowers on short stems. The seeds are feathery. Valerians are easy to grow, and they are a good choice for rock gardens and cracks between paving stones.

Popular species
Valeriana arizonica is hardy to zone 6. This clump-forming, rhizomatous plant grows up to 6 in (15 cm) tall and 9 in (23 cm) wide. It carries fresh green leaves and bears heads of pale pink flowers in late spring.
Valeriana montana usually grows 4 in (10 cm) high and spreads to about 6 in (15 cm). It has woody rhizomes and, from mid to late summer, bears flat heads of lilac, pink, or white flowers. The species is hardy to zone 6.

Cultivation
Plant valerians in mid to late fall or early spring in ordinary, well-drained soil in a sunny spot. They will tolerate light shade, and they thrive in alkaline soils.
Propagation Divide and replant in early fall or spring.
Pests/diseases Generally trouble free.

Verbascum
dwarf mullein

Verbascum 'Letitia'

- ❏ Height 10-12 in (25-30 cm)
- ❏ Spread 10-12 in (25-30 cm)
- ❏ Flowers early to late summer
- ❏ Any very well drained soil
- ❏ Sunny site
- ❏ Evergreen subshrub
- ❏ Hardy to zone 8

The tall border mulleins (*Verbascums*), many biennials among them, are noted for their large basal leaf rosettes and massive candelabras of flowers. These are Mediterranean plants that are only moderately cold hardy; however, they are extremely drought tolerant. The dwarf forms of mulleins are subshrubs, and they produce grayish hairy leaves and display yellow flowers in sprays or clusters.

Ideally, you should grow dwarf mulleins in scree beds and in other similar situations that allow for good drainage, even in winter. The site should be sunny and somewhat sheltered.

Verbascum dumulosum

Popular species and hybrids
Verbascum dumulosum forms a rounded shrub about 1 ft (30 cm) high and wide. The ovate leaves are covered with soft gray hairs. Sulfur-yellow flowers are borne in rounded clusters for most of the summer.

Verbascum 'Letitia' is a hybrid of *V. dumulosum*. It is a compact shrub that grows 10 in (25 cm) tall and wide, with gray-green, toothed leaves. Loose spikes of clear yellow flowers with brown basal blotches are carried from early to late summer.

Cultivation
Plant in spring in very well drained soil, such as a scree mixture. Crevices in rocks, drystone walls, and raised beds against sunny walls are all suitable sites. Deadhead after flowering. The hairy leaves easily fall prey to rot if the plants become waterlogged, especially in winter. Dwarf mulleins will flourish only in spots where they are not soaked for long periods of time. Cut away any dead growth in spring.

Propagation Take 2 in (5 cm) heel cuttings during summer and root in a cold frame or other protected spot.

Pests/diseases Generally trouble free.

Veronica
dwarf speedwell

Veronica cinerea

- ❏ Height 3-15 in (7.5-38 cm)
- ❏ Spread 8-18 in (20-45 cm)
- ❏ Flowers early spring and summer
- ❏ Any well-drained soil
- ❏ Sunny site
- ❏ Evergreen perennial
- ❏ Hardy to zone 3

Dwarf speedwells (*Veronica*) are hardy mat-forming plants ideal for troughs, scree beds, cracks in paving stones, and drystone walls. Their spikes of small, saucer-shaped flowers in shades of blue, pink, and white provide a mass of color throughout summer.

Popular species
Veronica armena is 4 in (10 cm) tall and 8 in (20 cm) wide. It has prostrate, branching stems with gray-green leaves. Bright blue flowers appear in late spring and early summer; it is hardy to zone 4.

Veronica cinerea, hardy to zone 5, grows 4 in (10 cm) tall and 16 in (40 cm) wide. It has toothed gray-green leaves; in early and mid summer pale blue flowers appear.

Veronica fruticans, syn. *V. saxatilis,* is hardy to zone 5. It is subshrubby, with oval leaves, and grows 6 in (15 cm) tall and 12 in (30 cm) wide. Deep blue flowers with red eyes bloom in summer.

Veronica gentianoides, hardy to zone 4, forms mats, 1½ ft (45 cm)

Vinca

lesser periwinkle

Veronica gentianoides

Vinca minor

❑ Height 2-4 in (5-10 cm)
❑ Spread 3-4 ft (90-120 cm)
❑ Flowers early spring to late summer
❑ Any well-drained soil
❑ Partially shaded or sunny site
❑ Evergreen subshrub
❑ Hardy zones 3-8

wide, of lance-shaped leaves. In early summer 15 in (38 cm) tall spikes of pale blue flowers appear. 'Variegata' has leaves marked with creamy white and is less vigorous. 'Nana' bears flower spikes only 9 in (23 cm) tall.
Veronica pectinata forms a 3 in (7.5 cm) tall and 15 in (38 cm) wide mat of gray-green leaves. Short spikes of blue flowers appear in late spring and early summer. 'Rosea' has pink flowers.
Veronica prostrata, syn. V. rupestris, grows as a leafy mat 16 in (40 cm) wide, with 8 in (20 cm) tall spikes of deep blue flowers in summer. It is hardy to zone 5. 'Trehane' has violet-blue flowers.

Cultivation
Plant in well-drained soil in a sunny site in fall or early spring. Deadhead after flowering.
Propagation Divide and replant in spring. Or take cuttings of lateral shoots in summer; root in a cold frame or other protected spot.
Pests/diseases Powdery mildew may affect the leaves.

Vinca minor (lesser periwinkle) is a hardy subshrub with trailing and creeping stems and glossy elliptical leaves. It grows up to 4 in (10 cm) tall and 4 ft (1.2 m) wide and makes an excellent ground cover in light shade or sun. Five-petaled flowers, usually blue and up to 1 in (2.5 cm) wide, appear from early spring to mid or late summer.

Among the numerous cultivars are 'Alba' (white), 'Bowle's Variety' (large, sky-blue), and 'Rosea' (violet-pink). Less vigorous forms with variegated leaves include 'Argenteo-variegata' (cream-white leaves, blue flowers) and 'Aureo-variegata' (golden-yellow leaf markings, blue flowers).

Cultivation
Plant in any well-drained soil in partial shade in fall or early spring. If necessary, trim the plants back in early spring to curb their spread.
Propagation Trailing stems, which are self-rooting at the leaf nodes, can be severed and replanted. Cuttings taken in early fall or early spring will root in open ground.
Pests/diseases Trouble free.

Veronica prostrata

Viola

viola, violetta, violet

Viola tricolor

Viola cornuta

- ❏ Height 2-10 in (5-25 cm)
- ❏ Spread 3-16 in (7.5-40 cm)
- ❏ Flowers late winter to midfall
- ❏ Fertile, moist soil
- ❏ Sunny or shady site
- ❏ Perennial
- ❏ Hardy zones 4-10

Violas are indispensable in rock gardens and scree beds. There are both sun- and shade-loving species with charming five-petaled flowers in a wide range of colors and a long-flowering season.

Popular species and cultivars

Viola aetolica, syn. *V. saxatilis aetolica,* forms 2 in (5 cm) high and 6 in (15 cm) wide clumps, with oval green leaves. Yellow flowers appear in late spring and early summer; it is hardy to zone 8.

Viola cornuta (horned violet) is hardy in zones 6-10. It makes 1 ft (30 cm) wide mats of oval- to lance-shaped leaves. From early summer to early fall, 10 in (25 cm) stems bear violet-purple, spurred flowers. Cultivars include 'Chantreyland' (apricot flowers), 'Scottish Yellow' (lemon-yellow), and 'White Perfection' (pure white).

Viola corsica, hardy to zone 9, grows to a height of 8 in (20 cm). The leaves are blackish green, and the squarish, bright purple flowers are borne from spring through fall. This species flourishes in shade or sun.

Viola gracilis is hardy to zone 7 and grows up to 6 in (15 cm) tall and 1 ft (30 cm) wide. It has oval leaves and, in summer, deep violet, long-spurred flowers.

Viola jooi is 3-4 in (7.5-10 cm) high, forming a basal rosette of small heart-shaped leaves. Fragrant pinkish-violet flowers bloom from spring through summer. It is hardy to zone 5.

Viola odorata (sweet violet) is hardy in zones 6-10 and thrives in partial shade. This species grows up to 6 in (15 cm) high, spreading by means of runners 1 ft (30 cm) or more wide. Fragrant violet-colored flowers appear from late winter to midspring above heart-shaped leaves. It has many cultivars, including 'Alba' (white), 'Royal Robe' (vibrant purple, with a white eye), and 'White Czar' (white veined with purple, a cream throat).

Viola pedata (bird's-foot violet) has divided leaves borne in a tuft 5 in (12 cm) high and 3 in (7.5 cm) wide. Violet-purple yellow-eyed flowers appear in mid and late spring. It is hardy to zone 4.

Viola sororia, syn. *Viola papilionacea,* has broad, heart-shaped leaves. Hardy to zone 4, it grows 8 in (20 cm) high and 1 ft (30 cm) wide. Dark blue or purple flowers appear from midspring to midsummer. Cultivars include 'Alice Witter,' which bears white flowers with wine-red centers, and 'Freckles,' which has white flowers with violet blotches. This species thrives in partial shade.

Viola tricolor (heartsease), hardy to zone 4, has naturalized in many parts of the northeastern United States and tolerates partial shade. It is a self-sowing annual or biennial or a short-lived perennial, and it grows up to 6 in (15 cm) high and wide. The flowers vary from cream and yellow to dark blue and purple-black; there are also bi- and tricolors. They bloom from midspring to midfall, often longer. Cultivars include 'Helen Mount' (violet, lavender,

Viola pedata

Viola sororia 'Freckles'

and yellow), 'Prince John' (yellow), and 'Blue Elf' (violet-blue).

Cultivation
In early and mid fall or early to mid spring, plant in fertile, moist but well-drained soil in a sunny or shady site. Deadhead regularly to extend the flowering season.
Propagation Sow seeds in early or mid spring in a moist, shady site outdoors or in a cold frame. Grow on in nursery rows or prick out seedlings into pots; plant out in early to mid fall. Or take basal-shoot cuttings in midsummer.
Pests/diseases Slugs, rust, and leaf spot harm leaves and flowers.

VITALIANA PRIMULIFLORA
— see *Douglasia vitaliana*

Waldsteinia
waldsteinia

Waldsteinia ternata

❑ Height 4 in (10 cm)
❑ Spread 1½ ft (45 cm)
❑ Flowers late spring and early summer
❑ Well-drained soil
❑ Sun or partial shade
❑ Evergreen perennial
❑ Hardy to zone 3

Ideal for ground cover, the hardy *Waldsteinia ternata,* syn. *W. trifolia,* spreads by means of woody rhizomes to wide mats of toothed, dark green, lobed leaves. In fall the foliage takes on bronzy tints. Clusters of buttercup-yellow, saucer-shaped flowers are borne freely from late spring onward.

Cultivation
Plant in fall or spring in any well-drained soil in sun or partial shade.
Propagation Divide and replant in fall or spring.
Pests/diseases Trouble free.

WALLFLOWER — see *Erysimum*
WHITLOW GRASS — see *Draba*
WILLOW, DWARF — see *Salix*
WILLOW HERB — see *Epilobium*
WINTER ACONITE — see *Eranthis*
WINTERGREEN — see *Gaultheria*
WOODRUFF — see *Asperula*
WOOD SORREL — see *Oxalis*
YARROW — see *Achillea*

Zauschneria
California fuchsia

Zauschneria californica

❑ Height 1-1½ ft (30-45 cm)
❑ Spread 1½ ft (45 cm)
❑ Flowers late summer to midfall
❑ Well-drained soil
❑ Sheltered, sunny site
❑ Shrubby perennial
❑ Hardy zones 8-10

Zauschneria californica (California fuchsia), syn. *Epilobium canum,* is a shrubby perennial that thrives in the mild climate of the Pacific Coast. Once established in the rock garden, it is long-lived and may prove invasive. It is valued for its fuchsialike flowers that appear at the end of summer and well into fall. Notably drought tolerant, it needs well-drained soil and full sun.

Clump-forming from a woody rootstock, the California fuchsia grows to a height and width of about 1½ ft (45 cm). The slender, arching stems are set with lance-shaped gray-green leaves. Vivid scarlet, tubular flowers, with flared mouths that are characteristic of some fuchsia species, are borne in loose sprays from late summer into fall. The subspecies

Z. californica microphylla (syn. *Zauschnesia cana, Epilobium canum* ssp. *canum*) has smaller, narrower gray leaves. *Z. californica latifolia (Epilobium canum* ssp. *latifolium)* is another subspecies; it has wider leaves.

Cultivation
Plant in fall or spring in well-drained soil in a sunny, sheltered site — at the back of a rock garden, on a retaining wall, or in a raised bed. With the exception of frost-free areas, protect the base of the plants with a winter mulch. In spring, cut back any winter-damaged stems to just above ground level.
Propagation You can divide and replant established clumps in midspring, but they do not split easily. It is easier to propagate from cuttings of basal shoots in late spring and root them in a propagation unit.
Pests/diseases Young growth may be attacked by aphids. In a severe infestation, leaves and stems can become distorted and may wilt and die.

Pool marginals These shallow-water plants — primulas and variegated water irises — are dwarfed by a huge *Gunnera manicata*.

A–Z of water plants

Plants are an essential part of every garden pool. They add to its decorative appeal and play an important role in creating a balanced environment for animal life.

Of the many plants that can be grown in or near water, water lilies *(Nymphaea)* are undoubtedly the best loved and most enchanting. Many species and hybrids are available in every color but blue. They grow in water depths ranging from 6 in (15 cm) to 3 ft (90 cm). Other deep-water aquatics include water hawthorn *(Aponogeton),* pond lilies *(Nuphar),* and golden club *(Orontium).*

Other plants that grow in deep water are known as floaters and oxygenators. Floaters, which include fairy moss *(Azolla)* and water hyacinth *(Eichhornia),* may be less spectacular than water lilies, but they are useful for covering the water surface and thus providing shade for fish. Oxygenators, which are submerged, include the pondweeds *(Elodea, Potamogeton)*; though invisible, they are essential for controlling algae and maintaining a balanced ecosystem in the pool.

Another, larger, group of water plants are the marginals, which grow in shallow water at the pool edge. Water irises, sweet flag *(Acorus),* marsh marigolds *(Caltha),* rushes *(Scirpus),* and arums *(Zantedeschia)* are just a few examples. Away from the water, in the boggy ground by streams and ponds, moisture-loving perennials find their perfect habitat — hostas, water avens *(Geum),* and hogweed *(Heracleum)* all grow more abundantly here than in dry garden borders.

A pool needs little attention once established. Lift, divide, and replant water lilies and marginals every few years, and if necessary, thin floating plants at the start of the growing season. Few pests trouble water plants, apart from water lily aphids and water lily beetles. Do not use insecticides, which can be harmful to fish; dislodge the pests with a forceful spray from a hose.

To help you determine if a particular plant will thrive in your area, we've given you zones that correspond to the plant hardiness map on page 176.

GROWING WATER PLANTS

**Garden pools contain both plant and animal
life — exotic lilies float on the surface and fish dart among
submerged oxygenating plants.**

For water plants to flower, site a garden pool in full sunlight. Keep the water clear, with about half its surface free of vegetation. Achieving a balance between plant and animal life is essential to maintain fresh, healthy water.

Murky, green water is caused by a buildup of algae — microscopic plants that thrive on sunlight and feed on mineral salts in the water. Because such salts are released when fallen leaves and other organic materials decompose, never add peat or garden compost to soil in which you plant aquatic plants. Oxygenators — plants that live beneath the water surface — suppress the growth of algae by removing nutrients that they need and by blocking sunlight. Oxygenators help the fish and other aquatic animals because they release into the water the oxygen these animals require.

Planting water lilies
The size and depth of the pool determine the type and number of water lilies *(Nymphaea)* it can hold. The numerous available cultivars are divided into categories. Miniature types require a water depth of 4-9 in (10-23 cm) and are ideal for tiny pools and tubs filled with water. They spread on the water surface 1-1½ ft (30-45 cm).

Small water lilies require water 6-12 in (15-30 cm) deep; they spread 1½-2½ ft (45-75 cm) wide. Medium types, 2½-3 ft (75-90 cm) wide, are suitable for large pools with water 6-18 in (15-45 cm) deep. Choose large water lilies for pools with a depth of 3 ft (90 cm) and a breadth wide enough to accommodate plants spreading up to 10 ft (3 m).

Water lilies and other true aquatics, such as aponogetons and cyperus, are best planted in

specially designed plastic baskets available from water-garden nurseries. Such aquatic baskets keep the plants from spreading out of control and make it harder for fish to disturb the soil. Large, established plants are sold in containers and can be added to a pool anytime in the growing season. However, you'll save money by buying young plants and setting them in the pool in spring.

Prepare a soil mixture of good, heavy loam in a bucket (avoid humus of any kind). Add a couple of handfuls of steamed bonemeal to each bucket, then enough water to make a pliable mixture.

Line the basket with burlap, plastic film, or the plastic fabrics

▼ **Pool harmony** Surface-floating water lilies and submerged oxygenators create a balanced ecosystem in which fish and other animal life flourish.

▲ Pool depths A series of pools of varied depths can accommodate aquatic plants of various types. The deepest pool is reserved for water lilies. The lush waterside planting includes rushes, ornamental grasses, and luxuriant clumps of hostas.

► Water iris The exquisitely flowered *Iris laevigata* thrives in the shallow water at pool margins. This plant colonizes readily and displays its rich violet-blue flowers in early summer, long before the water lilies open their exquisite flower cups.

▲ **Lily pads** The leaves alone can be just as charming as when the plants are in bloom. Here the lily pads contrast with duckweed, an invasive plant that should be discouraged from ornamental pools.

◄ **Bog plants** The shady, moist soil by a woodland stream is ideal for perennials, such as globe flowers *(Trollius)*, primulas, and ferns.

▼ **Crimson beauty** The brilliantly colored water lily *(Nymphaea)* 'James Brydon' and the creamy-flowered water hawthorn *(Aponogeton)* highlight this pool. Vertical contrast is provided by the variegated leaves of sweet flag *(Acorus calamus)*.

▲ **Poolside plants** Many garden perennials perform better in the moist soil by the water's edge than in ordinary flower beds. Notable examples here include hostas and astilbes, with tall, feathery plumes in shades of pink. The golden-yellow monkey flowers (*Mimulus luteus*) will also grow in shallow water.

◀ **Icy pond** In deepest winter, water continues to fascinate, mirroring in its glassy surface the surrounding landscape, rimmed with frost. Somber and still, conifers add touches of green.

sold as weed-suppressing mulch. Then fill it with the soil mixture to 1 in (2.5 cm) below the top. The roots of water lilies vary. Some are tuberous, with bulky anchorage roots and fibrous roots just below the crown; plant these vertically in the soil. Others are rhizomatous, with long, fleshy anchorage roots; plant these horizontally. For both types, make sure that the growing points of the shoots protrude just above the surface of the soil. Cover the points with a 1 in (2.5 cm) layer of fine gravel to keep fish from disturbing the soil.

Don't immerse newly planted water lilies to their final depth immediately. In an established pool, set the basket on a pile of bricks so that the shoots are just above the surface of the water. Remove a few bricks every few weeks as growth progresses until the basket is resting on the bottom of the pool.

▶ **Formal pool** The straight lines of a formal concrete pool can appear severe, but here the eye is irresistibly drawn to the focal point in one corner. An ornate urn holding a tall, spiky *Cordyline australis* perfectly complements a serene piece of statuary.

▼**Streamside planting** The banks of natural streams are ideal, semiwild habitats for moisture-loving plants, such as tall primulas, ferns, and self-sown Welsh poppies.

Cultivating oxygenators
Oxygenating plants spend their lives underwater. They are usually sold as bundles of unrooted cuttings. Plant the bottom ends in plastic pots filled with the same soil mixture used for water lilies.

Establishing floating plants
Floating water plants do not need planting at all. Simply place them on the surface of the pond; their trailing roots will absorb nutrients from the water.

Planting marginals
Marginal plants, which grow around the edge of the pool or in wet mud, prefer no more than 2-3 in (5-7.5 cm) of water above their roots. Most prefabricated pools are designed with a shelf around the edge to accommodate marginals. Like water lilies, they can be planted in aquatic baskets.

▲ **Arum lilies** The exotic marginal *Zantedeschia aethiopica* raises its glistening white spathes above the delicately patterned leaves of hostas.

◄ **Marsh marigolds** The golden buttercup heads of *Caltha palustris* are a familiar sight by the marshy edges of streams and ponds. The less common *Lysichiton americanum* (skunk cabbage) has striking golden spathes and leaves that can reach dramatic heights — it can be too large for small pools.

▼ **Primulas** A variety of primula species thrive in moist soil by a stream or pool, offering splashes of color in spring and summer.

Acorus

sweet flag

Acorus calamus 'Variegatus'

- ❏ Height 1-3 ft (30-90 cm)
- ❏ Water depth 3-5 in (7.5-13 cm)
- ❏ Foliage plant
- ❏ Sunny site
- ❏ Marginal aquatic
- ❏ Hardy to zone 3

The common name of *Acorus* — sweet flag — describes the plant well. Its foliage and form evoke the yellow flag iris, and when the leaves are crushed, they release a sweet, cinnamonlike aroma. This is one of the most fragrant, as well as striking, waterside plants.

Sweet flag is grown for its upright sword-shaped leaves, which form a dramatic edge to a pool. It bears flowers that resemble upright catkins in summer, but they are insignificant among the handsome leaves.

Popular species

Acorus calamus reaches 2-3 ft (60-90 cm) high and has dark green sword-shaped leaves. Plant it in water 3-5 in (7.5-13 cm) deep; it is hardy to zone 3. The rich green leaves of 'Variegatus' are striped with white.

Acorus gramineus (Japanese sweet flag) is hardy only through zone 6. It grows only 1 ft (30 cm) high and has narrow evergreen, grasslike leaves. Its minute flowers are insignificant.

Cultivation

Plant in early to mid spring in shallow water or moist, loamy soil by the pool edge in full sun.
Propagation Divide and replant clumps in spring.
Pests/diseases Trouble free.

Alisma

water plantain

Alisma plantago-aquatica

- ❏ Height 1½-2 ft (45-60 cm)
- ❏ Water depth 2-4 in (5-10 cm)
- ❏ Flowers in summer
- ❏ Sunny site
- ❏ Marginal aquatic
- ❏ Hardy to zone 6

Water plantain *(Alisma plantago-aquatica)* is a North American native that grows in muddy ground around pools, slow rivers, and canals. In water gardens it is a useful marginal aquatic — its loose spikes of small, pale pink or cream-white flowers will add a delicate touch to any planting arrangement.

The flowers open in summer. They are borne 1½-2 ft (45-60 cm) above lance- to oval-shaped, bright green leaves, which are arranged in a rosette at the base of the plant.

Cultivation

In early to mid spring, plant water plantains in loamy soil along the water's edge at a water depth of 2-4 in (5-10 cm), preferably in full sun. Alternatively, plant them in an aquatic basket or a crate, and sink it into the water.

Deadhead after flowering before the ripening seeds disperse.
Propagation Divide and replant overcrowded clumps in spring.
Pests/diseases Trouble free.

AMERICAN BURNET — see *Sanguisorba*

Aponogeton

Cape pondweed, water hawthorn

Aponogeton distachyus

- ❑ Spread 1½ ft (45 cm)
- ❑ Water depth 9-24 in (23-60 cm)
- ❑ Flowers early summer to early winter
- ❑ Sunny or shady site
- ❑ Deep-water aquatic
- ❑ Hardy to zone 10

The deep-water plant *Aponogeton distachyus* (Cape pondweed, or water hawthorn) is not winter hardy in most of the United States; you must replant it each year when the water warms to 65-70°F (18.5-21°C). It is worth the extra trouble and expense, however, because it is one of the few floating aquatics that tolerate shade. Unlike most other deep-water aquatics, which need to be kept in check, it is not invasive.

In spring Cape pondweed puts up floating oval green leaves. Soon afterward the flowers appear in a display that may last from midspring until early winter in milder regions. When they first open, the flowers are pure white with black anthers. After four or five days they turn cream-colored or green-white, then become completely green as they fade. The flowers have a waxy texture and measure up to 4 in (10 cm) wide. They are arranged in a V-shaped cluster held above the surface of the water. Their delicate but pervasive scent is especially strong in the evening. As cut flowers, the blossoms last several days.

Cultivation

Grow Cape pondweed in still or slow-moving water in neutral or slightly acid soil. It will tolerate partial shade, but the flowers are more profuse in full sun.

Set each tuber in an aquatic basket or crate of rich soil; cover with a mulch of fine gravel. Place them in the bottom of the pool at a depth of 9 in (23 cm) to ensure that the tubers survive winter.

Alternatively, push the tubers into the mud on the bottom of the pool or wrap each tuber in a small piece of sod, weigh it down with a

Aponogeton distachyus, flowers

stone, and drop it into place. In large pools, set the tubers at least 6 in (15 cm) apart.

Propagation Divide old tubers with several crowns in late spring and replant.

Pests/diseases Trouble free.

Arundo
giant reed

Arundo donax

- ❏ Height 10-20 ft (3-6 m)
- ❏ Spread 3 ft (1 m)
- ❏ Foliage plant
- ❏ Rich, moist soil
- ❏ Sunny, sheltered site
- ❏ Perennial
- ❏ Hardy to zone 6

The graceful giant reed *(Arundo donax)* comes from southern Europe. This plant is hardy as far north as zone 6, though it rarely produces its plumelike flowers in the North. It can reach a height of up to 20 ft (6 m) in one season. Giant reed thrives in rich, moist soil by the water's edge. It should be given a spot in full sun and sheltered from cold winds. The plant can be an aggressive spreader and will even grow wild in the eastern United States.

The thick stems bear broad, floppy blue-green leaves that are particularly ornamental in the cultivar 'Variegata,' which is broadly striped with creamy white. If these grasses have a good summer, they will produce dense sprays of yellow-green spikelets in early fall.

Cultivation
Plant in midspring in rich, deep, moist soil in a sunny, sheltered site. Cut the stems back to ground level in midfall and cover the crowns with a deep winter mulch of leaf mold or leaves.
Propagation Divide and replant the roots in late spring.
Pests/diseases Trouble free.

Asclepias
swamp milkweed

Asclepias incarnata

- ❏ Height 4 ft (1.2 m)
- ❏ Spread 2 ft (60 cm)
- ❏ Flowers midsummer to early fall
- ❏ Moist, acid soil
- ❏ Sunny site
- ❏ Perennial
- ❏ Hardy to zone 3

Most species of milkweed are vigorous, spreading plants that are best suited to wild gardens. However, the species *Asclepias incarnata* (swamp milkweed) thrives in the boggy ground by a pool or stream. It is easy to grow and, like other milkweeds, exudes a milky sap when cut. The stout, erect stems carry lance-shaped, rich green leaves. In mid and late summer the stems are topped with showy clusters of horned, reflexed rosy-pink flowers. These are followed by large, hairy seedpods.

Cultivation
Plant in midfall or midspring in rich, moist, preferably acid soil in full sun. Cut the stems back to ground level in late fall.
Propagation Divide and replant in fall or spring. Or sow seeds in spring.
Pests/diseases Trouble free.

Astilbe
astilbe

Astilbe x arendsii 'Cattleya'

- ❏ Height 2-3 ft (60-90 cm)
- ❏ Spread 1-2 ft (30-60 cm)
- ❏ Flowers early to late summer
- ❏ Rich, moist soil
- ❏ Sunny or lightly shaded site
- ❏ Perennial
- ❏ Hardy zones 4-8

The elegant astilbes are popular plants for flower borders, but they flourish most luxuriantly in boggy ground in close proximity to water. In such conditions, their deeply cut, rich green foliage, which is bronze-colored in spring, becomes particularly lush, and the tall, fluffy flower spikes are especially dense and long-lasting. The flowers will often fade to an attractive russet color; they can be dried for winter decoration.

Astilbe × arendsii is a hybrid of vigorous plants and is available in a range of pastels as well as in strong colors. It includes 'Bressingham Beauty' (rich pink), 'Cattleya' (pale pink), 'Irrlicht' (creamy white), and 'Ostrich Plume' (deep coral-pink).

Cultivation
Plant astilbes in mid to late fall or early spring. They need rich, permanently moist soil in sun or light shade. Cut the plants down to ground level in midfall.
Propagation Divide and replant in early to mid spring. Shade the new divisions until they are growing strongly and make sure that they do not dry out.
Pests/diseases Trouble free.

Azolla

fairy moss

Azolla caroliniana

❑ Surface-floating
❑ Any water depth
❑ Foliage plant
❑ Sunny site
❑ Floating aquatic
❑ Hardy to zone 6

Fairy moss *(Azolla caroliniana)* is a native of eastern North America. This tiny plant measures only ½-1 in (1.25-2.5 cm) wide. However, it multiplies rapidly, particularly during a long, hot summer, when it can take over an entire garden pool.

The tiny fronds — this plant is a true fern — float on the surface of still water, forming a dense pale green carpet. In late summer and early fall, they may be tinted a very attractive pinkish-red. With the onset of cold weather, the plant will sink to the bottom, resurfacing only when the water warms up.

Cultivation
Scatter the plants over the surface of the water in late spring or early summer. Control their spread by scooping up unwanted plants with a net.
Propagation You can buy new stock from a nursery, or transfer plants from one pool to another with a net.
Pests/diseases Trouble free.

BOGBEAN — see *Menyanthes*
BULRUSH — see *Scirpus*

Buphthalmum

buphthalmum

Buphthalmum speciosum

❑ Height 4-5 ft (1.2-1.5 m)
❑ Spread 3-4 ft (0.9-1.2 m)
❑ Flowers late summer
❑ Moist, poor soil
❑ Sunny site
❑ Perennial
❑ Hardy to zone 6

A member of the daisy family, *Buphthalmum speciosum,* syn. *Telekia speciosa,* is a robust, strong-growing plant. It is suited to boggy ground near woodland streams, where it can be allowed to spread by its invasive underground runners. Given plenty of room, this is a magnificent perennial with medium-green, coarsely toothed leaves that are heart-shaped at the basal rosettes and oval on the branching stems.

In late summer the stems are topped with large, rich yellow daisylike flowers with centers of darker yellow.

Cultivation
In midfall or early spring, plant buphthalmums in a sunny site in moist to boggy soil by the edge of the water. Avoid rich soils, which encourage the plants' natural tendency to spread.
Propagation Even if you do not want new plants, lift and divide buphthalmums every few years, in fall or spring, in order to keep them under control.
Pests/diseases Trouble free.

Butomus

flowering rush

Butomus umbellatus

❑ Height 3 ft (90 cm)
❑ Water depth up to 6 in (15 cm)
❑ Flowers early to mid summer
❑ Sunny site
❑ Marginal aquatic
❑ Hardy to zone 6

The flowering rush *(Butomus umbellatus)* is a gorgeous water-side plant. In spring it pushes up 3 ft (90 cm) tall spears of sword-shaped, rushlike green leaves that have sharp edges and may be tinged with purple.

In early to mid summer, tall flower spikes rise above the foliage. The sight is reminiscent of a large-flowered allium — slender stems carrying open heads of rose-pink, cup-shaped flowers. Each flower head may have up to 30 blooms, 4-6 in (10-15 cm) wide.

This plant thrives in the mud alongside a stream or pool. Because it is not especially robust, take care to keep more vigorous neighbors from smothering it.

Cultivation
Plant in early to mid spring at the margins of pools or on the muddy banks of slow-moving streams. Plant directly in the ground or use an aquatic basket or container and sink it into the water. The plants will tolerate a water depth of up to 6 in (15 cm), and they thrive in a sunny site.
Propagation Increase by dividing and replanting the rootstock of mature plants in spring.
Pests/diseases Trouble free.

BUTTERCUP— see *Ranunculus*

Calla

calla lily, water arum

Calla palustris

❏ Height 10 in (25 cm)
❏ Water depth 2-4 in (5-10 cm)
❏ Flowers late spring to early summer
❏ Sunny or partially shaded site
❏ Marginal aquatic
❏ Hardy to zone 2

Where the water merges imperceptibly with the land, at the edge of a shallow pool, the lovely calla lily *(Calla palustris)* can add much to the scenery. Its creeping stems grow through the marshy soil and shallow water to send up thick, glossy, heart-shaped leaves that stand 10 in (25 cm) high.

The display of small white arum flowers is full of charm. Flowering starts in late spring and continues through early summer. Each of the blooms will last for a couple of weeks. The flowers are followed by bright red or orange seed heads. There may be a second show of flowers in late summer.

Cultivation
Plant in late spring in fertile soil at the edge of a pool up to a water depth of 2-4 in (5-10 cm). A sunny or partially shaded site is suitable.
Propagation To increase calla lilies, divide and replant mature or crowded clumps in midspring.
Pests/diseases Trouble free.

CALLA LILY — see *Calla*, *Zantedeschia*

Caltha

kingcup, marsh marigold

Caltha palustris 'Flore Pleno'

❏ Height 1-2 ft (30-60 cm)
❏ Water depth up to 6 in (15 cm)
❏ Flowers midspring to early summer
❏ Sunny or lightly shaded site
❏ Marginal aquatic
❏ Hardy to zone 3

In late winter few sights are more encouraging along the poolside than the newly emerging heart-shaped leaves of marsh marigold *(Caltha)*. The splendid golden, buttercuplike flower heads follow in spring on thick, fleshy stems. However, because the foliage dies back to the ground in summer, it is unwise to devote large areas solely to this species.

This is a remarkably adaptable plant that is native to wetlands from Labrador to Alaska and as far south as the Carolinas.

Popular species
Caltha palustris will grow into a clump of dark green, heart-shaped leaves, 1-1½ ft (30-45 cm) high. It bears a profusion of single golden-yellow flowers. Among the popular cultivars are 'Alba' (white flowers) and 'Flore Pleno' (syn. 'Multiplex'; double golden-yellow flowers).

Caltha palustris 'Alba'

Cultivation
Plant in early spring in sun or light shade in water 6 in (15 cm) deep. Or plant above the water level, but keep the soil moist.
Propagation Divide and replant the roots between late spring and early summer.
Pests/diseases Rust may develop on the foliage.

CANADIAN PONDWEED — see *Elodea*
CAPE PONDWEED — see *Aponogeton*

Cardamine
cuckooflower

Cardamine pratensis 'Flore Pleno'

- ❑ Height 12-18 in (30-45 cm)
- ❑ Spread 1 ft (30 cm)
- ❑ Flowers late spring and early summer
- ❑ Moist soil
- ❑ Partially shaded site
- ❑ Perennial
- ❑ Hardy to zone 5

Cuckooflower *(Cardamine pratensis),* or lady's-smock, is a native wildflower commonly found on wet meadowlands. The cultivar usually available in water gardens is 'Flore Pleno,' a clump-forming perennial with basal rosettes of medium-green leaves divided into numerous leaflets. From late spring onward, slender and wiry, leafy stems bear loose spikes of delicate lilac-pink flowers.

Cardamines are valued for their early flowering. They thrive in moist or wet ground on streamside banks and in bog gardens.

Cultivation
Plant in fall or early spring in any type of soil that is wet or permanently moist. Flowering is most profuse in partial shade.
Propagation Divide and replant established clumps after flowering or in late winter, just as the plants start to grow.
Pests/diseases Trouble free.

CARDINAL FLOWER — see *Lobelia*
CATTAIL — see *Typha*
CINQUEFOIL, MARSH — see *Potentilla*

Claytonia
spring beauty

Claytonia virginica

- ❑ Height 2-6 in (5-15 cm)
- ❑ Spread 8 in (20 cm) or more
- ❑ Flowers in early spring
- ❑ Fertile, moist soil
- ❑ Shady site
- ❑ Evergreen perennial
- ❑ Hardy to zone 6

The hardy little spring beauty *(Claytonia virginica)* is aptly named, as the plant unfolds its cup-shaped flowers at the first touch of spring sun. These flowers are white or pale pink with deep pink stripes, and they are carried on branching stems that are clothed with narrowly spoon-shaped, near-succulent leaves. The evergreen foliage is bronzy-red when young but later turns bright, glossy green.

Claytonia, a creeping, spreading plant, is a native of eastern North America from Canada to Texas. It is an ideal ground cover for moist, shady woodlands, wild gardens, and boggy areas.

Cultivation
Plant claytonias in good, moist soil in a shady site in midfall. They are tuberous-rooted plants and are sometimes slow to become established; however, once they are, they spread rapidly.
Propagation Offsets are formed on mature clumps. Lift them in early to mid fall, separate the offsets, and replant immediately.
Pests/diseases Slugs and snails are the chief enemies.

COMMON ARROWHEAD — see *Sagittaria*
COTTON GRASS — see *Eriophorum*
COW LILY — see *Nuphar*
CREEPING JENNY — see *Lysimachia*

Cyperus
umbrella palm, papyrus

Cyperus alternifolius

- ❑ Height 1-8 ft (30-240 cm)
- ❑ Water depth up to 6 in (15 cm)
- ❑ Flowers summer to early fall
- ❑ Sunny or partially shaded site
- ❑ Marginal
- ❑ Hardy to zone 10

Umbrella palm *(Cyperus alternifolius)* is a sedge, a grasslike plant that needs moisture around its roots. Whorled flower heads are borne on 5 ft (1.5 m) stems. North of zone 10, grow it in a submerged tub so that you can bring it indoors in wintertime. The dwarf 'Nana' is 1-2 ft (30-60 cm) tall.

Cyperus papyrus (papyrus plant) is equally exotic-looking and even more expansive. It can reach 8 ft (2.4 m) high. The foliage is reduced to sheaths that enfold the stems, but the stems end in airy bursts of green flowers borne in heads 1 ft (30 cm) wide. Grow it in a submerged tub so that you can bring it indoors at the first hint of frost.

Cultivation
Plant cyperus in sun or partial shade between midspring and early summer by the margin of a pool or in an aquatic basket filled with rich soil and lowered into the water, no more than 6 in (15 cm) below the surface.

Cut down and clean up old foliage in fall; move plants indoors before the first frost.
Propagation Lift established plants in mid to late spring. Cut off young rooted growths; replant, discarding the old woody centers.
Pests/diseases Trouble free.

Cypripedium
lady's slipper

Cypripedium reginae

Cypripedium calceolus

❑ Height 1-2 ft (30-60 cm)
❑ Spread 1 ft (30 cm)
❑ Flowers late spring to midsummer
❑ Moist, humus-rich soil
❑ Partial shade
❑ Perennial
❑ Hardy to zone 3

Lady's slippers are among the most spectacular of our native American wildflowers. Unfortunately, they have suffered greatly as a result of their beauty. Until recently, nurseries did not know how to propagate them, so they simply collected plants from wild populations. Rarely did such collected stock survive the transfer to the garden. Although cypripediums can be prolific once they are established in an environment that suits them, they are extremely difficult to transplant — some species cannot survive except in partnership with special strains of soil-borne fungi, and these are rarely found in a backyard setting. All in all, the popularity of cypripediums has led to their near-extermination.

The two species listed here are the ones that can succeed in a garden; both are available as nursery-propagated stock that is not collected from the wild. But before buying these plants from any nursery or garden center, check with a local chapter of a native plant or wildflower society to make sure that the nursery is not selling collected plants. A reliable source is the New England Wildflower Society in Framingham, Massachusetts. It keeps an updated list of nurseries that propagate all the plants they sell.

These orchids thrive by a bog or stream. The stems are sheathed with lance-shaped medium-green leaves that are pleated or prominently ribbed. The flowers have a conspicuous pouch or slipperlike lip beneath the spreading, fused petals and sepals.

Popular species
Cypripedium calceolus (yellow lady's slipper) grows best in slightly acid to neutral soil. It is 1-1½ ft (30-45 cm) tall. In late spring each erect stem bears up to three blossoms with twisted maroon-purple sepals and petals and a large, pale yellow lip. The variety *pubescens* has hairy leaves and stems and purple-flushed brown lips and yellowish petals.
Cypripedium reginae (showy lady's slipper), syn. *C. spectabile*, is 2 ft (60 cm) high. The stems are enfolded by broad, densely hairy, pleated leaves, usually in pairs. The fragrant flowers, borne one to three per stem, are pure white; the large lip is heavily streaked and mottled with rose-purple.

Cultivation
Moist, loose, humus-filled soils are a must for cypripediums; a shady location is also essential. Although *C. calceolus* thrives as far south as New Mexico and Louisiana, *C. reginae* is a northern plant that needs a cool spot. The north side of a wall or building is an ideal location if the soil is properly prepared and kept continuously moist.

Plant nursery-grown cypripediums in early or mid spring. Set the roots about 2 in (5 cm) deep for *C. calceolus*, 1 in (2.5) deep for *C. reginae*. Mulch annually with well-rotted garden compost or leaf mold.
Propagation As the clumps become established, they spread and form new rhizomes; divide and replant them in spring.
Pests/diseases Aphids and scale insects infest the leaves. Discoloration and leaf spot are caused by unsuitable growing conditions.

Eichhornia
water hyacinth

Eichhornia crassipes

❏ Height 6-9 in (15-23 cm)
❏ Water depth 6-18 in (15-45 cm)
❏ Flowers in summer
❏ Sunny site
❏ Floating evergreen aquatic
❏ Hardy to zone 8

Eichhornia crassipes, syn. *E. speciosa*, is a native of the tropics that has escaped to Florida and other parts of the Southeast, where it is a serious pest. Do not plant it where it is winter hardy and can escape from cultivation. It is suitable for the North, where it makes a lovely aquatic that can be overwintered in a tub indoors or started afresh each summer.

Water hyacinths bear glossy dark green leaves, and in summer, lavender-blue flowers. The inflated stems act as floats, keeping the plants buoyant.

These floating plants will also grow in mud.

Cultivation
Place the plants on the surface of the pool in early summer. The soil at the bottom of the pool should be rich and at least 2 in (5 cm) deep. Full sun is essential. Bring the plants into a greenhouse or other sunny but heated spot in early fall and overwinter in wet soil at 55-61°F (13-16°C).
Propagation New plants are borne on runners in summer. When a young plant has several well-formed leaves, detach it.
Pests/diseases Trouble free.

Elodea
Canadian pondweed

Elodea canadensis

❏ Any water depth
❏ Foliage plant
❏ Sun or partial shade
❏ Submerged aquatic
❏ Hardy to zone 3

Canadian pondweed *(Elodea canadensis*, syn. *Anacharis canadensis)* belongs to the group of aquatic plants known as oxygenators. These are essential in any still-water pool because they add oxygen to the water and consume some of the carbon dioxide emitted by fish and plants. They discourage the growth of algae, promote the existence of beneficial microscopic animals, and provide shade and shelter for fish.

Canadian pondweed is a vigorous submerged perennial whose fleshy stems and dark green, lance-shaped leaves are rarely seen on the pool's surface. Tiny white, purple-tinged flowers are borne throughout summer.

Cultivation
Plant in midspring, inserting small bundles of unrooted cuttings, popularly known as slips, into the mud at the bottom of the pool or in aquatic baskets of loamy compost lowered into place. The plants are prolific and need thinning out in late fall. Use a rake to pull out surplus growth.
Propagation If necessary, take cuttings in midspring and plant as you would the slips (see above).
Pests/diseases Trouble free.

Eriophorum
cotton grass

Eriophorum angustifolium

❏ Height 1-1½ ft (30-45 cm)
❏ Planting depth up to 6 in (15 cm)
❏ Flowers mid to late spring
❏ Sunny site
❏ Marginal aquatic
❏ Hardy to zone 4

This attractive low-growing perennial is ideal for moist soil around the edge of a pool. Cotton grass *(Eriophorum angustifolium)* will also grow in water up to 6 in (15 cm) deep. A European native, it grows naturally on damp moorland and is useful as a ground cover on exposed ground, where few other marginals thrive.

Cotton grass has dense tufts of rushlike foliage and attractive tassels of cotton-woollike flower heads. They are borne in mid to late spring and will grow 1-1½ ft (30-45 cm) above the ground.

Cultivation
Plant in moist soil along the water's edge in spring. Ideally the site should be sunny.
Propagation Multiply in fall or spring by lifting, dividing, and replanting mature plants.
Pests/diseases Trouble free.

FAIRY MOSS — see *Azolla*
FLOATING HEART — see *Nymphoides*
FLOWERING RUSH — see *Butomus*
FORGET-ME-NOT — see *Myosotis*

Geum
water avens

Geum rivale

❏ Height 1 ft (30 cm)
❏ Spread up to 1½ ft (45 cm)
❏ Flowers late spring to late fall
❏ Moist soil
❏ Sunny site
❏ Perennial
❏ Hardy to zone 3

Flowering almost continuously from late spring well into fall, water avens *(Geum rivale)* is invaluable for providing color in boggy ground or at the margins of a pool. It grows to a height of 1 ft (30 cm) or more and is clump-forming, with medium-green, strawberrylike leaves. The nodding bell-shaped flowers have purple-red calyxes and pink to yellow petals veined with purple.

The cultivar 'Leonard's Variety' bears rose-pink blossoms flushed with golden-yellow.

Cultivation
Plant water avens in fall or early spring in any fertile, moisture-retentive soil, preferably in full sun. In late fall, or when flowering has finished, cut the stems back to ground level.
Propagation Divide and replant established clumps every three or four years in early or mid spring.
Pests/diseases Trouble free.

GIANT HOGWEED — see *Heracleum*
GIANT REED — see *Arundo*

Glyceria
manna grass, reed sweetgrass

Glyceria maxima 'Variegata'

❏ Height 4-6 ft (1.2-1.8 m)
❏ Water depth up to 6 in (15 cm)
❏ Flowers in summer
❏ Sunny site
❏ Marginal aquatic
❏ Hardy zones 5-10

The bright green *Glyceria maxima*, a 4-6 ft (1.2-1.8 m) tall plant that thrives in wet meadows and by watersides, is too invasive for the average garden.

The cultivar 'Variegata,' however, is shorter and more decorative than the species. It will grow in a dry site, although the leaves tend to lose their color as the summer progresses. The water's edge or shallow water up to a depth of 6 in (15 cm) is ideal. In spring, young green leaf shoots emerge; they have pink stripes that are flushed with white. As the long, narrow leaves open out, the pink fades and the grassy inflorescences of cream flowers appear, waving in the breeze.

Cultivation
Plant in early fall or spring in a sunny site by the water's edge or in aquatic baskets submerged in water to a depth of 6 in (15 cm). If you plant above the water level, make sure that the soil will retain moisture.
Propagation Lift, divide, and replant in spring.
Pests/diseases Trouble free.

GOLDEN CLUB — see *Orontium*

Heracleum
giant hogweed

Heracleum mantegazzianum

❏ Height 10-16 ft (3-4.9 m)
❏ Spread 4-6 ft (1.2-1.8 m)
❏ Flowers mid and late summer
❏ Deep, moist soil
❏ Sun or partial shade
❏ Perennial
❏ Hardy zones 3-9

Giant hogweed *(Heracleum mantegazzianum)* is truly gigantic, often growing to a height of 16 ft (4.9 m) in a season. While it is too large for a small pool, it is impressive by a large pond or lake in a semiwild setting. Its stout fluted stems, often spotted with purple, shoot upward and are clothed with enormous, deeply lobed, medium-green leaves. Huge round heads, up to 18 in (45 cm) wide, of starry white flowers are borne in mid and late summer.

Giant hogweed is a short-lived perennial, and often of biennial growth, but it seeds itself freely and can become a nuisance unless it is deadheaded before the seeds ripen in early fall.

Cultivation
In mid to late fall or early spring, plant giant hogweeds in any deep, moist soil in full sun or light shade. Cut the tall stems back to ground level after flowering.
Propagation Sow seeds in an outdoor nursery bed in spring and transplant the seedlings to their growing positions in fall.
Pests/diseases Trouble free.

Hosta
hosta, plantain lily

Hosta ventricosa 'Aureo-marginata'

Hosta plantaginea

- ❑ Height 1½-3 ft (45-90 cm)
- ❑ Spread 1½-2 ft (45-60 cm)
- ❑ Flowers midsummer to fall
- ❑ Moist, rich soil
- ❑ Partial shade or sunny site
- ❑ Perennial
- ❑ Hardy zones 3-9

Hostas are grown primarily for their striking foliage, which comes in an array of colors, shapes, and textures. The large leaves are heart- or lance-shaped and crinkled, smooth, or prominently veined. They vary in color from the palest green to blue and are edged or overlaid with white, gold, or silver. The tall, slender stems bear loose clusters or spikes of bell- or funnel-shaped flowers that are white or in shades of pink, purple, and mauve.

Hostas grow well in flower borders but are particularly vigorous and luxuriant in moist soil at the margins of pools and streams. In such situations they form increasing clumps of foliage. They retain their leaf colorings best in dappled shade.

Popular species
Hosta plantaginea is a distinctive all-green species that is 1½-2 ft (45-60 cm) high. It bears long-stemmed, glossy, bright green, heart-shaped leaves from which stems topped with pure white flowers rise in late summer.
Hosta sieboldii, syn. *H. albomarginata*, grows about 1½ ft (45 cm) tall. It has narrow, lance-shaped, glossy green leaves with thin but distinctive white margins. The funnel-shaped flowers, lilac striped with violet, bloom from mid to late summer. 'Louisa' is a white-flowered cultivar.
Hosta ventricosa, syn. *H. caerulea*, is a vigorous species that grows up to 3 ft (90 cm) high. It bears heart-shaped blue-green leaves; mauve to violet flower spikes appear in late summer. The cultivar 'Aureo-marginata' produces leaves that are prominently splashed with yellow.

Cultivation
Plant in midfall or early spring in rich, moist but not waterlogged soil. Hostas prefer a site in dappled shade. If the site is sunny, make sure the roots do not dry out. Set the plants 1½ ft (45 cm) apart (2 ft/60 cm for *H. ventricosa*) and place the crowns flush with the surface of the soil. Deadhead the plants after they flower, and clear away any dead and rotting leaves in fall.
Propagation Division in early spring, just as growth starts, is the usual method. Ideally, hostas should be left undisturbed; they are long-lived and in time develop tough, woody crowns that are difficult to split. For propagation purposes, divide and replant hostas while they are still young.
Pests/diseases Slugs and snails can destroy the leaves.

Hosta sieboldii 'Louisa'

Houttuynia
houttuynia

Iris
iris

Iris laevigata 'Rose Queen'

❑ Height 1-6 ft (30-180 cm)
❑ Water depth 2-18 in (5-45 cm)
❑ Flowers late spring to summer
❑ Sunny site or dappled shade
❑ Marginal aquatic
❑ Hardy zones 3-10

Houttuynia cordata 'Variegata'

❑ Height 1-1½ ft (30-45 cm)
❑ Water depth 1-2 in (2.5-5 cm)
❑ Flowers in summer
❑ Dappled shade
❑ Marginal aquatic
❑ Hardy zones 6-10

Houttuynia cordata is a hardy herbaceous perennial that thrives in boggy ground or shallow water. Unlike most aquatics, it needs a site in dappled shade. It spreads rapidly by means of underground stems and can be invasive.

Upright bright red stems bear pointed, heart-shaped leaves that are blue-green and have a metallic appearance; the leaves may be flushed with red. Small spikes of white flowers with white bracts appear in summer. 'Flore Pleno' is a cultivar with large white bracts; 'Variegata' (syn. 'Chamaeleon') has cream-and-red leaves.

Cultivation
Plant in spring or fall in soft, moist soil or in shallow water to a depth of 2 in (5 cm). Dappled shade is essential. Plant dormant runners horizontally, about 3 in (7.5 cm) deep. Plant container-grown plants at the same depth as they were in the pots.
Propagation Divide in spring or fall. Pot up pieces of underground stem, each with a growing point or developed shoot, in potting soil; grow on until well rooted. Transplant to the growing position.
Pests/diseases Trouble free.

Houttuynia cordata

There are irises for every garden situation, including the aquatic types. *Iris laevigata* and *Iris ensata* flourish in shallow water and at the margins of streams and pools; *Iris pseudacorus* thrives in deep water. The Louisiana irises and *Iris versicolor* thrive in soils that range from wet to merely moist (the Louisiana irises also tolerate dry and alkaline soils). All have upright sword-shaped foliage and bear typical iris flowers from late spring to summer.

Popular species and hybrids
Iris brevicaulis occurs naturally from Kentucky to Kansas and southward into Louisiana and is hardy to zone 5. It grows 12-18 in (30-45 cm) high and bears up to six blue-purple flowers per stem. *Iris ensata* (Japanese water iris), hardy in zones 5-10, grows 2-3 ft (60-90 cm) high; it thrives in wet or moist soil and in shallow water, and flowers in summer. The cultivars have flowers that are purple, blue, pink, yellow, or white. *Iris fulva,* native to the wetlands of the Southeast, is hardy only to zone 7. It grows 2-3 ft (60-90 cm) high and in late spring bears flowers that range in color from coppery orange to salmon-pink.

Iris laevigata

Iris pseudacorus 'Variegata'

Iris pseudacorus

Iris giganticaerulea is hardy to zone 7 and may reach a height of 6 ft (1.8 m). It displays fragrant violet-blue flowers in June.

Iris laevigata, hardy to zone 5, does best in water to 6 in (15 cm) deep. The smooth, pale green leaves are 1½-2 ft (45-60 cm) long. Two to four violet-blue flowers open at the tip of each stem in early summer. Popular cultivars include 'Regal' (cyclamen-red), 'Rose Queen' (rose-pink), and 'Variegata' (soft blue flowers; white-and-green-striped leaves).

Iris × 'Louisiana' is a group of hybrids that grow 3-4 ft (90-120 cm) high. The 3-4 in (7.5-10 cm) wide flowers may be white, yellow, red, bronze, blue, or purple. 'Inner Beauty' is a cultivar with purple-and-yellow flowers. Hardy in

zones 5-10, the Louisiana irises thrive in well-watered garden soil enriched with organic matter. They also flourish in the wet soil at the edge of a pond or stream.

Iris pseudacorus (yellow flag, or flag iris) is hardy in zones 4-9. It thrives in a water depth to 1½ ft (45 cm) and is 3-4 ft (90-120 cm) or more high. It has blue-green, distinctly ridged leaves, and the branching, shiny stems carry five or more yellow flowers, usually marked with brown veins, in late spring and early summer. Cultivars include 'Golden Queen' (golden flowers) and 'Variegata' (golden-and-green leaves).

Iris versicolor (blue flag) is hardy in zones 3-9 and flourishes in wet or soggy soil. It forms vigorous clumps of sword-shaped leaves up

to 2 ft (60 cm) or more tall. The flowers, which open in late spring or early summer, may be lavender, blue, violet, or purple.

Cultivation
In early to mid spring, plant the rhizomes along the margins of pools or streams in good, deep moist soil in full sun or light shade. Or plant directly in muddy soil beneath shallow water or in aquatic baskets lowered to the bottom in deeper pools.

Propagation Divide the rhizomes after flowering every three years. Replant immediately.

Pests/diseases Iris borers feed on the foliage.

159

Iris 'Inner Beauty'

Juncus
soft rush

Juncus effusus 'Spiralis'

❑ Height 15-18 in (38-45 cm)
❑ Water depth up to 3 in (7.5 cm)
❑ Foliage plant
❑ Sunny or partially shaded site
❑ Marginal aquatic
❑ Hardy zones 7-9

Most species of the *Juncus* genus are too coarse and rampant for the water garden, but *Juncus effusus* 'Spiralis' (soft rush) is sufficiently ornamental to merit a position around the garden pool. It is a sprawling, untidy plant, but the virtually leafless stems — dark green and with a twist that varies from tight curls to perfect spirals — are interesting. The brown flower clusters, borne in early to mid summer, are insignificant. Soft rush grows 15-18 in (38-45 cm) high.

Cultivation
In mid to late spring, plant in the margins of a pool in 3 in (7.5 cm) deep water, in a sunny or partially shaded site. Any soil, even the poorest, is suitable.

Thin congested plants by removing individual stems, and cut out any that fail to develop a spiral shape.
Propagation Increase by dividing and replanting clumps in mid to late spring. Use a sharp knife to sever the tough rootstocks.
Pests/diseases Trouble free.

KINGCUP — see *Caltha*
LADY'S SLIPPER — see *Cypripedium*
LADY'S SMOCK — see *Cardamine*

Lobelia
cardinal flower

Lobelia siphilitica

❑ Height 1-3 ft (30-90 cm)
❑ Spread 12-15 in (30-38 cm)
❑ Flowers midsummer to fall
❑ Rich, moist soil
❑ Lightly shaded, sheltered site
❑ Perennial
❑ Hardy zones 2-9

Lobelias are hardy, tall, branching perennials with spikes of two-lipped tubular flowers; they grow naturally in boggy ground.

Popular species
Lobelia cardinalis is hardy in zones 2-9. A short-lived, clump-forming species, it is 2½ ft (75 cm) high and has green or coppery lance-shaped foliage. Spikes of red flowers bloom in summer.
Lobelia siphilitica grows 2-3 ft (60-90 cm) high. It has narrowly oval green leaves; spikes of blue flowers appear in midsummer to fall. It is hardy in zones 4-9.
Lobelia splendens, syn. *L. fulgens*, resembles *L. cardinalis* but has bronze-purple leaves and showier flower spikes on thick stems. It is hardy in zones 7-9.

Cultivation
Plant in midspring in rich, moist to wet soil in a sheltered site in sun or partial shade; in cold climates cover with a mulch in winter.
Propagation Divide and replant mature clumps in spring. Alternatively, increase *L. cardinalis* from stem cuttings in summer.
Pests/diseases Trouble free.

LOOSESTRIFE — see *Lythrum*

Lobelia splendens

Lysichiton
skunk cabbage

Lysichiton americanum

- ❏ Height 2-4 ft (60-120 cm)
- ❏ Crown level with the water's surface or moist soil
- ❏ Flowers early to late spring
- ❏ Sunny or partially shaded site
- ❏ Marginal aquatic
- ❏ Hardy to zone 6

Despite the unattractive odor of their flowers, skunk cabbages have ornamental value. They produce 1 ft (30 cm) wide, waxy arumlike flower spathes in early to late spring. The leaves, which unfurl afterward, will grow up to 4 ft (1.2 m) long.

These are dramatic and long-lived plants that thrive in the deep, rich, moist soil around pools and streams. *Lysichiton americanum,* a species native to the western United States, can be obtained from native-plant suppliers. Its Asian relative is available from aquatic-plant nurseries.

Popular species
Lysichiton americanum reaches 2-4 ft (60-120 cm) high. It has grass-green leaves and bears deep golden-yellow spathes. In mid to late summer the ripening seed heads provide another attraction. *Lysichiton camtschatcense,* a native of eastern Asia, is similar to *L. americanum* but smaller. It grows 2-3 ft (60-90 cm) high and

Lysichiton camtschatcense

bears pure white odorless or sweet-scented flowers that do not seed. The leaves are blue-green.

Cultivation
Plant container-grown specimens in midspring to early summer in sun or partial shade; take care not to damage the fleshy roots. They need a soil depth of at least 12 in (30 cm) and rich, moist loam.
Propagation Division is the easiest method, but divided plants may take two or three years to establish themselves. Remove the young plants that form around the rhizomes; pot up in loamy compost. Plant out in spring.
Pests/diseases Trouble free.

Lysimachia
creeping Jenny, moneywort

Lysimachia nummularia 'Aurea'

- ❏ Height 1-2 in (2.5-5 cm)
- ❏ Spread 1½ ft (45 cm) or more
- ❏ Flowers early and mid summer
- ❏ Any moist soil
- ❏ Sunny or partially shaded site
- ❏ Evergreen perennial
- ❏ Hardy to zone 3

Creeping Jenny *(Lysimachia nummularia)* is a hardy prostrate evergreen plant much used for ground cover in rock gardens, on banks, and in borders; yet it is a true waterside perennial that thrives in moist soil or shallow water. The prostrate stems will spread and trail indefinitely, rooting where they touch the soil or spilling over the water's edge. The stems are clothed with tiny, rounded medium-green leaves and are studded in summer with bright yellow cup-shaped flowers. The cultivar 'Aurea' produces soft yellow-green foliage.

Cultivation
In mid to late fall or early to mid spring, plant creeping Jenny in shallow, moist soil at the margins of a pool or close to the pool's rim, where the shoots can trail over the water. This plant does equally well in full sun or dappled shade, but the yellow-leaved 'Aurea' tends to lose its bright color in a shady site.
Propagation In midspring or early fall, take 3-4 in (7.5-10 cm) long stem sections and insert them directly in the growing site, where they will root readily.
Pests/diseases Generally trouble free.

Lythrum
purple loosestrife

Lythrum salicaria 'Firecandle'

- ❏ Height 2-5 ft (60-150 cm)
- ❏ Spread 1½ ft (45 cm)
- ❏ Flowers summer and fall
- ❏ Moist soil
- ❏ Sunny or partially shaded site
- ❏ Perennial
- ❏ Hardy zones 3-10

The tall red-purple flower spikes of purple loosestrife *(Lythrum salicaria)* are beautiful; however, this European plant aggressively invades American wetlands. Cultivars are often less invasive, but check with your county's Cooperative Extension Service before you plant them; in some states planting them is prohibited.

The 2-5 ft (60-150 cm) high flower spikes are borne among green lance-shaped foliage from early summer to early fall.

Popular cultivars
'Firecandle' displays purple-pink flower spikes.
'Morden's Pink,' one of the least invasive types, has pink flowers.
'Purple Spires' produces fuchsia-purple flowers.
'Robert' has vivid rose-red flowers.

Cultivation
Plant in fall or spring in wet soil by a garden pool or stream in sun or partial shade. Cut back in fall.
Propagation Divide and replant in fall or spring.
Pests/diseases Trouble free.

MANNA GRASS — see *Glyceria*
MARSH MARIGOLD — see *Caltha*

Mentha
water mint

Mentha aquatica

- ❏ Height 1 ft (30 cm)
- ❏ Water depth 2-5 in (5-13 cm)
- ❏ Flowers in late summer
- ❏ Sunny or shady site
- ❏ Marginal aquatic
- ❏ Hardy zones 6-11

Water mint *(Mentha aquatica)* is a versatile plant that thrives in wet mud or on the surface of shallow pools. It grows in sun or shade. In shade the hairy oval leaves of water mint are bright green; in full sun they turn purple.

Small mauve-lilac flowers are arranged in tight, rounded clusters; they appear in late summer. A distinctive characteristic of the plant is its strong minty smell.

Cultivation
Water mint is an invasive plant, so it is advisable to plant it in an aquatic basket and sink the basket into wet mud or shallow water at the margins of a pool or stream. Plant in spring or fall in a sunny or shady site.
Propagation Increase by removing rooted suckers and replanting in late spring to early summer.
Pests/diseases Trouble free.

Menyanthes
bogbean

Menyanthes trifoliata

- ❏ Height 10 in (25 cm)
- ❏ Water depth up to 4 in (10 cm)
- ❏ Flowers in early summer
- ❏ Sunny site
- ❏ Marginal aquatic
- ❏ Hardy to zone 3

Bogbean *(Menyanthes trifoliata)* grows wild in the northern parts of North America. Its scrambling stems make this a suitable plant for covering the margins of garden pools. Mud just covered with water provides the best growing conditions for bogbean.

Thick green trailing stems carry three-lobed cloverlike leaves. Bare flower stalks appear in early summer, producing pinkish-tinged buds that open into spikes of pure white, heavily fringed flowers. They are particularly charming when massed together.

Bogbean will spread, but it is rarely invasive.

Cultivation
Plant the rhizomes in spring in a sunny site. Set them 1 ft (30 cm) apart in wet soil at the pool's edge so that their roots can grow into the water. Bogbean will also grow in water up to 4 in (10 cm) deep.
Propagation Divide the rhizomes into sections, each with a healthy growing tip, and replant immediately.
Pests/diseases Trouble free.

MILKWEED, SWAMP — see *Asclepias*

Mimulus
monkey flower

Mimulus luteus

❏ Height 12 in (30 cm)
❏ Water depth up to 3 in (7.5 cm)
❏ Flowers late spring to late summer
❏ Sunny or lightly shaded site
❏ Marginal aquatic
❏ Hardy zones 6-9

Monkey flower *(Mimulus luteus)* is excellent for providing color throughout summer. It belongs to a genus composed of both annuals and perennials, all of which require moist soil. Monkey flower is a true aquatic and will grow in water up to 3 in (7.5 cm) deep.

It carries medium-green oval leaves and bears snapdragonlike golden-yellow flowers that are sometimes marked with maroon or crimson-brown spots.

Cultivation
Plant monkey flower in spring in moist soil at the margins of a pool or stream. It will thrive in water up to a depth of 3 in (7.5 cm). It does equally well in a sunny or lightly shaded site. Cut down faded flower stems in late fall.
Propagation Divide and replant in spring. Alternatively, sow seeds indoors in late winter. Prick out the seedlings into cell packs or peat pots. Harden off before planting out in late spring or early summer.
Pests/diseases Trouble free.

Miscanthus
silver grass

Miscanthus sinensis 'Gracillimus'

❏ Height 4-6 ft (1.2-1.8 m)
❏ Spread 3 ft (90 cm)
❏ Foliage plant
❏ Rich, moist soil
❏ Sunny site
❏ Perennial
❏ Hardy zones 5-9

These tough, robust grasses make admirable shelter plants by the waterside and create handsome focal points where space allows. They grow rapidly, to 6 ft (1.8 m) tall or more each season, if given deep, rich, and moist soil.

Popular species
Miscanthus sacchariflorus (amur silver grass, silver banner grass), a rhizomatic, slowly spreading species, can form dense colonies. The stout stems bear narrow arching leaves that are medium green with paler midribs. They persist into fall, turning russet-brown before dying.
Miscanthus sinensis, syn. *Eulalia japonica,* grows to 5 ft (1.5 m) and forms wide-spreading clumps. It has arching blue-green grassy leaves with white midribs. In early to mid fall, it occasionally bears feathery flower panicles. 'Gracillimus,' which grows 4 ft (1.2 m) high, has very narrow leaves and sometimes white inflorescenses in fall. The free-flowering 'Silver Feather' displays tall, silky flower plumes that fade to bronzy-red in fall. 'Variegatus' is outstanding for its green leaves striped with bright primrose-yellow.

Cultivation
In early to mid spring, plant in deep, rich, moist soil in a sunny site. For a dramatic effect, set miscanthus where its graceful outline is reflected in water. In late fall or early spring, cut all stems and dead foliage back to ground level.
Propagation Divide and replant during early and mid spring.
Pests/diseases Older clumps may die out at the center; lift and divide every four years or so.

MONKEY FLOWER — see *Mimulus*
MONEYWORT — see *Lysimachia*

Miscanthus sacchariflorus

Myosotis
forget-me-not

Myosotis scorpioides

- ❏ Height 9 in (23 cm)
- ❏ Water depth up to 3 in (7.5 cm)
- ❏ Flowers midspring to midsummer
- ❏ Sunny or partially shaded site
- ❏ Marginal aquatic
- ❏ Hardy to zone 5

The well-known group of forget-me-not includes one moisture-loving species — *Myosotis scorpioides* (syn. *M. palustris*). This hardy evergreen flourishes in moist soil that is found along the edges of a pool or stream. It will also grow in shallow water up to a depth of 3 in (7.5 cm).

Between midspring and midsummer numerous pale blue flowers with pale yellow eyes are carried in sprays at the tips of long stems. They are set off by a foil of spoon-shaped green leaves covered with rough hairs. The plants grow 9 in (23 cm) high. 'Mermaid' bears deep blue flowers with a deep yellow eye and narrow dark green leaves.

Cultivation
Plant these forget-me-nots in deep, fertile soil at water level or covered by up to 3 in (7.5 cm) of water in mid to late spring or early to mid fall. They thrive in full sun or partial shade. To prolong the flowering season, trim off flower heads as they fade.

Propagation Increase forget-me-nots by sowing seeds or taking cuttings. Sow the seeds in mid to late spring in a cold frame or other protected spot. Prick out the seedlings into an outdoor nursery bed and grow them on. Transplant to the flowering sites in early fall.

Alternatively, take basal cuttings in early spring or late summer to early fall. Root them in a protected bed of a moist, loose mix of sphagnum peat, perlite, and loam, making sure that the bed never dries out. When the cuttings are well rooted, plant out in the permanent positions.

Pests/diseases Botrytis can cause the flowers to rot, and mildew may appear as a white, powdery coating on the stems and the leaves.

Nuphar
cow lily

Nuphar lutea

- ❏ Surface floater
- ❏ Water depth to 4 ft (1.2 m) or more
- ❏ Flowers in summer
- ❏ Sunny or partially shaded site
- ❏ Aquatic
- ❏ Hardy to zone 3

Cow lilies resemble true water lilies *(Nymphaea)* but are coarser and inferior in bloom. Like water lilies, they have thick, leathery leaves, up to 16 in (40 cm) wide, that float on the water's surface, as well as fernlike and translucent submerged foliage. However, the flowers, usually yellow or orange, are much smaller and more rounded, with fewer petals. The flowers have an unpleasant smell and will self-seed readily.

These characteristics notwithstanding, nuphars do have their strong points: they thrive where water lilies would not succeed — in running water, deep ponds, and shady sites.

The European cow lily *(Nuphar lutea)* is hardy to zone 4 and spreads to at least 5 ft (1.5 m). It should be introduced only to large pools and natural ponds and streams. A native American species, *Nuphar advena* (spatterdock cow lily), is hardy to zone 3 and also expansive.

Cultivation
Plant the rhizomes in spring, setting them in the muddy soil at the bottom of a large pool or lowering them in aquatic baskets. Nuphars will do well in either sun or shade, but they will grow most vigorously in full sun. Remove the flowers as they fade.

Propagation Divide congested clumps periodically in spring.

Pests/diseases Trouble free.

Nymphaea

water lily

Nymphaea tetragona 'Helvola'

- Surface floater
- Water depth 6-48 in (15-120 cm)
- Flowers in summer
- Sunny site
- Shallow- and deep-water aquatics
- Hardy zones 3-10

Water lilies *(Nymphaea)* are the marvels of the ornamental water garden, with their elegant blooms that appear over a long period in the summer. An enormous range of cultivars offers the gardener a choice of sizes and flower colors. Water lilies are planted in the mud at the bottom of a pool or in aquatic baskets, but the flowers and leaves float on the surface of the water. They are easy to grow, are long-lived, and demand little attention, although the larger types can be invasive.

The cup-shaped flowers have several rows of petals. The outer petals lie almost flat as the inner ones open. The shape varies from cultivar to cultivar; some have pointed petals that give the flowers a starry appearance. The central boss of stamens is usually orange or yellow. A few blooms are almost completely double.

The glossy, leathery leaves are pale to medium green, sometimes splashed or flushed with maroon.

In spring the rounded or heart-shaped leaves unfurl and float on the water, except where overcrowding forces them above the surface. Leaf size is determined by the vigor of the plant.

Popular species and cultivars
Water lilies are categorized according to size and required water depth. Miniature, small, and medium types are suitable for the average-size garden pool.

MINIATURE TYPES require 6-9 in (15-23 cm) deep water. They spread 1-1½ ft (30-45 cm) on the surface and have leaves 2-3 in (5-7.5 cm) wide. One popular cultivar is *Nymphaea tetragona* (syn. *N. pygmaea*) 'Helvola'; it produces maroon-spotted leaves and sulfur-yellow star-shaped flowers. Popular hybrids include 'Aurora' (maroon-mottled foliage; yellow flowers that age to orange and then dark red) and 'Paul Hariot' (orange flowers; leaves spotted with maroon).

SMALL TYPES have a spread of 1½-2½ ft (45-75 cm) and require a water depth of 1-1½ ft (30-45 cm). The leaves are 4-7 in (10-18 cm) wide. The most commonly grown species is *N. candida* (white flowers). Hybrids include 'Albatross'

Nymphaea x marliacea 'Albida'

(pure white flowers, prominent golden centers), 'Fire Crest' (rich pink flowers, orange stamens), 'Froebelii' (rich red flowers), *N. × laydekeri* 'Purpurata' (wine-red flowers), *N. × marliacea* 'Chromatella' (large primrose-yellow flowers), 'Rose Arey' (scented cerise-pink flowers), and 'Sioux' (yellow flowers flushed with red). **MEDIUM TYPES** will spread 2½-3½ ft (75-105 cm) on the water's surface; they need water at a depth of 1½-2 ft (45-60 cm). The

Nymphaea 'Attraction'

Nymphaea 'General Pershing'

Nymphaea 'Gladstone'

leaves are 7-10 in (18-25 cm) wide. Cultivars include 'Attraction' (white-tipped deep red flowers), 'Comanche' (warm rose flowers darkening to red), 'Conqueror' (large deep red blooms flecked with white), 'Escarboucle' (deep crimson-red flowers), 'General Pershing' (wine-red flowers), 'Gladstone' (large pure white flowers), 'Gloire de Temple sur Lot' (double cream-white flowers), 'James Brydon' (pinkish-red flowers; purple young leaves), 'Joey Tomocik' (rich yellow flowers), *N.* × *marliacea* 'Albida' (white flowers), *N.* × *marliacea* 'Carnea' (pale pink flowers), 'Moorei' (yellow flowers; spotted brown leaves), 'Sunrise' (golden-yellow, fragrant flowers; leaves flecked with brown), and 'William Falconer' (dark ruby-red flowers, golden anthers).

Cultivation

Choose a sunny site for water lilies. Plant directly in the mud at the bottom of a pool or in aquatic baskets that are then sunk into position. For both methods, use fertile, loamy soil. Mix light or clay soil with rotted cow manure or coarse bonemeal.

Miniature types need soil at a depth of 3-4 in (7.5-10 cm); small types, 4-6 in (10-15 cm); and medium types, 6-8 in (15-20 cm).

Plant the tubers or rhizomes between midspring and early summer. If using the aquatic baskets, set the tubers or rhizomes so that the soil is level with the growing point of the rootstock. When planting directly in the mud, reach down and push the rootstocks into the soft mud.

Water lilies require little attention after planting. If necessary, remove excessively large leaves. Thin plants in small pools in mid to late spring; drain off the water or lift out the basket and examine the rootstock. Use a sharp knife to sever strong-growing tubers and rhizomes 6-8 in (15-20 cm) from the growing point; trim off the true roots beneath. Use the severed pieces for propagation.

Propagation After thinning in spring, replant the severed sections or remove offsets from the main rootstock with a sharp knife. Insert the offsets in small pots of loamy soil mix and stand them in a bowl or tank of water just covering the rim of the pot. Keep in full sun, and plant out when fully rooted.

Pests/diseases Water lily aphids infest leaves and flowers, and water lily beetles eat strips out of the leaves. Leaf spot and stem rot are the chief diseases.

Nymphaea x marliacea 'Carnea'

Nymphoides
floating heart

Nymphoides peltata

❑ Surface floater
❑ Water depth 6-18 in (15-45 cm)
❑ Flowers in summer
❑ Sunny site
❑ Aquatic
❑ Hardy to zone 6

Floating heart, which strongly resembles the water lily, is ideal for new pools because it spreads quickly, providing interest while other water plants are still establishing themselves.

Nymphoides peltata bears dainty yellow cup-shaped flowers with fringed petals that are held well above the water's surface in summer. The floating rounded leaves are similar to those of the water lily, but they are smaller — just 2 in (5 cm) wide. They are light green mottled with maroon and brown, with wavy margins.

Cultivation
In midspring and early summer, plant directly in the mud at the bottom of the pool or in loam-filled aquatic baskets, which can then be sunk into position. A water depth of 6-18 in (15-45 cm) is ideal. Control their spread by thinning them in late spring.
Propagation Floating heart is best increased by removing offsets from the main rootstock with a sharp knife in late spring. Insert offsets in pots of loamy compost and stand them in a bowl of water just covering the rim of the pot. Plant out when fully rooted.
Pests/diseases Water lily aphids may infest the leaves and flowers. Leaf spot and stem rot can also be problems.

Orontium
golden club

Orontium aquaticum

❑ Surface floater
❑ Water depth up to 1½ ft (45 cm)
❑ Flowers late spring to early summer
❑ Sunny site
❑ Aquatic
❑ Hardy to zone 7

Golden club (*Orontium aquaticum*) is a plant native to North America that grows wild in slow-moving streams and swamps in the South. It is hardy as far north as New York and adapts well to widely differing environments. However, its appearance differs according to the conditions.

When grown in shallow water or at the margins of pools, golden club produces a profusion of large, sturdy oval to round leaves that are coated with a bluish-green water-repellent wax. The leaves are borne on tough stalks up to 1½ ft (45 cm) tall.

In deep water, however, the leaves float on the surface in near-circular clumps. The leaves are strap-shaped instead of oval and retain their attractive appearance well into fall.

The flowers, which appear from late spring into early summer, reveal the golden club's relationship with the arum family, although they lack the usual white-spathe wrapping. The flowers are bright golden, slightly knobbly spikes borne on white-tipped, pencil-thick stalks that rise gracefully from the leaf bases before arching outward.

Cultivation
Plant the tubers from early spring to early summer, ideally in good, loamy soil at the bottom of the pool. Water depth should be up to 1½ ft (45 cm).

Alternatively, plant golden club in boggy ground at the pool's edge. The roots penetrate deeply and need plenty of soil depth.

Remove the faded spikes after flowering and rake out the yellowing foliage in fall before it can foul the water.
Propagation As established clumps become overgrown, you should lift and divide them in early spring, after flowering, or in

Pontederia

pickerelweed

Orontium aquaticum, flowers

early fall. Use a sharp knife to cut through the tough rootstock; discard the old woody centers and replant outer, younger sections immediately.

Alternatively, sow fresh seeds in early summer. Sow them in shallow boxes of loamy seed compost and keep the pans submerged until seedlings appear. Transplant the seedlings individually to small pots that are kept in water up to their rims, and grow on until the young plants are sturdy enough to be planted out in the pool.

Pests/diseases Generally trouble free, although water lily aphids and water lily beetles can sometimes be troublesome.

Pontederia cordata

❏ Height 2-2½ ft (60-75 cm)
❏ Water depth 3-9 in (7.5-23 cm)
❏ Flowers midsummer to early fall
❏ Sunny site
❏ Aquatic
❏ Hardy to zone 3

Pickerelweed (*Pontederia cordata*) is one of the few blue-flowered aquatic plants. For this reason alone it is well worth growing in a water garden. It will do well in boggy ground by the pool's edge, but it flourishes in shallow water, where the blue flowers are patterned with light reflected off the ripples below.

The plants root in mud, from which their smooth, fleshy stems grow 2-2½ ft (60-75 cm) high. Flower spikes of small purple-blue blooms, which are surrounded by soft hairs, push through the membranes at the bases of the upward-pointing heart-shaped leaves. They come into full color in midsummer, often until fall.

Cultivation
Plant from midspring to early summer in a layer of loam 4-6 in (10-15 cm) deep; cover with 3-9 in (7.5-23 cm) of water. Position in full sun at the margins of a pool or slow-flowing stream.

Propagation Lift the plants in spring; cut off side branches with a sharp knife. Replant, pushing the rootstock 2 in (5 cm) into the loam. Do not cover with more than 3 in (7.5 cm) of water until the plants are well established.

Pests/diseases Trouble free.

Potamogeton
pondweed

Potamogeton

❑ Any water depth
❑ Foliage plant
❑ Sunny or shady site
❑ Submerged aquatic
❑ Hardy to zone 5

Not one of the pondweeds *(Potamogeton)* can be called beautiful, but in small pools in particular they are valuable. As oxygenators, they absorb from the water the carbon dioxide emitted by fish and algae, and they release oxygen into the water, thus keeping the underwater environment healthy. The leaves provide shelter for fish and help to block the sunlight, thus discouraging the growth of algae.

Several pondweeds are native to North America or have escaped from garden ponds and aquariums to flourish in the wild here. One of the natives is *Potamogeton nodosus,* also known as *Potamogeton americanus.* This plant has both submerged and floating leaves; those below the surface are lanceolate (thin and pointed), while those on the surface are small and oval.

Also available is *Potamogeton pectinatus* (fennel pondweed), which grows below the surface of the water and has dark green threadlike leaves and stems.

Cultivation
Plant in spring in mud at the bottom of the pool. These plants are vigorous and will spread rapidly. If necessary, thin by pulling plants out by hand or with a rake.
Propagation If necessary, take cuttings in spring and insert bunches of them in the mud at the bottom of the pool.
Pests/diseases Trouble free.

Potentilla
marsh cinquefoil

Potentilla palustris

❑ Height 1 ft (30 cm)
❑ Spread 1 ft (30 cm) or more
❑ Flowers early to late summer
❑ Moist or wet, acid soil
❑ Sunny site
❑ Perennial
❑ Hardy to zone 3

The little marsh cinquefoil *(Potentilla palustris)* grows wild across the northern half of the United States. It is easy to grow in shallow water at the margins of pools or in permanently boggy ground by ponds and streams. It has strawberrylike medium to dark green hairless leaves.

From early summer onward, slender stems carry loose clusters of buttercuplike flowers that open out to stars; they are purple surrounded by maroon sepals. The plant self-seeds and spreads by means of underground runners.

Cultivation
In mid to late fall or in early and mid spring, plant in shallow water or in constantly wet ground. Marsh cinquefoils will not tolerate alkaline soil, and they often fail to grow in hard (limey) water. Choose a site in full sun. Cut the faded stems back to ground level after flowering.
Propagation Detach rooted runners from established plants in early spring and replant at once.
Pests/diseases Trouble free.

Primula
primula, primrose

Primula prolifera

❑ Height 6-48 in (15-120 cm)
❑ Spread 5-15 in (13-38 cm)
❑ Flowers early to late spring and early to late summer
❑ Fertile, moist or boggy soil
❑ Light shade
❑ Perennial
❑ Hardy zones 5-9

All primulas thrive in moist soil, but certain species are particularly associated with boggy conditions and are invaluable for colonizing by watersides. From early spring into midsummer their graceful spikes provide swaths of color.

Primulas do not appreciate waterlogged soil, but they thrive in permanently moist ground, preferably in light shade. They are hardy plants, with basal rosettes of oval, coarsely textured leaves that range in color from pale to medium and dark green.

Popular species
Primula beesiana is hardy in zones 5-9. It is one of the finest species for moist soil. It is a candelabra type, bearing 2 ft (60 cm) high spikes of fragrant yellow-eyed rose-carmine flowers in early and mid summer. The pale green, slightly mealy leaf rosettes spread to 1 ft (30 cm).
Primula bulleyana, another candelabra primula, has dark green leaves with red midribs. Clump-forming to 1 ft (30 cm) wide, it carries 2½ ft (75 cm) high stems set with tiers of golden-yellow flowers from reddish buds in early summer. It is hardy to zone 6.

Primula denticulata

Primula beesiana

Primula denticulata (drumstick primula), hardy to zone 5, grows 1 ft (30 cm) tall and 9 in (23 cm) wide. It flowers from early to late spring, carrying ball-shaped pale lilac to deep purple flower clusters on sturdy stems. White, blue, and red cultivars are available.

Primula florindae (giant cowslip) is one of the tallest species, up to 4 ft (1.2 m) high, and will grow in shallow water at the pool's edge. It is hardy in zones 6-9 and forms wide clumps of large medium-green heart-shaped leaves. In midsummer tall stems rise from the leaves, terminating in loose clusters of scented nodding, bell-shaped soft yellow flowers.

Primula japonica grows to 2½ ft (75 cm) high and 1 ft (30 cm) wide. Tier upon tier of yellow-centered crimson-purple flowers bloom from late spring on. It is hardy in zones 5-9. The cultivars may be pink, red, blue, or white.

Primula prolifera, a candelabra-type species, is 2-3 ft (60-90 cm) tall and spreads to 10 in (25 cm). It is hardy to zone 7 and often retains its pale green, glossy leaves throughout winter. Tall-stemmed tiers of golden-yellow flowers are borne in summer.

Primula pulverulenta resembles P. japonica, but it has mealy flower stems with dark-eyed wine-red to crimson flower clusters. It is hardy to zone 6. The pink-flowered 'Bartley' cultivar is particularly fine.

Primula rosea rarely grows more than 6 in (15 cm) high and wide. Hardy in zones 6-9, it is ideal for carpeting boggy ground by the waterside. It bears clusters of deep rose-pink flowers in early and mid spring.

Primula sikkimensis (Himalayan cowslip) is an outstanding species up to 1½ ft (45 cm) high and 12 in (30 cm) wide. Hardy to zone 6, it has long, narrow pale green leaves that are finely toothed along the margins. It flowers from early to late summer, producing slender spikes of fragrant pale yellow bell flowers.

Cultivation

In mid to late fall or early spring, plant primulas in rich, boggy but not waterlogged soil by the edges of pools and streams. A lightly shaded site is ideal, but P. japonica will tolerate the sun.

Deadhead after flowering. Primulas will often self-seed and hybridize with other species, producing flowers in colors different from those of their parents.

Propagation Primulas spread rapidly and should be regularly divided and replanted every three or four years, after flowering.

New plants are easily raised from seeds sown as soon as they mature in early fall. Sow seeds in shallow pots; overwinter in a cold frame or other protected spot. Prick out the seedlings into small pots, plunge them outdoors, and keep them moist until planting out in fall or the following spring.

Pests/diseases Aphids distort flowering stems, and caterpillars, slugs, and snails feed on the foliage. Fungal rots may attack underground tissues of plants and cause them to collapse. Various virus diseases, for which there is no cure, cause stunting of growth and distortion of flowers. Destroy affected plants.

Primula pulverulenta

Ranunculus
buttercup, spearwort

Sagittaria
common arrowhead

Ranunculus lingua 'Grandiflora'

Sagittaria sagittifolia

❏ Height 2 ft (60 cm)
❏ Water depth up to 1½ ft (45 cm)
❏ Flowers mid to late summer
❏ Sunny site
❏ Aquatic
❏ Hardy to zone 6

The main attraction of *Sagittaria sagittifolia* is its elegant arrow-shaped foliage. In spring it emerges as long, grasslike, almost translucent leaves below the water's surface. As the season progresses, triangular arrowlike leaves rise above the water on stout stems up to 2 ft (60 cm) high. The foliage is pale green, sometimes spotted with brown.

Loose clusters of three-petaled white flowers with yellow-brown centers are borne in mid to late summer. The plants spread rapidly and should not be introduced into small pools.

Cultivation
Plant in early to mid spring along the margins of slow-moving ponds or streams. A water depth of up to 1½ ft (45 cm) is suitable, above fertile soil at least 6 in (15 cm) deep. Push the tubers 2-3 in (5-7.5 cm) deep into the soft mud; take care not to damage growing shoots. Thin out in the growing season by uprooting unwanted specimens.
Propagation In early to mid summer, remove and replant the smallest of the young offsets.
Pests/diseases Aphids, particularly water lily aphids, may infest leaves and flowers.

❏ Height 1-5 ft (30-150 cm)
❏ Water depth 4-6 in (10-15 cm)
❏ Flowers midspring to early fall
❏ Sunny or partially shaded site
❏ Marginal aquatic
❏ Hardy to zone 4

The buttercups, a familiar flower of meadows and rocky slopes, offer a couple of species ideal for the margins of the water garden.

Popular species
Ranunculus lingua (spearwort), a tall perennial, spreads by means of underground runners. It grows in shallow water and is hardy to zone 4. Narrow 1 ft (30 cm) long blue-green leaves are borne on 3 ft (90 cm) high pinkish-green stems. Elegant sprays of glossy, large golden flowers appear from late spring until early fall. 'Grandiflora' is a popular cultivar.

Ranunculus septentrionalis (swamp buttercup) is hardy to zone 4 and thrives in moist soil. It is 1-3 ft (30-90 cm) tall and bears three-segmented leaves on short stalks. Yellow flowers appear from midspring to early summer.

Cultivation
Plant in fall or spring in constantly wet soil or in water up to a depth of 6 in (15 cm). *R. lingua* spreads quickly and can become invasive. In small pools thin it annually in fall or early spring.
Propagation Lift and divide the rhizomes in spring and replant immediately.
Pests/diseases Trouble free.

REED SWEETGRASS — see *Glyceria*
RUSH, ZEBRA — see *Scirpus*

Sanguisorba

American burnet

Sanguisorba canadensis

- ❏ Height 4-5 ft (1.2-1.5 m)
- ❏ Spread to 2 ft (60 cm)
- ❏ Flowers late summer to fall
- ❏ Moist or boggy soil
- ❏ Sun or partial shade
- ❏ Perennial
- ❏ Hardy zones 3-8

Often called American burnet, *Sanguisorba canadensis* is native to North America from Labrador to Illinois and south to Georgia. It reaches a height of as much as 5 ft (1.5 m) and has long-stemmed, bright green feathery leaves composed of oblong leaflets that are 2-3 in (5-7.5 cm) long. The bottle-brushlike spikes of flowers appear in fall. Although they are not especially dramatic, they bloom when little else is in flower and so are a welcome addition to a pool-side planting.

Cultivation

American burnet thrives in either sun or partial shade and is tolerant of most soils. It is most vigorous, however, in moist or even boggy ground.

Propagation Lift and divide established plants in spring. Alternatively, collect seeds in the fall and sow in early spring in a cold frame or other protected spot.

Pests/diseases None serious.

SCHOENOPLECTUS — see *Scirpus*

Scirpus

bulrush

Scirpus lacustris tabernaemontana 'Zebrinus'

- ❏ Height 6-60 in (15-150 cm)
- ❏ Water depth up to 6 in (15 cm)
- ❏ Foliage plant
- ❏ Sunny or partially shaded site
- ❏ Marginal aquatic
- ❏ Hardy zones 5-10

Botanists differ as to whether bulrushes should be classified as *Scirpus* or *Schoenoplectus*. These grasslike plants are native to wetlands in almost every region of North America. They are prized for the striking vertical accent they can provide around pools or along streams.

It is best to investigate the local species, since they are apt to be particularly well adapted to their climate. The plants listed here are cultivated types with outstanding decorative value.

Popular species

Scirpus cernuus forms dense tufts of foliage, 6-12 in (15-30 cm) tall, with bright green grasslike leaves. In summer the leaves are capped by terminal spikes of small white flowers that cause the foliage to bend over. This plant is best situated where it can spill over rocks or the edge of a pool. It requires wet soil and thrives in full sun or light shade. It is hardy in zones 9-10.

Scirpus cyperinus (wool grass), hardy to zone 7, grows 40-60 in (1-1.5 m) tall and is native to the eastern states. Plumes of woolly flowers appear in late summer.

Scirpus lacustris tabernaemontana, syn. *Schoenoplectus tabernaemontana,* is hardy to zone 5 and has cylindrical leaves that grow 2-4 ft (60-120 cm) tall. Of outstanding ornamental value is 'Zebrinus' (banded bulrush, or zebra rush), which is hardy in zones 7-9. Its green leaves are marked by horizontal bands of yellow, and it looks striking growing along the water's edge, where it forms expanding clumps.

Cultivation

Plant in good, loamy soil around the margins of a pool or the edge of a stream in mid to late spring.

Sun is essential to the zebra rush if the variegations are to be strong, but in hot areas the plant grows best in afternoon shade. Zebra rush thrives in water up to 6 in (15 cm) deep. In zone 7 it needs a sheltered site.

Bulrushes spread vigorously. Unless you want a large colony, confine the roots within a bottomless container and sink it into the ground so that the top is flush with the surface of the soil.

Cut back *S. cernuus* in late winter to 2-3 in (5-7.5 cm) tall to promote fresh new growth.

Propagation Increase by lifting and dividing mature clumps in early spring; use a sharp knife to cut the tough rootstock. Replant the divided pieces immediately.

Pests/diseases Trouble free.

Typha
cattail

Typha minima

- ❏ Height 1-6 ft (30-180 cm)
- ❏ Water depth up to 6 in (15 cm)
- ❏ Flowers in summer
- ❏ Sunny site
- ❏ Marginal aquatic
- ❏ Hardy to zone 3

Cattails *(Typha)*, familiar water-side plants, have brown, poker-like flower heads. They are too big for any but large pools and can be invasive if not kept in check.

Popular species
Typha latifolia grows about 6 ft (1.8 m) high and forms large clumps of blue-green foliage. *Typha minima*, at just 1½-2½ ft (45-75 cm) high, is smaller and more suitable for the average-size pool. It produces grasslike green leaves and slender flower heads.

Cultivation
Plant in mid to late spring in rich, deep soil along the water's edge or in water 6 in (15 cm) deep.
Propagation Cut the rhizomes into 1-3 in (2.5-7.5 cm) pieces in spring and replant.
Pests/diseases Trouble free.

UMBRELLA PALM — see *Cyperus*
WATER AVENS — see *Geum*
WATER HAWTHORN — see *Aponogeton*
WATER HYACINTH — see *Eichhornia*
WATER LILY — see *Nymphaea*
WATER MINT — see *Mentha*
WATER PLANTAIN — see *Alisma*

Zantedeschia
calla lily

Zantedeschia aethiopica 'Green Goddess'

- ❏ Height 2-3 ft (60-90 cm)
- ❏ Spread 1-2 ft (30-60 cm)
- ❏ Water depth 6-12 in (15-30 cm)
- ❏ Flowers late spring to early summer
- ❏ Sunny site
- ❏ Marginal perennial
- ❏ Hardy zones 8-10

The stately calla lily *(Zantedeschia aethiopica)* is a magnificent and exotic perennial that thrives by the pool's edge or in shallow water in the South. Its large arrow-shaped, glossy dark green leaves, which grow in dense rosettes, are handsome. From late spring into early summer, tall flower stems rise above the foliage. Each is topped with a dazzling white spathe (a hoodlike leaf) surrounding a golden spadix.

The cultivars are often hardier than the species and will grow in drier sites. They include 'Giant White' and 'Green Goddess.'

Cultivation
Plant calla lilies in spring in good but not overrich, moist soil or in shallow water in mild areas. Where freezes are likely in winter, protect the fleshy crowns with a loose mulch of straw or pine needles; or lift them and store in pots in a frost-free place.
Propagation Divide and replant the rhizomes in spring.
Pests/diseases Corm rot may occur in heavy, cold soil. Various virus diseases cause mottling of the foliage and distort flowers.

Zantedeschia aethiopica

Plant Hardiness Zone Map

Selecting plants suitable for your climate is half the secret to successful gardening. The U. S. Department of Agriculture (USDA) has created a plant hardiness zone map as a guide. Each zone is based on an average minimum winter temperature. Most nurseries and mail-order companies have adopted this map and indicate zones for their plants. Once you identify the zone you live in, buy only plants that are recommended for that zone. Local conditions, such as a garden near a pond or in a higher mountainous elevation, can affect the climate and the zone. In such cases, contact your local Cooperative Extension Service for assistance in adapting the map to your garden.

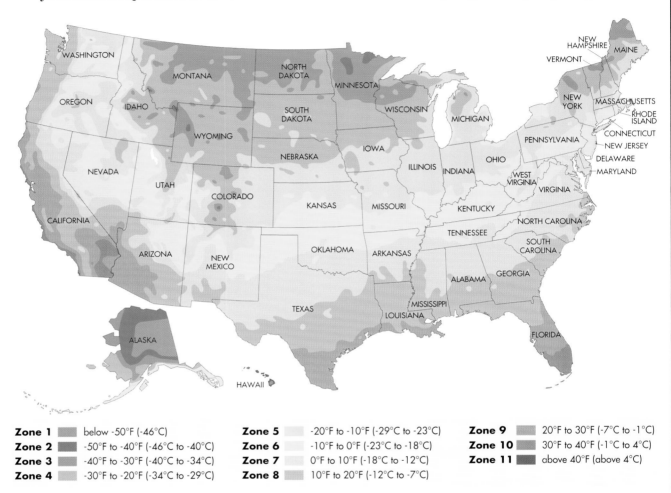

Zone 1	below -50°F (-46°C)	**Zone 5**	-20°F to -10°F (-29°C to -23°C)	**Zone 9**	20°F to 30°F (-7°C to -1°C)
Zone 2	-50°F to -40°F (-46°C to -40°C)	**Zone 6**	-10°F to 0°F (-23°C to -18°C)	**Zone 10**	30°F to 40°F (-1°C to 4°C)
Zone 3	-40°F to -30°F (-40°C to -34°C)	**Zone 7**	0°F to 10°F (-18°C to -12°C)	**Zone 11**	above 40°F (above 4°C)
Zone 4	-30°F to -20°F (-34°C to -29°C)	**Zone 8**	10°F to 20°F (-12°C to -7°C)		

ACKNOWLEDGMENTS

Photo credits
A-Z Botanical 107(r), 153(c); Agence Bamboo 17(l), 57(r), 98(b), 106(l), 110(l), 111(t), 112(l), 114(r), 149(t), 151(l), 155(l), 175(l); Gillian Beckett 34(r), 37(l), 39(r), 40(b), 43(b), 45(l), 46(c), 52(tl), 54(tr), 59(l), 65(br), 67(tr), 73(tr), 74(b), 78(l), 84(b), 87(l), 99(b,r), 111(b), 127(l), 128(l); Biofotos (Heather Angel) 89(c), 144(tr), 148(r), 149(r), 163(c), 169(l), 171(l,c), 173(r); Ruth Rogers Clausen 52(b); Bruce Coleman Picture Library 155(c); Eric Crichton, front cover (bc), 14(l), 15(t), 18(tl), 19(l,br), 23(b), 24(r), 25(tr), 26(tc), 29(r), 33(l), 36(tl), 40(tr), 41(l), 48(r), 49(r), 50(bl), 53, 54(l,br), 58(r), 60(r), 64(t), 66(t), 68(bl), 70(br), 71(l), 72(br), 75(l), 76(r), 78(tr), 81(l), 82(tl), 83(r), 85(t), 87(tr), 88(l), 89(l,r), 90(l), 93(r), 95(tr), 96(r), 97, 100(c), 101(tl), 105(l), 107(b), 108(l), 109(r), 110(r), 112(r), 115(l), 118(l), 119(r), 121(bl), 122(l,br), 126(tl), 128(tr), 129(r), 130(t), 132(b,tr), 133(tr), 136(b,r), 137, 151(l,c), 152(l), 158(t,b), 159(br), 164(l), 168(b), 173(l); Earth Scenes (Patti Murray) 55(r), (Ken Lewis) 76(c); Thomas Eltzroth 174(l); Derek Fell 90(tr), 99(tl), 133(b), 175(t); Philippe Ferret 148(l), 152(tr), 155(r), 162(b), 167, 168(tl), 170(r); Andrew Gagg (Photoflora) 26(tr); Garden Picture Libary (J. Ainsworth) 110(br), 117(tr), (Brian Carter) 13(b), 18(cl), 20(tl), 21(r), 24(bl), 31(l), 32(l), 42(r), 43(tl), 47(tr), 86(tr), 91(r), 102(bl,tr), 108(bl), 131(c), 162(tr), 168(r), 169(r), (John Elliot) 82(b), 85(bl), 135(tl), (Chris Fairweather)

171(r), (John Glover) front cover (c), 47(b), (Marijke Heuff) 120(r), (Clive Nichols) back cover, (Joanne Pavia) 8, 124(b), (S. Sira) 90(b), (David Russell) 157(tr), 164(b), (Ron Sutherland) 172(b), (Brigitte Thomas) 2-3; John Glover, front cover (bl), 11(t,bl), 12(bl), 33(c), 145, 147(bl), 175(b); Derek Gould 15(b), 18(br), 23(r), 26(l); Grant Heilman Photography, Inc. (Jane Grushow) 17(r), (Lever/Grushow) 109(l); Pamela Harper 103(r), 120(l), 129(l); Jerry Harpur 13(t), 144(tl); Robert E. Heapes 34(l); Patrick Johns 28(r), 69(l), 84(tl); Panayoti Kelaidis 60(tl), 65(tr), 71(r), 74(tl); Michelle Lamontagne 22, 25(br), 33(l), 44(c), 51(tr), 63(l,r), 66(c), 67(br), 70(t), 96(l), 100(r), 104(tl), 122(tr), 135(bl), 136(tl); Andrew Lawson 109(br), 133(l), 139(r); Lilypons Water Gardens 174(l); Charles Mann 73(tl), 103(l); Elvin McDonald 21(l); Tania Midgley, front cover (cr), 10, 14(b), 44(r), 51(bl), 58(l), 64(b), 80(b), 84(tl), 114(tl), 124(tl), 140, 147(l), 152(l), 156(l), 163(r); Natural Image 24(tl), 25(cr), 36(b), 76(c), 85(br), 92(r), 93(l), 94(t), 108(r), 114(b), 118(r), 123(r), 124(r), 125(l), 126(c,r), 128(b); Clive Nichols, front cover (br), 1, 4-7, 11(br), 143; Muriel Orans 45(r); Photo/Nats, Inc. (Liz Ball) 92(l), (Bill Larkin) 138(t), (Jerry Pavia) 38(l), (Ann Reilly) 36(r), (Les Saucier) 125(r), (David M. Stone) 138(b); Photos Horticultural, front cover (t), 12(tl), 14(tr), 16(t), 20(r), 23(tl), 27, 28(l), 29(l), 30, 35(t), 37(r), 39(l), 40(l), 43(tr), 46(r), 48(l), 50(l), 51(tl), 52(r), 56(l), 59(r), 60(b), 61(r), 62, 63(c), 67(l), 68(r), 75(r), 77, 78(b), 79(l,b), 80(l), 82(r), 83(l), 86(l), 91(l), 92(tr), 94(b), 95(b), 98(tl),

101(b), 102(tl), 104(b), 105(r), 106(r), 107(tl), 116(t), 121(t), 127(r), 130(b), 131(l), 132(tl), 134, 135(r), 139(l), 142, 147(br), 150, 153(l), 154(t), 156(c,r), 157(l,b), 159(t), 161(tr), 162(tl), 163(l), 165, 166(b), 172(t); Photo Researchers, Inc. (Michael Giannechini) 119(tl), (K.H. Jacobi/Okapia) 65(l), (Dr. Eckhart Pott) 74(r), (David Weintraub) 56(r); William Probeck 25(tl); Reader's Digest Plant Photo Library, London 96(b), 158(r); R.W. Redfield 101(r); Richard Shiell 47(l), 72(l), 153(r); Harry Smith Collection, front cover (cl), 12(r), 16(br), 17(c), 18(tr), 19(tr), 20(b), 26(b), 32(r), 35(b), 38(r), 42(l), 44(l), 46(tl), 50(r), 55(l), 61(l), 69(r), 72(tr), 73(bl), 76(l), 81(r), 87(b), 88(b), 93(c), 95(l), 98(l), 100(1), 104(r), 113, 115(r), 116(b), 117(l), 123(tl), 125(b), 146, 161(l,b), 164(tr), 170(l); Michael S. Thompson 41(b), 49(l), 57(l), 68(tl), 79(tr), 131(r), 160; John N. Trager 105(c); judywhite 31(l), 41(tr), 166(t).

Illustrator
Gill Tomblin – Reader's Digest 144

Reader's Digest Production
Assistant Production Supervisor: Mike Gallo
Electronic Prepress Support: Karen Goldsmith
Quality Control Manager: Ann Kennedy Harris
Assistant Production Manager: Dexter Street
Book Production Director: Ken Gillett
Prepress Manager: Garry Hansen
Book Production Manager: Joe Leeker
U.S. Prepress Manager: Mark P. Merritt